WAR IS BORING

BORED STIFF, SCARED TO DEATH
IN THE WORLD'S WORST WAR ZONES

WAR IS BORING

DAVID AXE AND MATT BORS

 NEW AMERICAN LIBRARY

New American Library
Published by New American Library, a division of
Penguin Group (USA) Inc., 375 Hudson Street,
New York, New York 10014, USA
Penguin Group (Canada), 90 Eglinton Avenue East, Suite 700, Toronto,
Ontario M4P 2Y3, Canada (a division of Pearson Penguin Canada Inc.)
Penguin Books Ltd., 80 Strand, London WC2R 0RL, England
Penguin Ireland, 25 St. Stephen's Green, Dublin 2,
Ireland (a division of Penguin Books Ltd.)
Penguin Group (Australia), 250 Camberwell Road, Camberwell, Victoria 3124,
Australia (a division of Pearson Australia Group Pty. Ltd.)
Penguin Books India Pvt. Ltd., 11 Community Centre, Panchsheel Park,
New Delhi - 110 017, India
Penguin Group (NZ), 67 Apollo Drive, Rosedale, North Shore 0632,
New Zealand (a division of Pearson New Zealand Ltd.)
Penguin Books (South Africa) (Pty.) Ltd., 24 Sturdee Avenue,
Rosebank, Johannesburg 2196, South Africa

Penguin Books Ltd., Registered Offices:
80 Strand, London WC2R 0RL, England

First published by New American Library,
a division of Penguin Group (USA) Inc.

First Printing, August 2010
10 9 8 7 6 5 4 3 2 1

 REGISTERED TRADEMARK–MARCA REGISTRADA

Printed in the United States of America

PUBLISHER'S NOTE
While the author has made every effort to provide accurate telephone numbers
and Internet addresses at the time of publication, neither the publisher nor the
author assumes any responsibility for errors, or for changes that occur after publication. Further, publisher does not have any control over and does not assume
any responsibility for author or third-party Web sites or their content.

For Moqtar Hirabe, gunned down by Somali insurgents in Mogadishu in June 2009—and for all the other fixers, stringers, interpreters, drivers and guards who've risked their lives, and sometimes given them, to help us reporters do our jobs.

INTRODUCTION

BY TED RALL

Like a moth to the flame.

Every year or so, David Axe seeks out the world's hottest and nastiest conflict zones. He doesn't exactly try to get himself killed. But he's not afraid of dying.

Invariably, the good bad times end. Sometimes peace breaks out. More often, things get too hot. Money runs out. Armed goons who call themselves the authorities deport him. David heads home. And it's good.

It's good. For a while. Maybe only a few days. If war is boring, peace is stultifying. Or is it America? Or home?

Whatever the reason, David soon finds himself working the phones, dialing for expense-account dollars so he can get himself shot at by, usually, who knows?

And it's partly my fault. Not David's death wish—whether this cynical young man was hard-wired for fatalism or his parents did something to him, it has nothing to do with me—but his novel means of expressing it. War first found me drinking Nes café at an outdoor café in Kazakhstan; Western troops were fighting a bizarre secret war against the Islamic Movement of Uzbekistan, who were attacking a British Petroleum oilfield. Two years later, I blundered into the start of the Kargil Conflict, also known as the Third Kashmir War, in a high-altitude village along the Karakoram Highway.

As I feasted on hard naan bread and Kashmiri chai served in a banged-up metal cup, an Indian mortar smashed into a store up the street. The proprietor of the tea house ran outside, shaking his fist. "Indian motherfuckers!" he screamed in Urdu. He stolled to my table. "Another Coke?" he asked, his seconds-old rage instantly cooled.

I loved that. Death and life, hatred and normalcy, so closely intertwined. That's what you find in Third World shitholes, particularly Third World shitholes where people are shooting at one another. In America, of course, death is always present. But we don't see it. When is the last time you saw a body lying in the street? Or anywhere? Reality is best when it's out in the open.

Another couple of years, then 9/11. I went to Afghanistan to cover the U.S. invasion. That's true. I went to learn the truth. That's also true. But I mainly went to test myself. To risk death. To get that thrill, that "War Fix" as David called it in his previous tome, that comes with a close brush with

The End. I got what I came for. I dodged mortars, bombs, bullets, and a couple of ambushes. I have never felt more alive.

Which is the flip side of David's death wish. He doesn't really want to die. He really wants to live. To feel alive.

Maybe just to feel.

The typical existence of a generic middle-class American citizen doesn't allow anyone to feel anything: bland, dull, cut-and-pasted, like the mall zombies in *Dawn of the Dead*. Rage, terror, vengeance, giddiness aren't allowed. Must. Maintain. Calm.

I came back from Afghanistan. I wrote a book. People bought it. David was one of them.

My book wasn't the only reason he wanted to become a war correspondent (or "war tourist," as I call it). But it was a contributing factor.

What if David dies in some war zone? I may feel guilty, but I doubt it. Not a day passes without me wishing I was in the shit somewhere, miserable and scared and bored. How could I begrudge my friend the same thrill?

Ted Rall *is a cartoonist, columnist, and author of* To Afghanistan and Back: A Graphic Travelogue, *and* Silk Road to Ruin: Is Central Asia the New Middle East?

WAR IS BORING

PROLOGUE

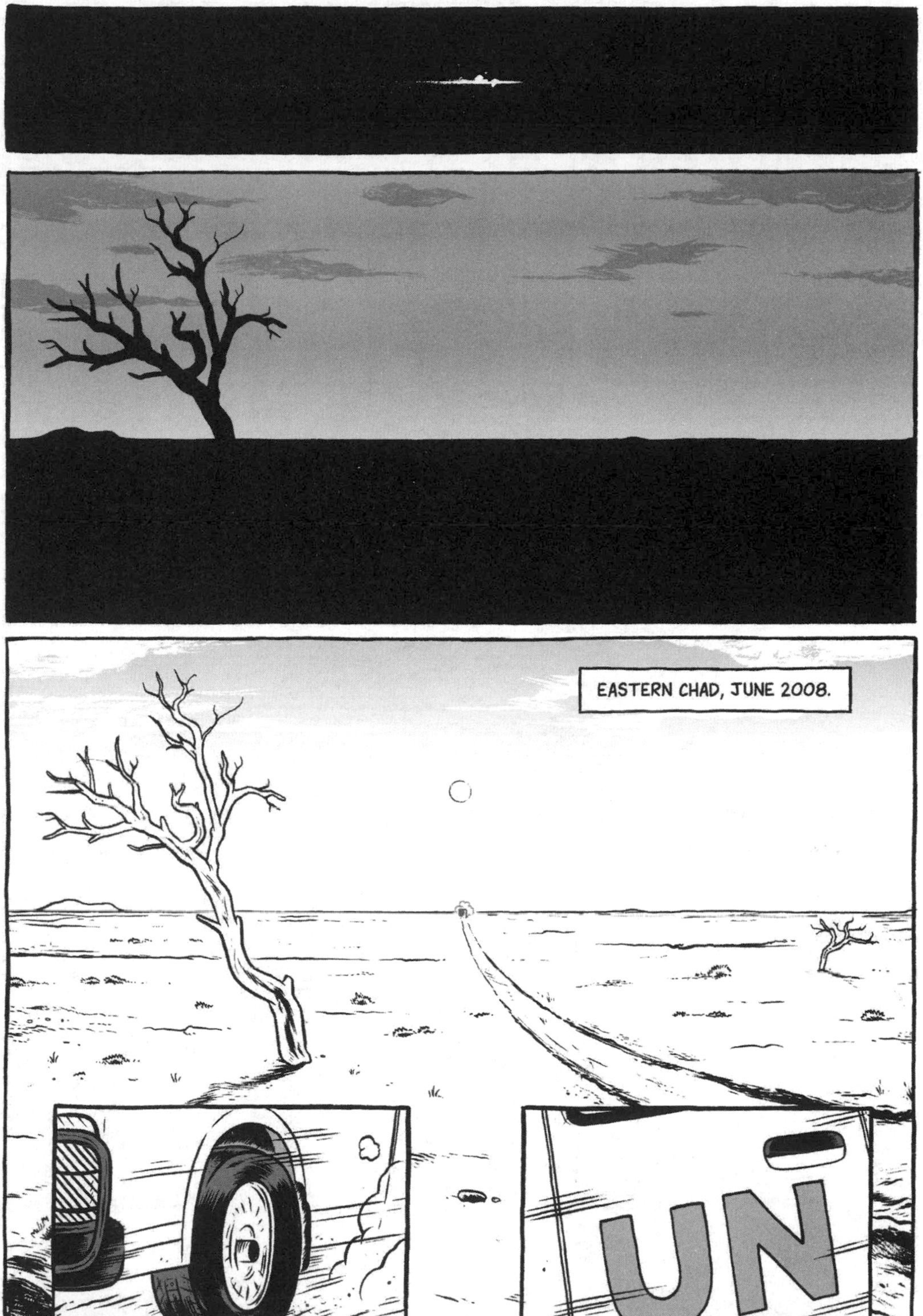
EASTERN CHAD, JUNE 2008.
UN

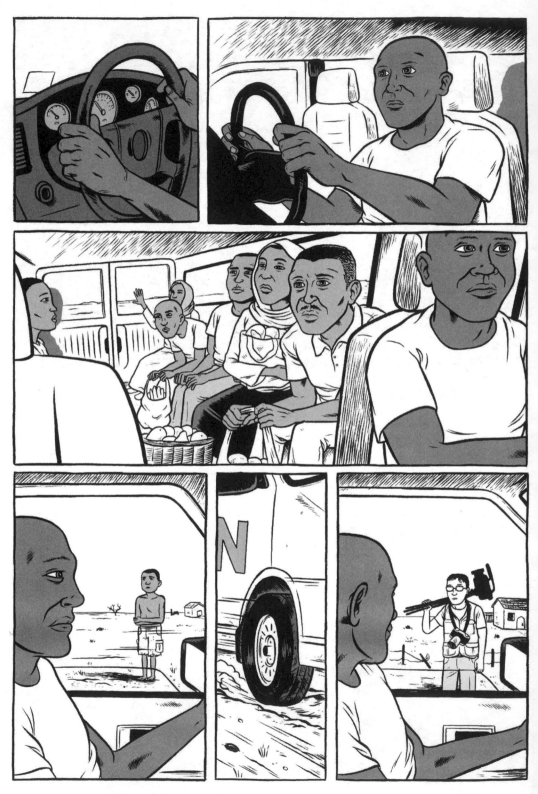

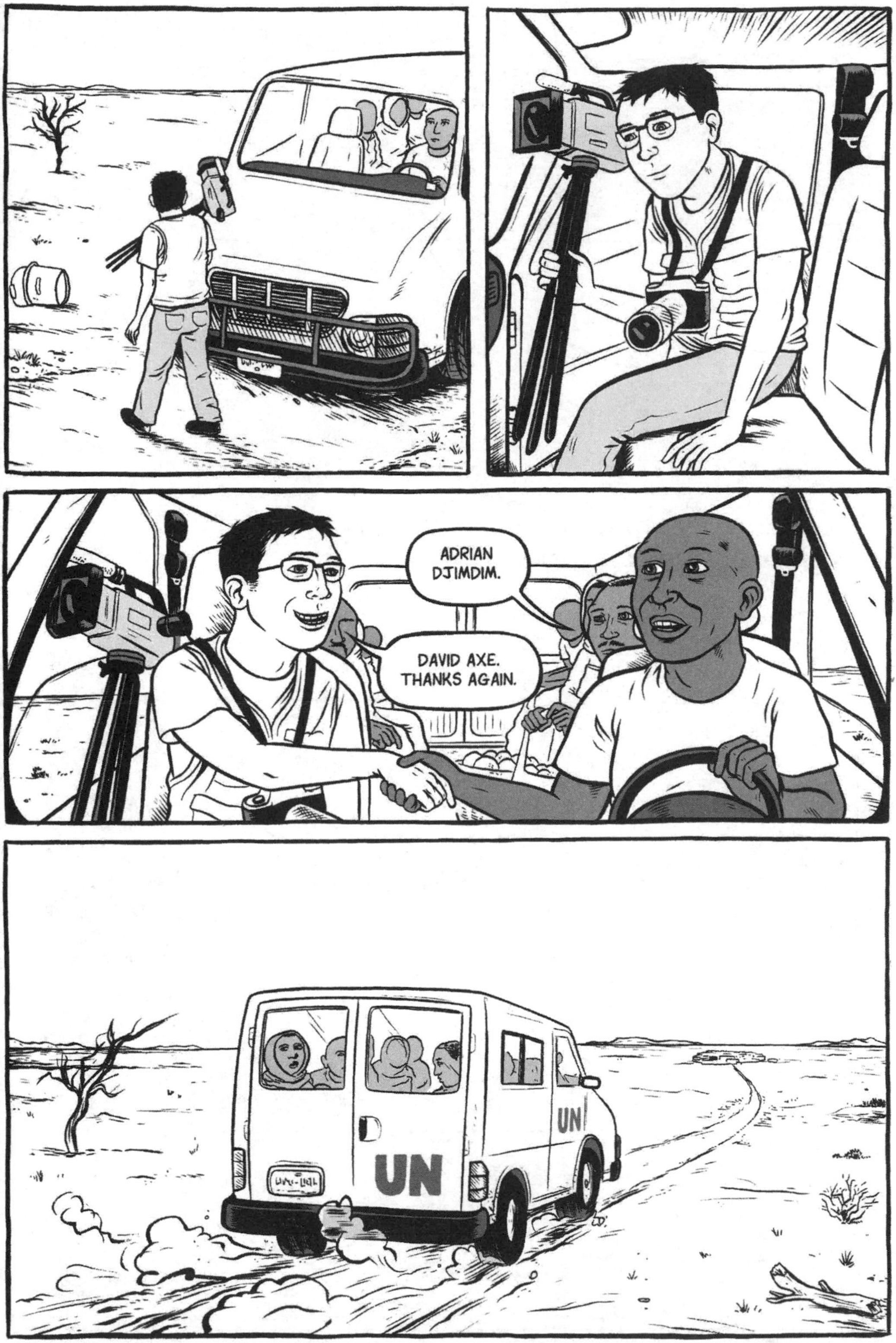
ADRIAN DJIMDIM.
DAVID AXE. THANKS AGAIN.
UN
UN

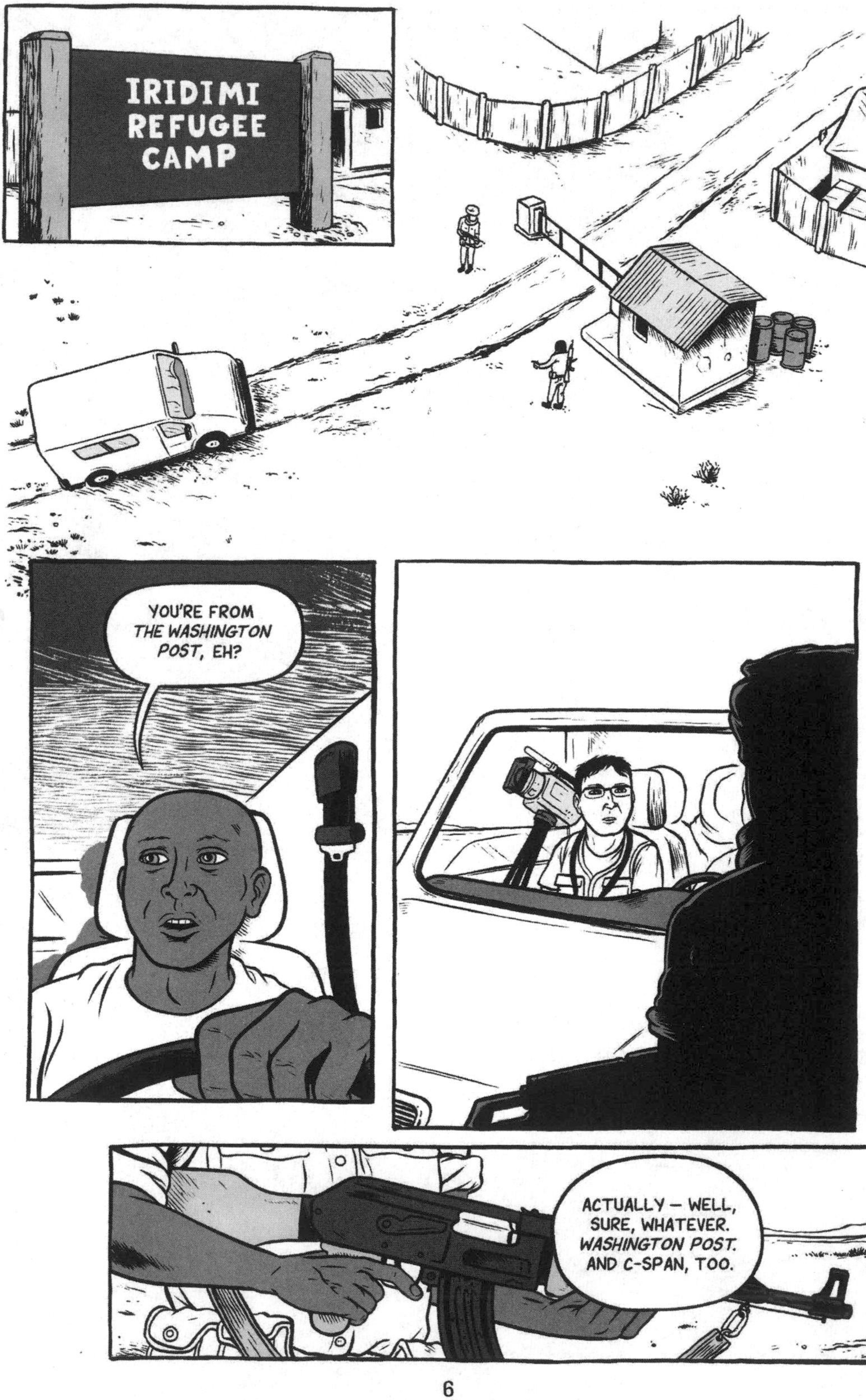
IRIDIMI REFUGEE CAMP
YOU'RE FROM *THE WASHINGTON POST*, EH?
ACTUALLY — WELL, SURE, WHATEVER. *WASHINGTON POST.* AND C-SPAN, TOO.

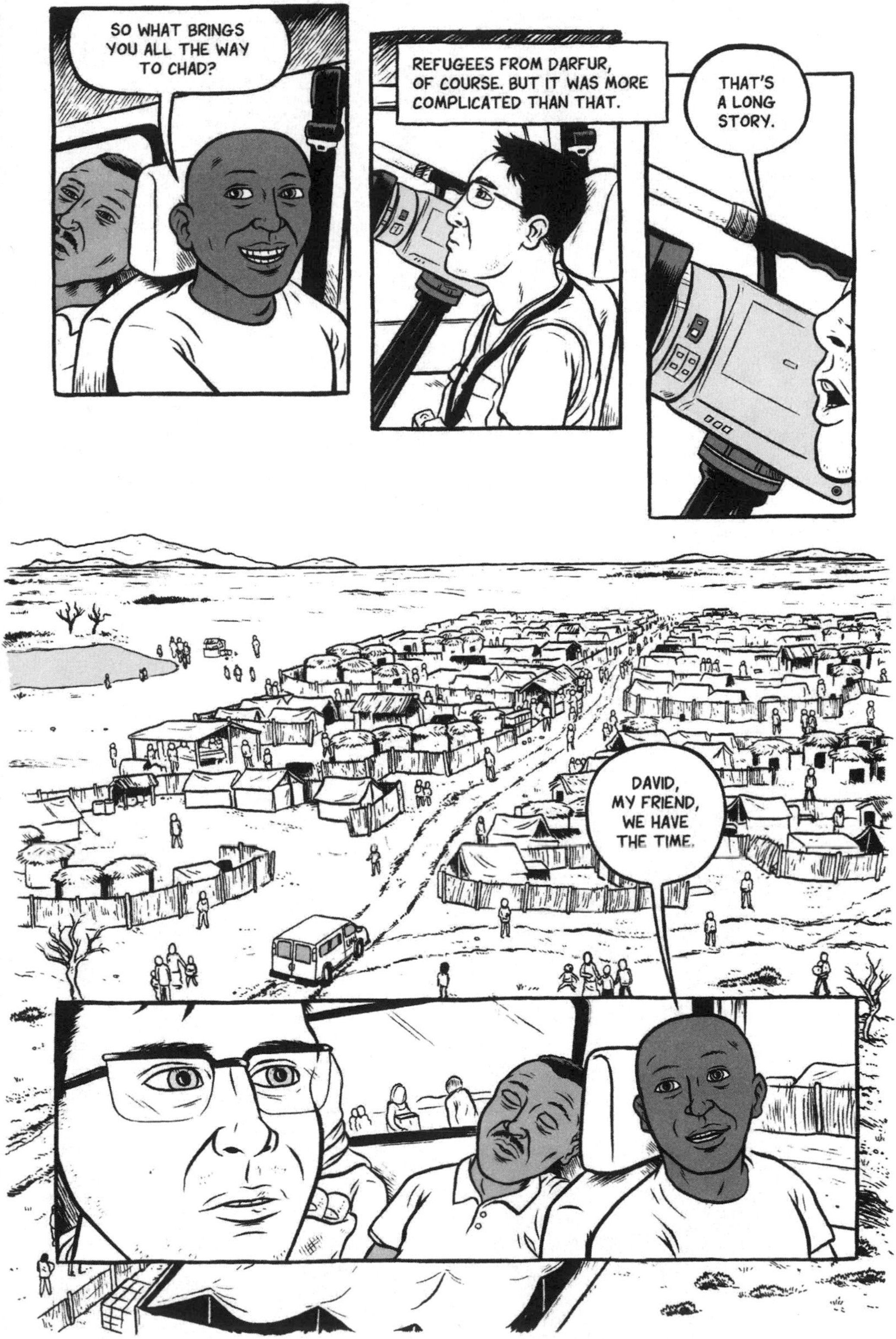
SO WHAT BRINGS YOU ALL THE WAY TO CHAD?
REFUGEES FROM DARFUR, OF COURSE. BUT IT WAS MORE COMPLICATED THAN THAT.
THAT'S A LONG STORY.
DAVID, MY FRIEND, WE HAVE THE TIME.

IRAQ

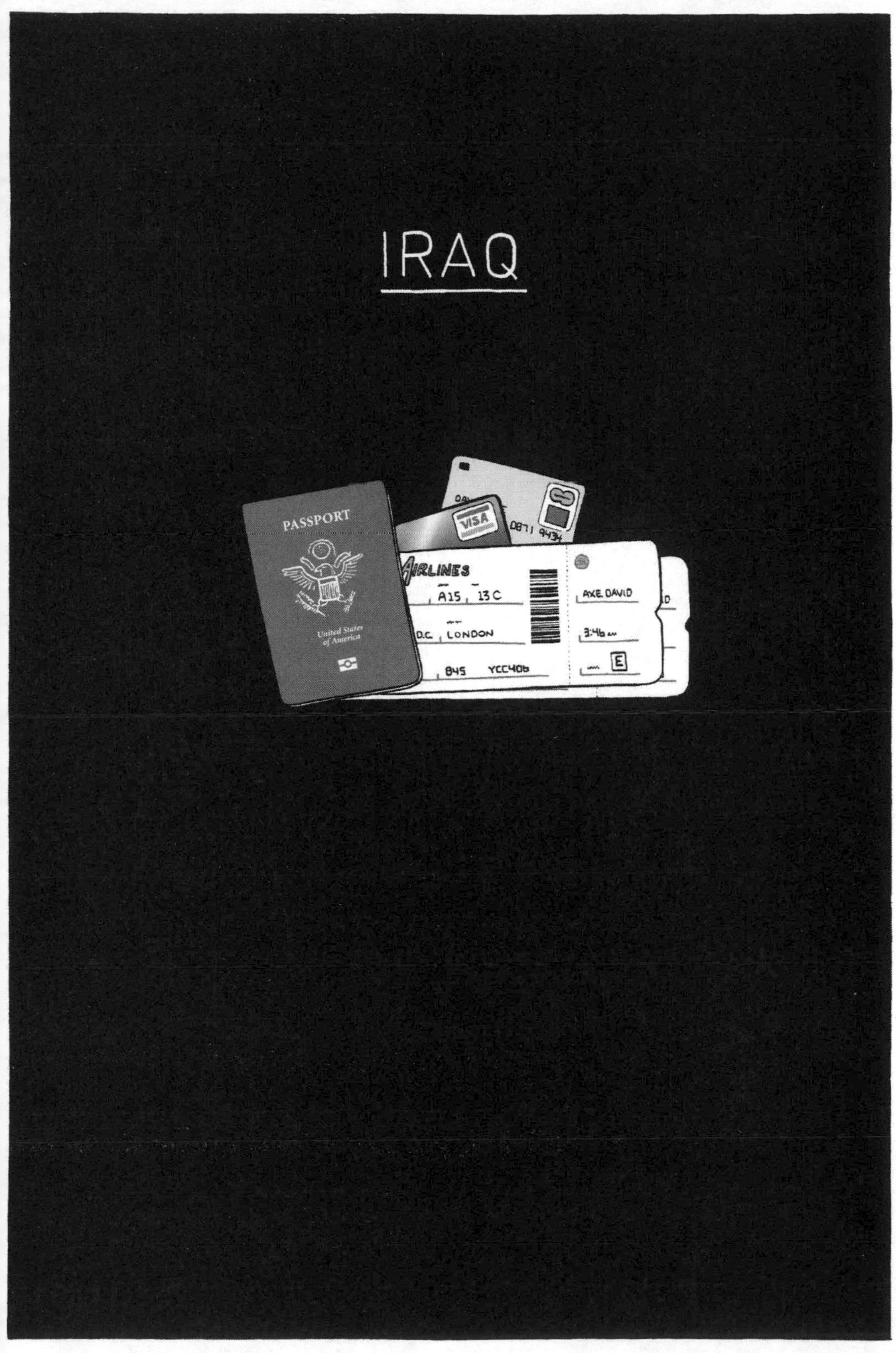
PASSPORT
United States of America
VISA
0871 9434
AIRLINES
A15
13C
D.C.
LONDON
845
YCC406
AXE, DAVID
3:46
E

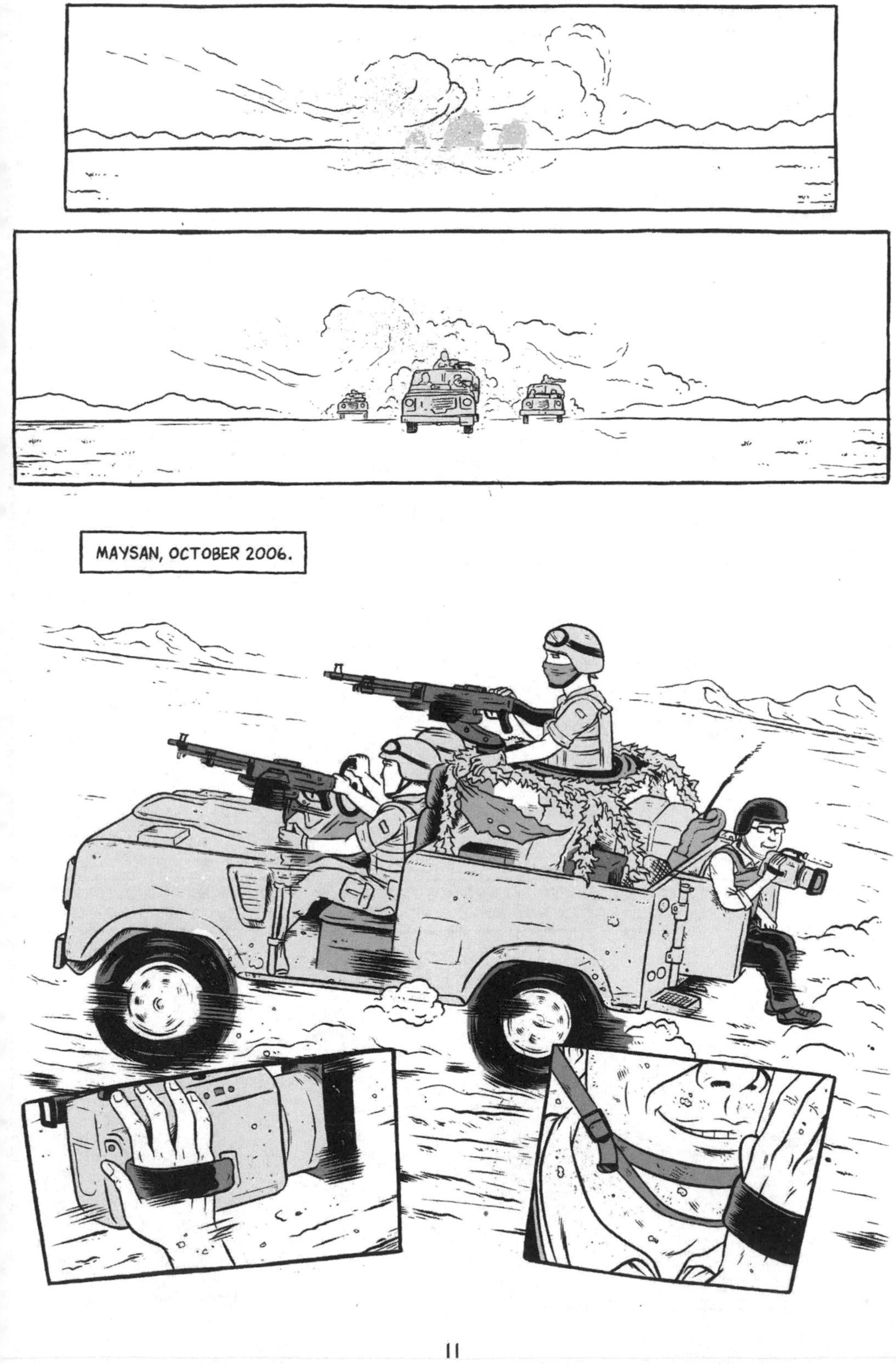
MAYSAN, OCTOBER 2006.

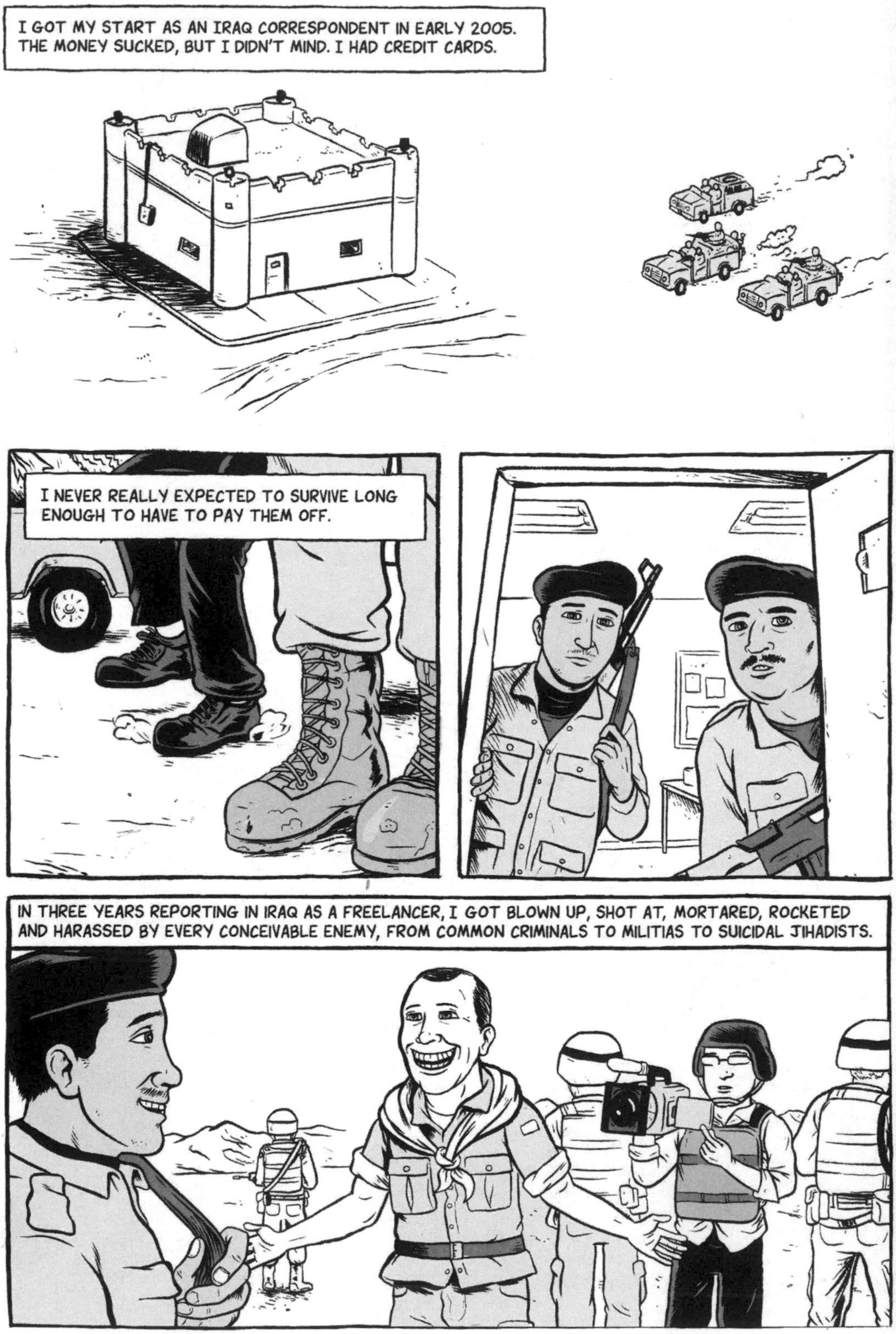
I GOT MY START AS AN IRAQ CORRESPONDENT IN EARLY 2005. THE MONEY SUCKED, BUT I DIDN'T MIND. I HAD CREDIT CARDS.
I NEVER REALLY EXPECTED TO SURVIVE LONG ENOUGH TO HAVE TO PAY THEM OFF.
IN THREE YEARS REPORTING IN IRAQ AS A FREELANCER, I GOT BLOWN UP, SHOT AT, MORTARED, ROCKETED AND HARASSED BY EVERY CONCEIVABLE ENEMY, FROM COMMON CRIMINALS TO MILITIAS TO SUICIDAL JIHADISTS.

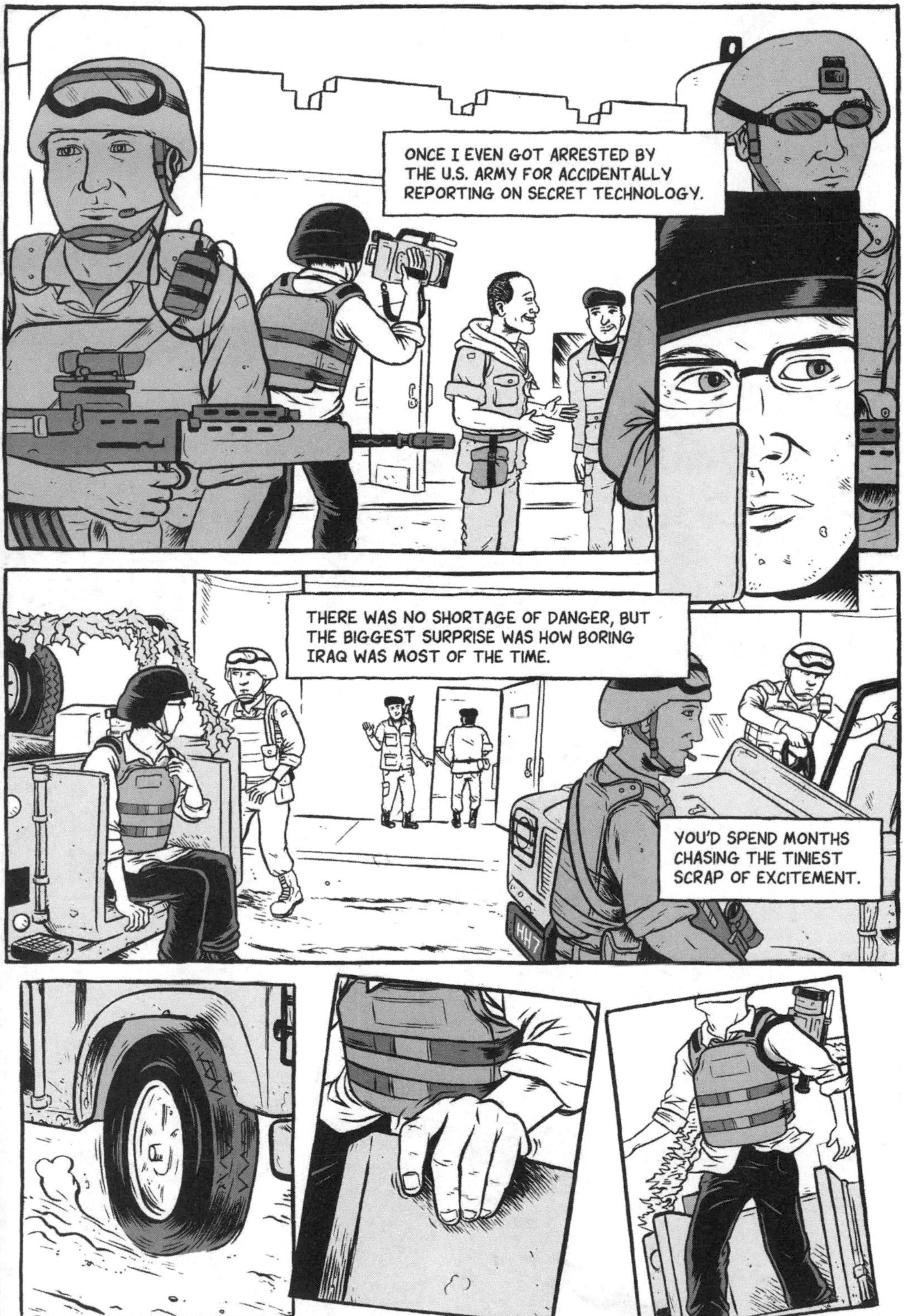
ONCE I EVEN GOT ARRESTED BY THE U.S. ARMY FOR ACCIDENTALLY REPORTING ON SECRET TECHNOLOGY.
THERE WAS NO SHORTAGE OF DANGER, BUT THE BIGGEST SURPRISE WAS HOW BORING IRAQ WAS MOST OF THE TIME.
YOU'D SPEND MONTHS CHASING THE TINIEST SCRAP OF EXCITEMENT.
HH7

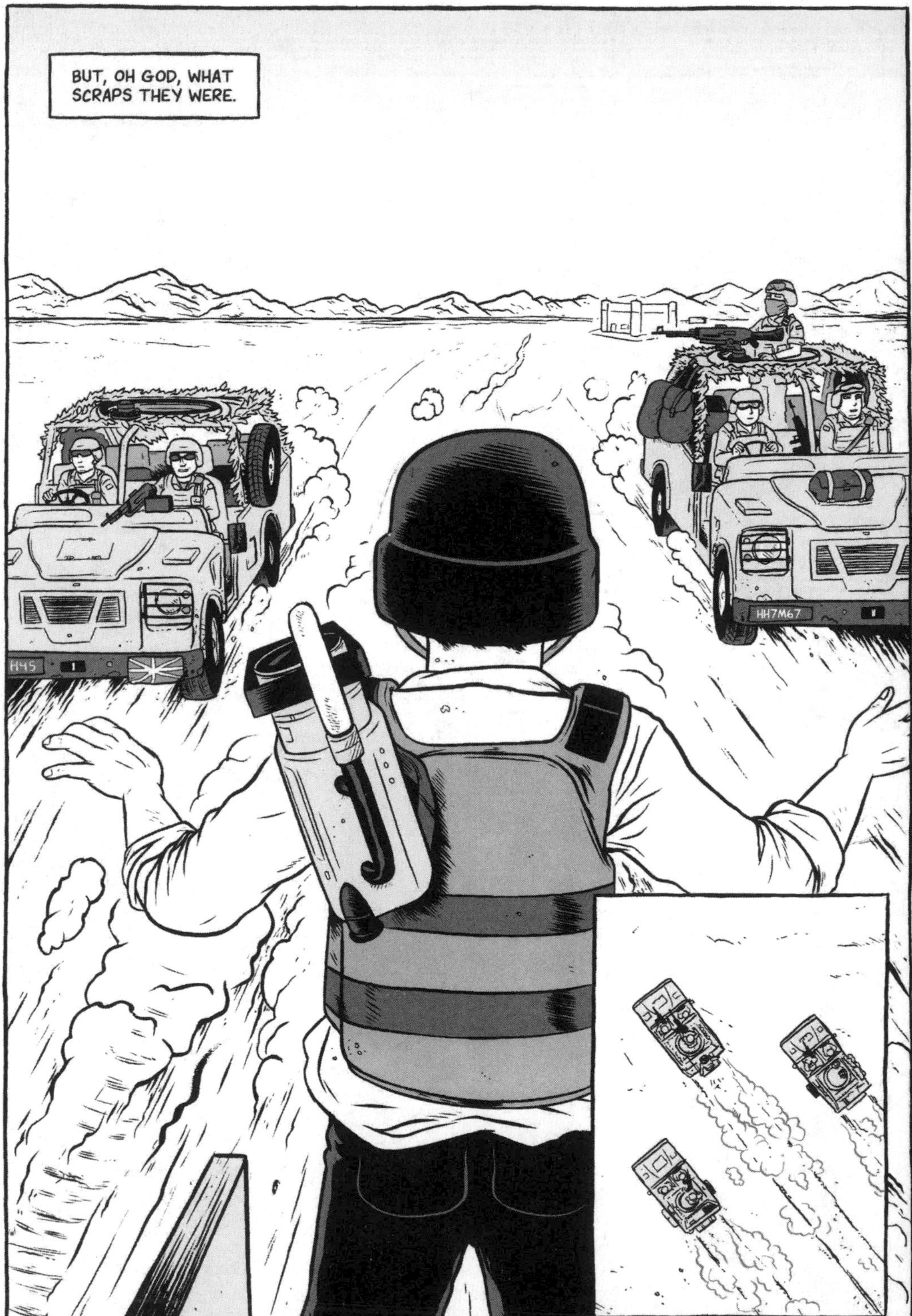
BUT, OH GOD, WHAT SCRAPS THEY WERE.
H45
HH7M67

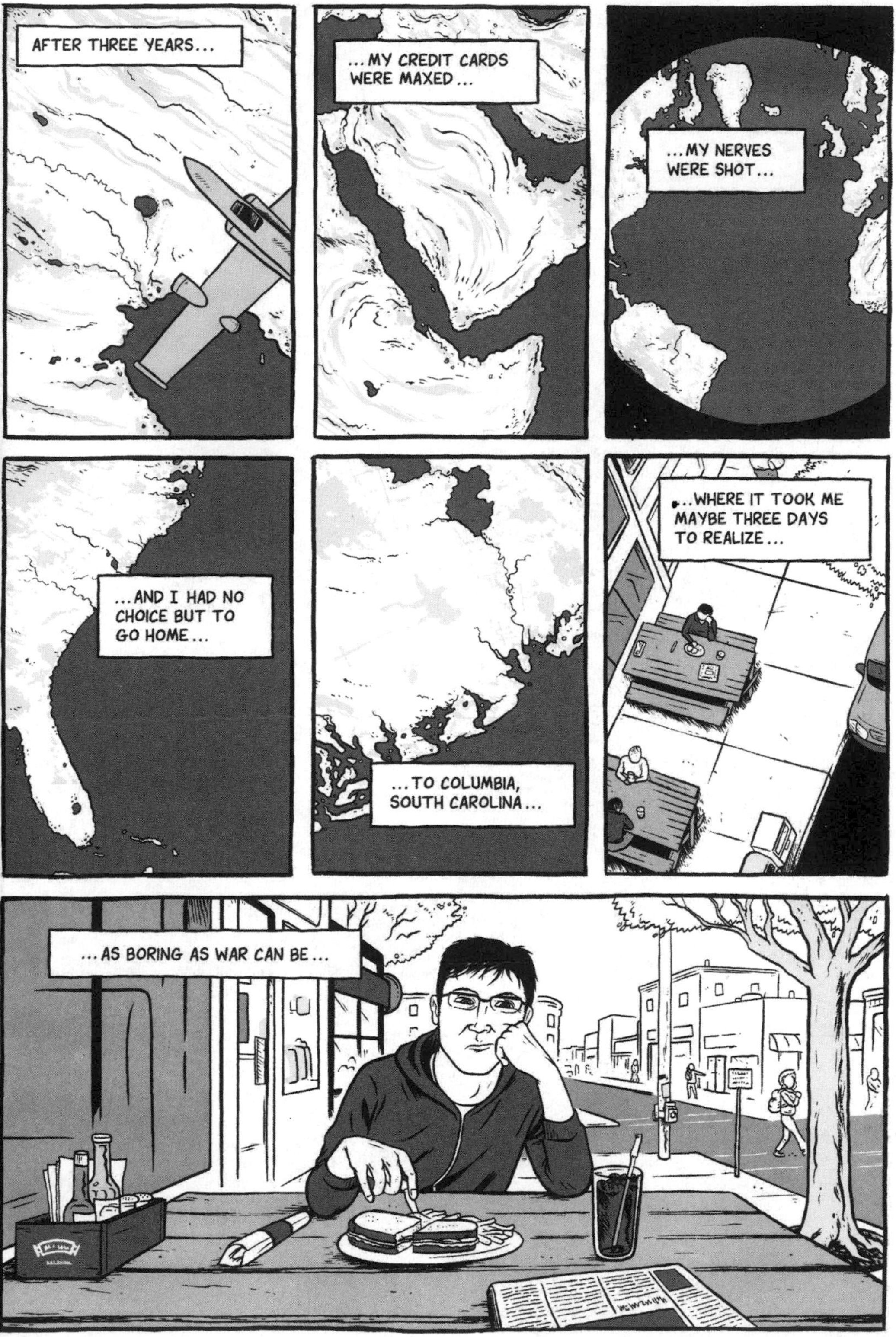
AFTER THREE YEARS...
...MY CREDIT CARDS WERE MAXED...
...MY NERVES WERE SHOT...
...AND I HAD NO CHOICE BUT TO GO HOME...
...TO COLUMBIA, SOUTH CAROLINA...
...WHERE IT TOOK ME MAYBE THREE DAYS TO REALIZE...
...AS BORING AS WAR CAN BE...

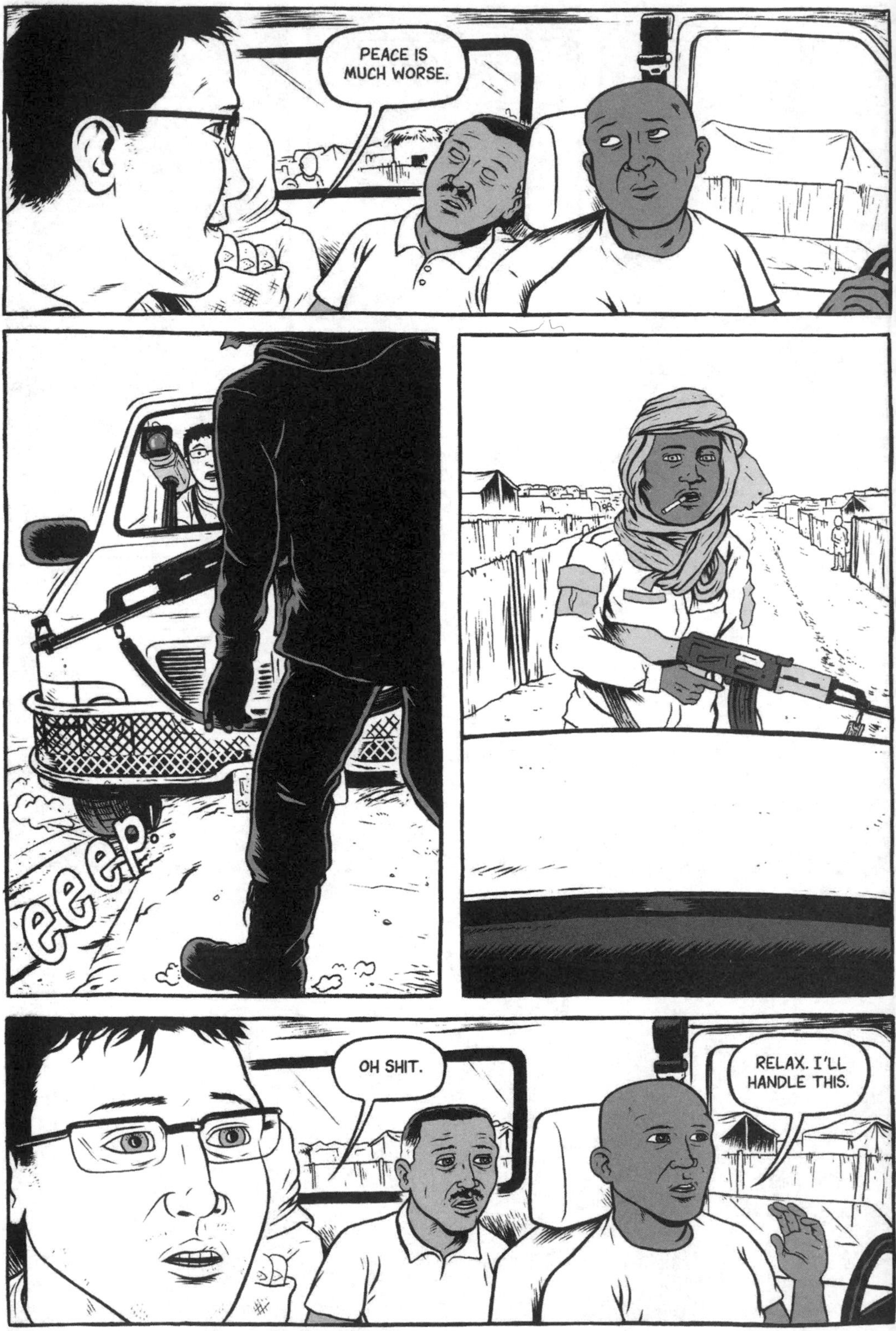
PEACE IS MUCH WORSE.
EEEEP
OH SHIT.
RELAX. I'LL HANDLE THIS.

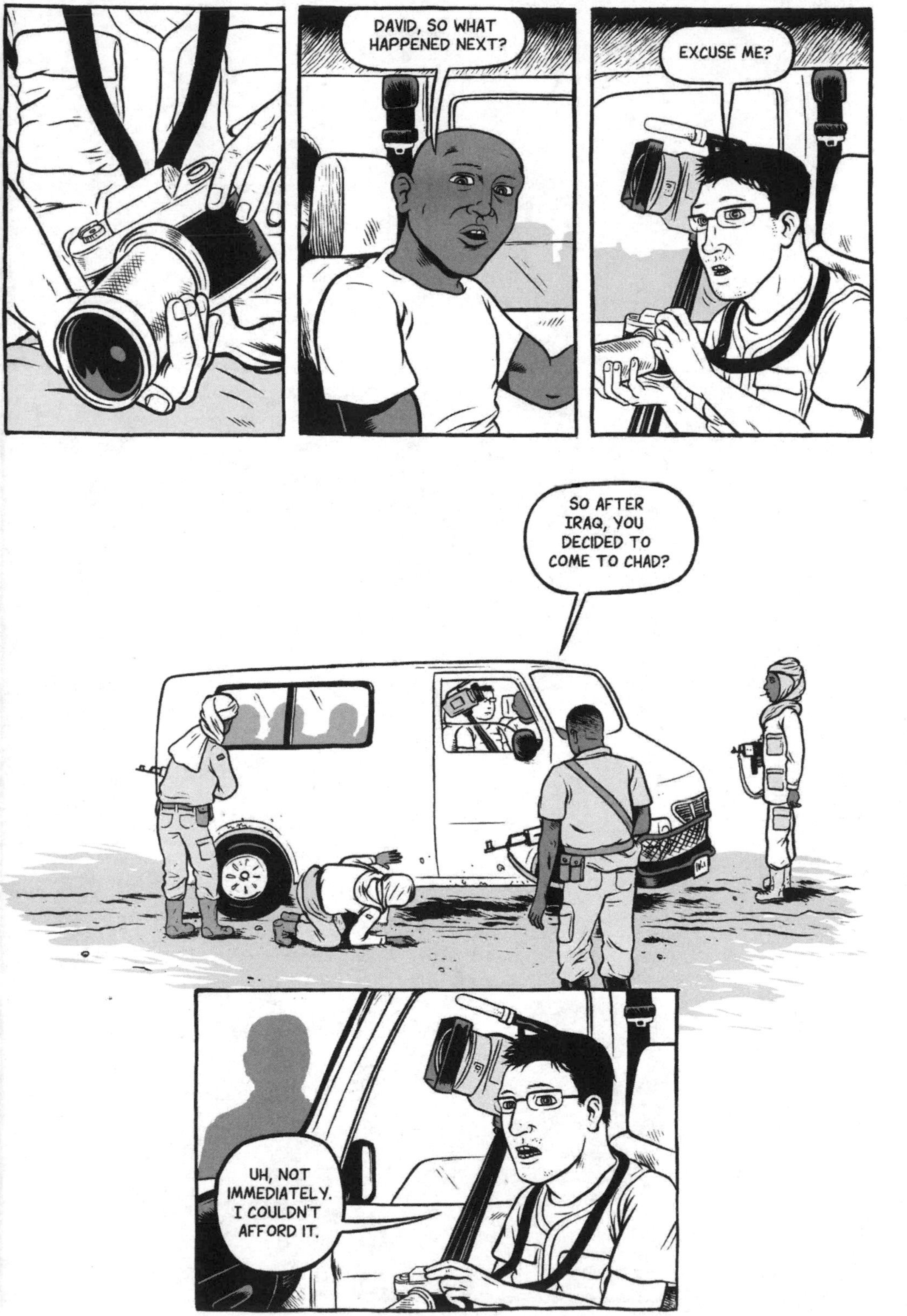
DAVID, SO WHAT HAPPENED NEXT?
EXCUSE ME?
SO AFTER IRAQ, YOU DECIDED TO COME TO CHAD?
UH, NOT IMMEDIATELY. I COULDN'T AFFORD IT.

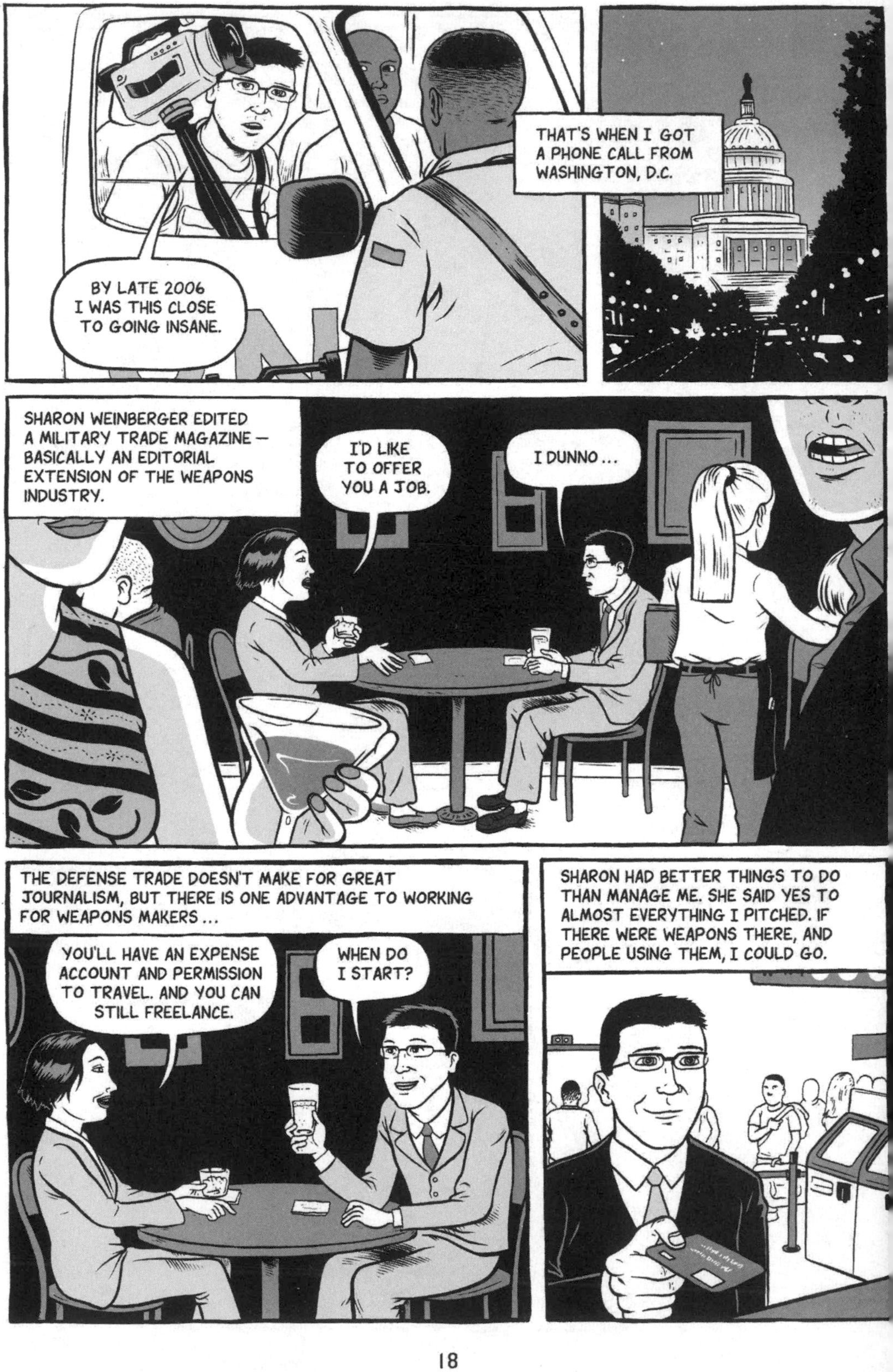
BY LATE 2006 I WAS THIS CLOSE TO GOING INSANE.
THAT'S WHEN I GOT A PHONE CALL FROM WASHINGTON, D.C.
SHARON WEINBERGER EDITED A MILITARY TRADE MAGAZINE — BASICALLY AN EDITORIAL EXTENSION OF THE WEAPONS INDUSTRY.
I'D LIKE TO OFFER YOU A JOB.
I DUNNO ...
THE DEFENSE TRADE DOESN'T MAKE FOR GREAT JOURNALISM, BUT THERE IS ONE ADVANTAGE TO WORKING FOR WEAPONS MAKERS ...
YOU'LL HAVE AN EXPENSE ACCOUNT AND PERMISSION TO TRAVEL. AND YOU CAN STILL FREELANCE.
WHEN DO I START?
SHARON HAD BETTER THINGS TO DO THAN MANAGE ME. SHE SAID YES TO ALMOST EVERYTHING I PITCHED. IF THERE WERE WEAPONS THERE, AND PEOPLE USING THEM, I COULD GO.

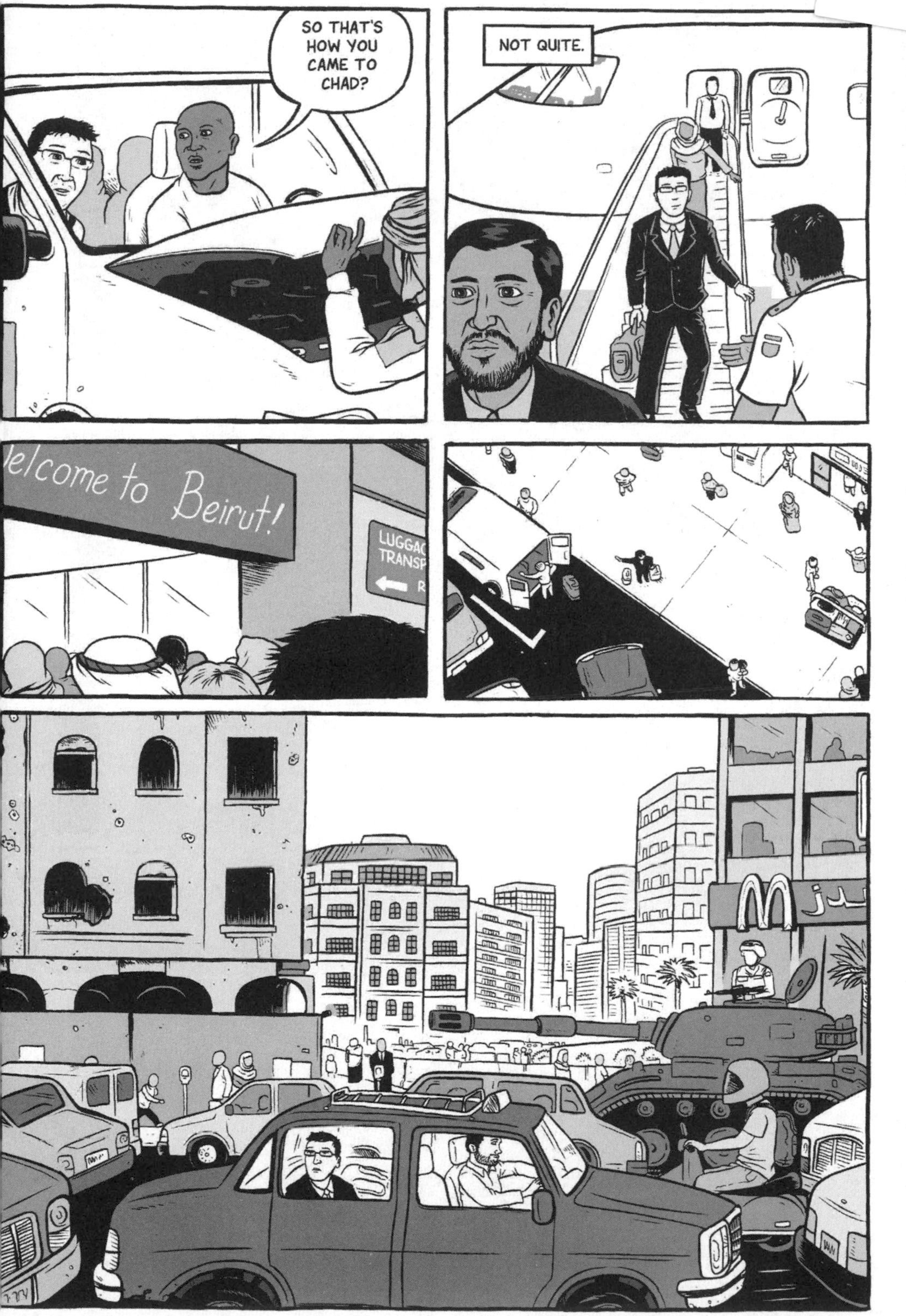
SO THAT'S HOW YOU CAME TO CHAD?
NOT QUITE.
Welcome to Beirut!

LEBANON

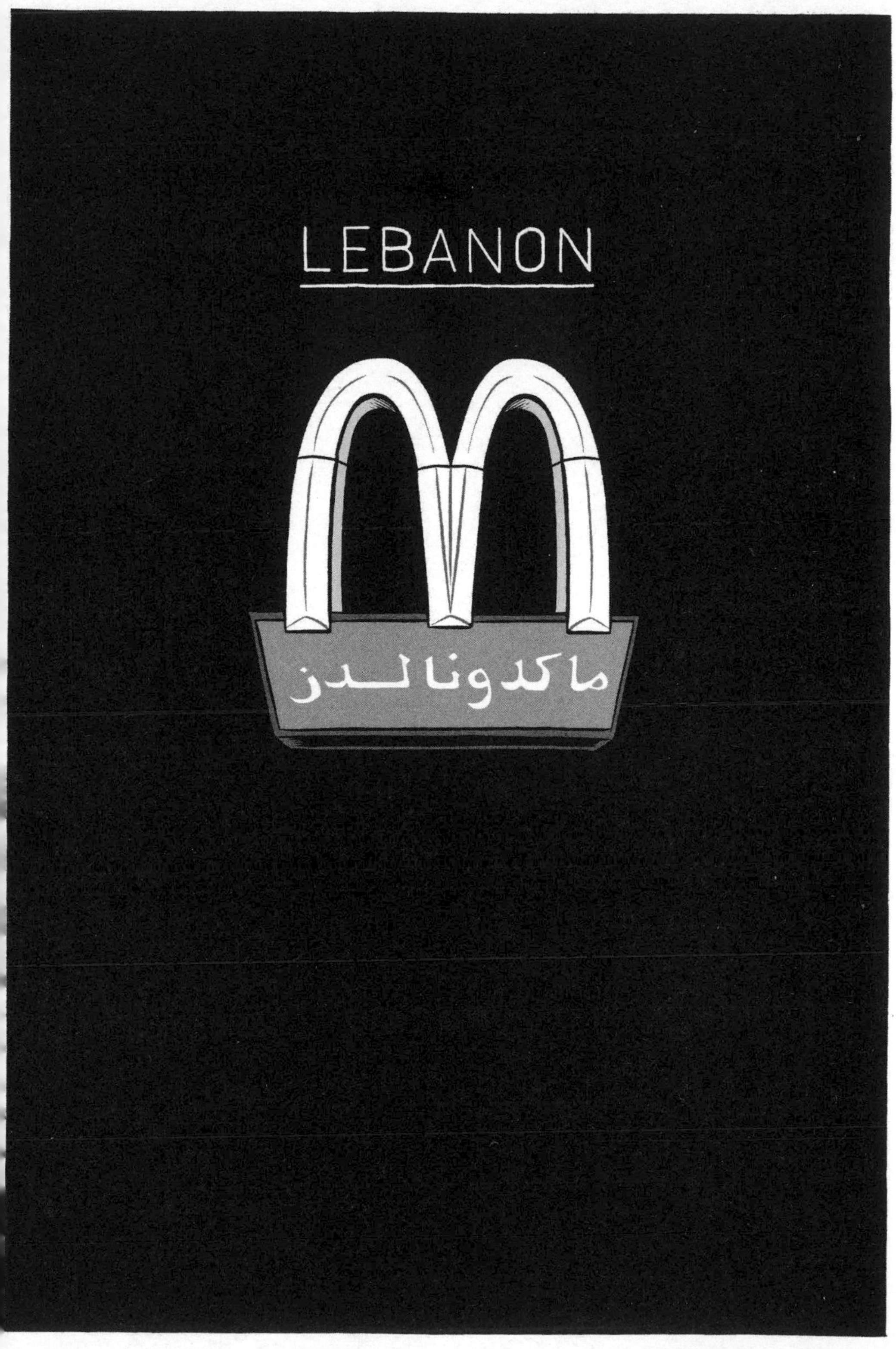
ماكدونالدز

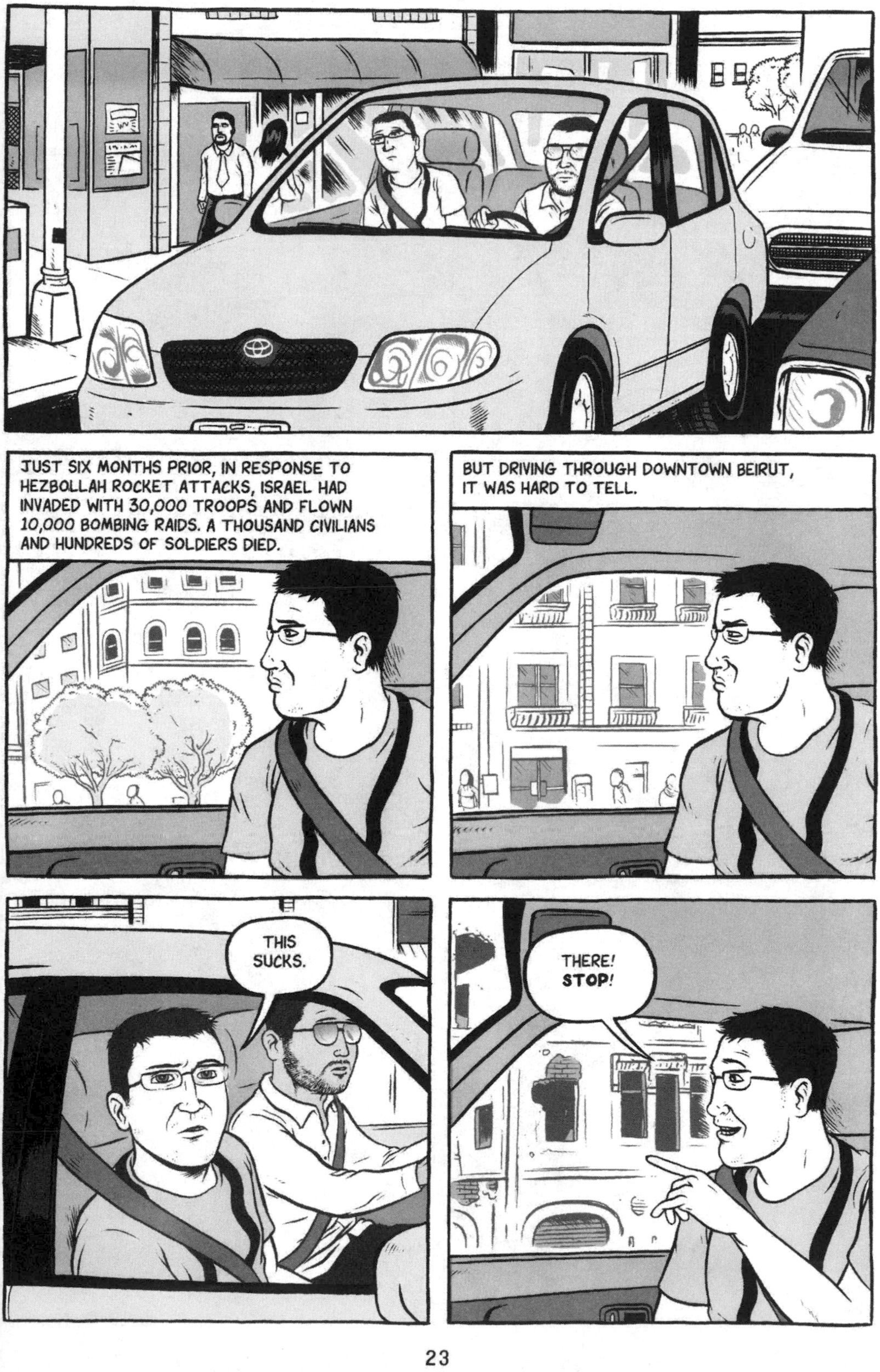
JUST SIX MONTHS PRIOR, IN RESPONSE TO HEZBOLLAH ROCKET ATTACKS, ISRAEL HAD INVADED WITH 30,000 TROOPS AND FLOWN 10,000 BOMBING RAIDS. A THOUSAND CIVILIANS AND HUNDREDS OF SOLDIERS DIED.
BUT DRIVING THROUGH DOWNTOWN BEIRUT, IT WAS HARD TO TELL.
THIS SUCKS.
THERE! **STOP!**

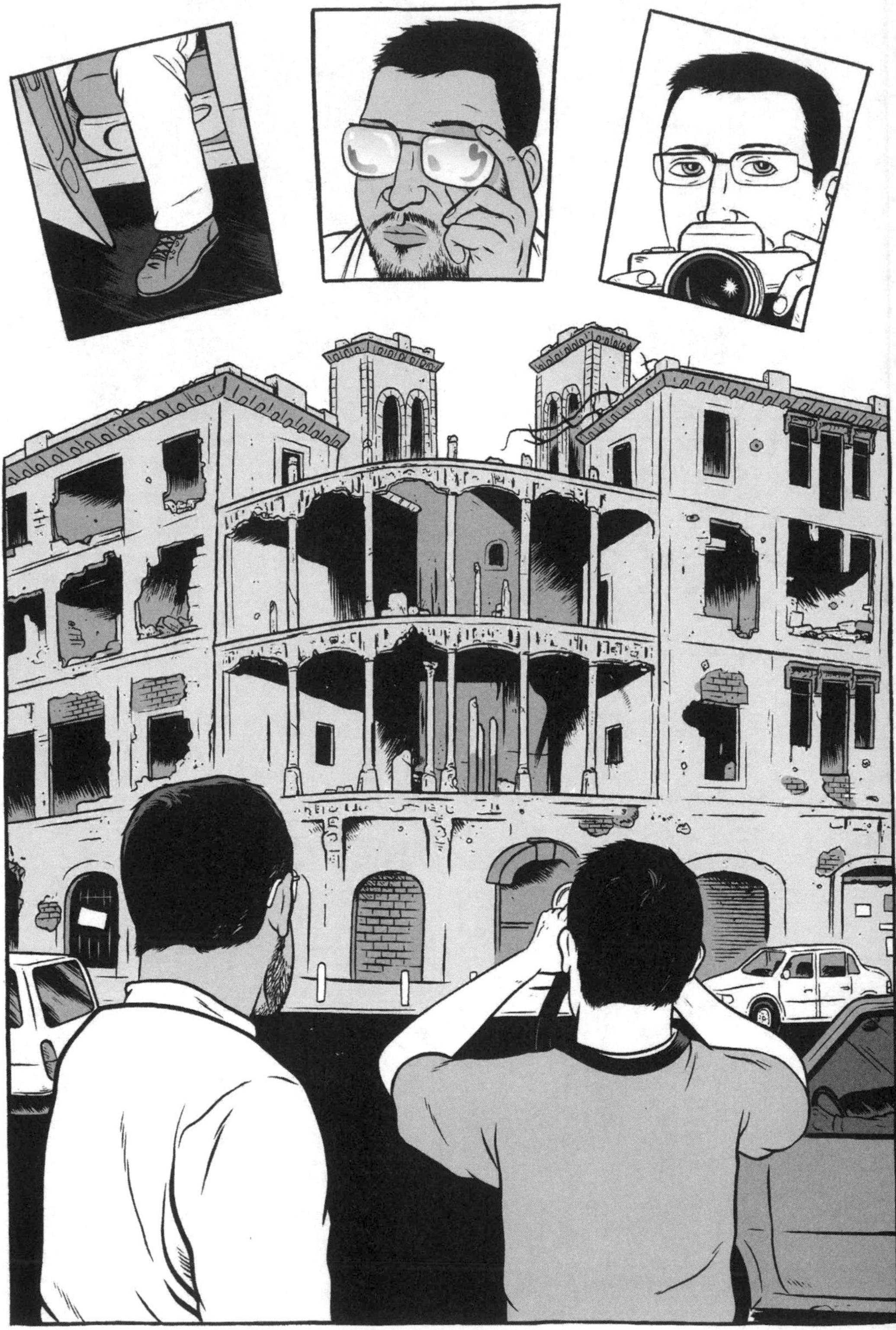

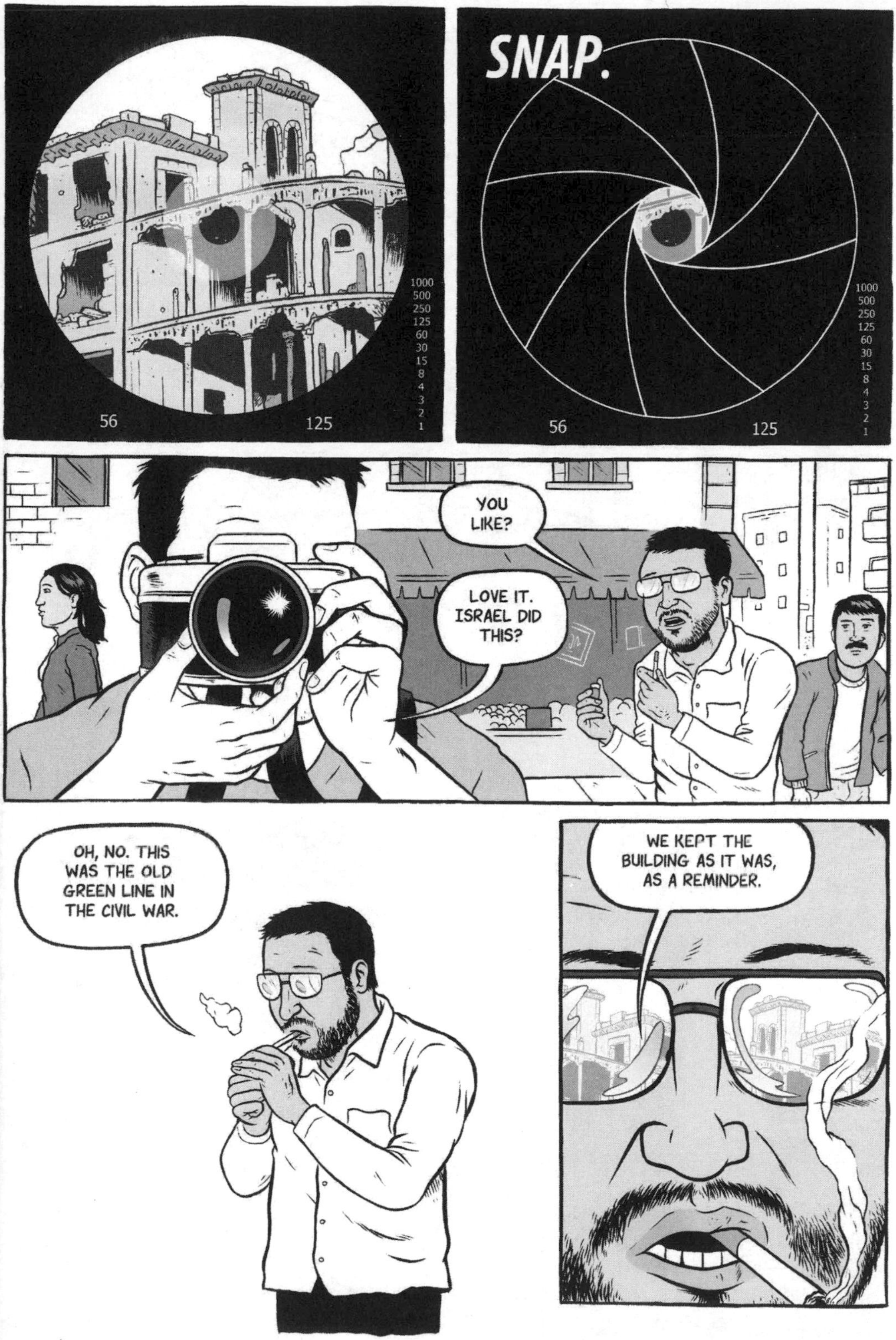
56
125
1000 500 250 125 60 30 15 8 4 3 2 1
SNAP.
56
125
1000 500 250 125 60 30 15 8 4 3 2 1
YOU LIKE?
LOVE IT. ISRAEL DID THIS?
OH, NO. THIS WAS THE OLD GREEN LINE IN THE CIVIL WAR.
WE KEPT THE BUILDING AS IT WAS, AS A REMINDER.

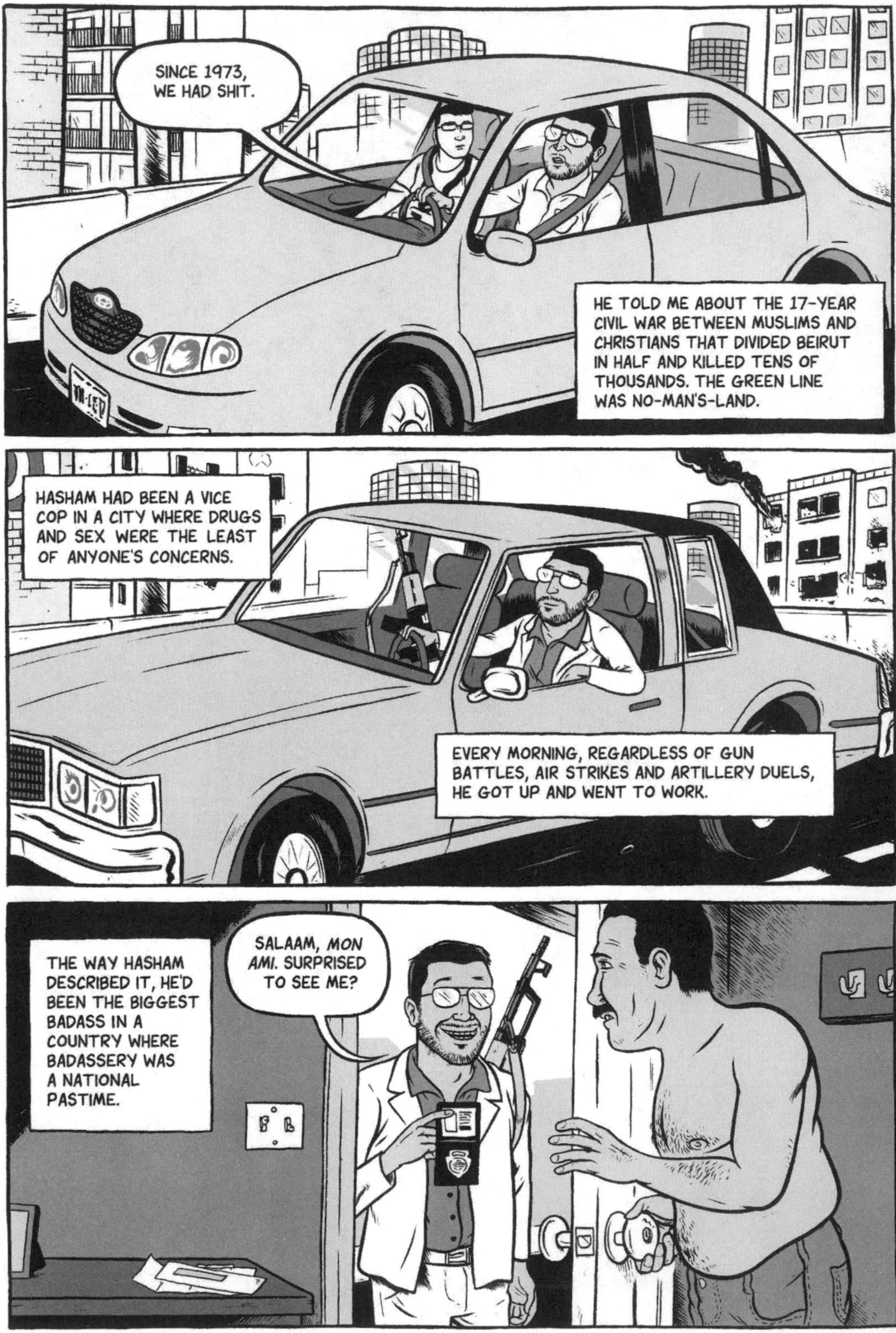
SINCE 1973, WE HAD SHIT.
HE TOLD ME ABOUT THE 17-YEAR CIVIL WAR BETWEEN MUSLIMS AND CHRISTIANS THAT DIVIDED BEIRUT IN HALF AND KILLED TENS OF THOUSANDS. THE GREEN LINE WAS NO-MAN'S-LAND.
HASHAM HAD BEEN A VICE COP IN A CITY WHERE DRUGS AND SEX WERE THE LEAST OF ANYONE'S CONCERNS.
EVERY MORNING, REGARDLESS OF GUN BATTLES, AIR STRIKES AND ARTILLERY DUELS, HE GOT UP AND WENT TO WORK.
THE WAY HASHAM DESCRIBED IT, HE'D BEEN THE BIGGEST BADASS IN A COUNTRY WHERE BADASSERY WAS A NATIONAL PASTIME.
SALAAM, *MON AMI*. SURPRISED TO SEE ME?

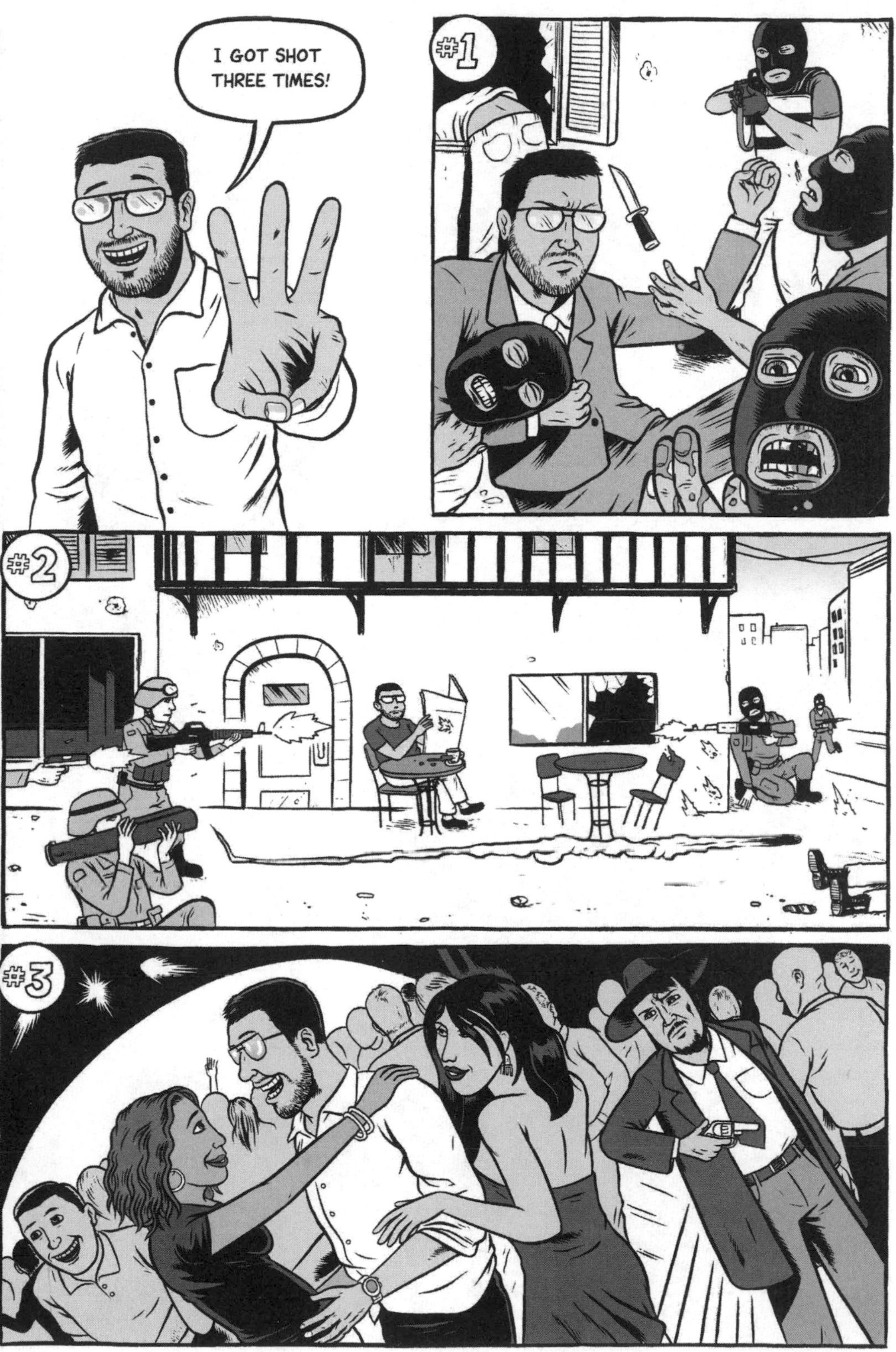
I GOT SHOT THREE TIMES!
#1
#2
#3

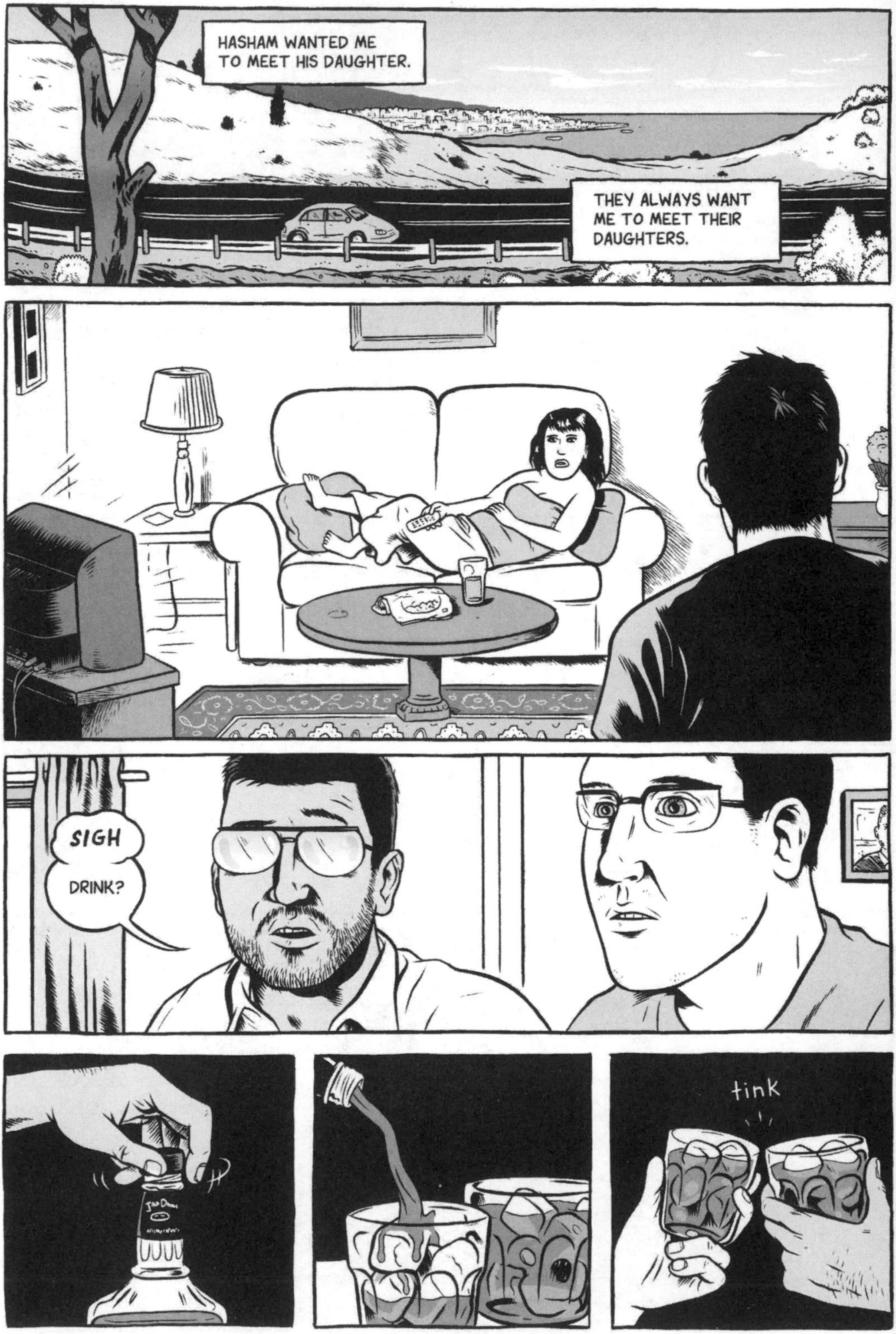
HASHAM WANTED ME TO MEET HIS DAUGHTER.
THEY ALWAYS WANT ME TO MEET THEIR DAUGHTERS.
SIGH
DRINK?
tink

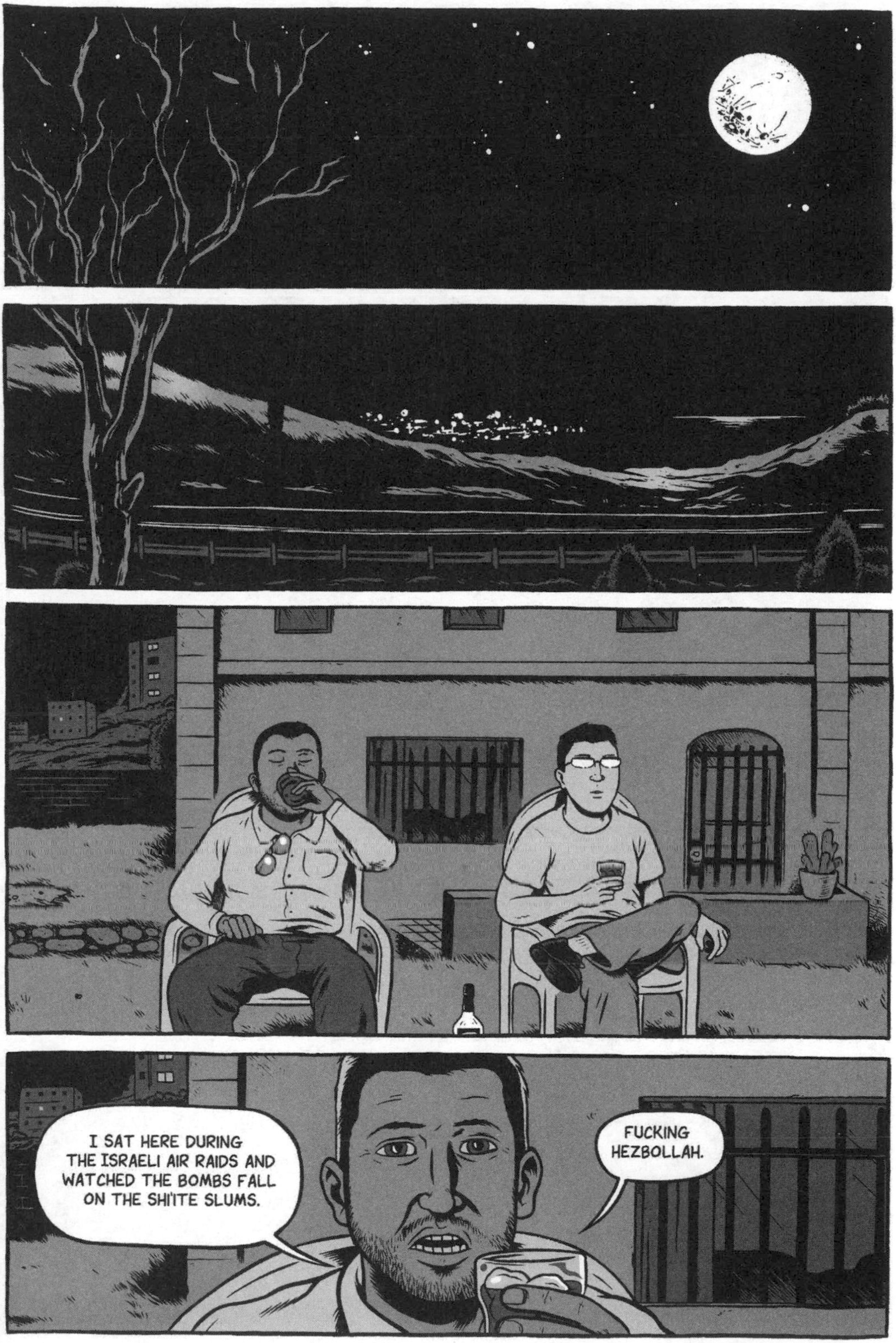
I SAT HERE DURING THE ISRAELI AIR RAIDS AND WATCHED THE BOMBS FALL ON THE SHI'ITE SLUMS.
FUCKING HEZBOLLAH.

THE PLAN I'D SOLD SHARON ON WAS SIMPLE. TRAVEL SOUTH THROUGH HEZBOLLAH TERRITORY TO NAQOURA, ON THE ISRAELI BORDER, WHERE THOUSANDS OF U.N. PEACE-KEEPERS WERE TRYING TO PREVENT A REPEAT OF THE PREVIOUS YEAR'S FIGHTING.

LEBANON

Beirut

Damour

Beit ed
Dine

Barja

Sidon

Qaraaoun

Ad

Tyre

SYR

Naqoura

Qatana

ISRAEL

Gadot

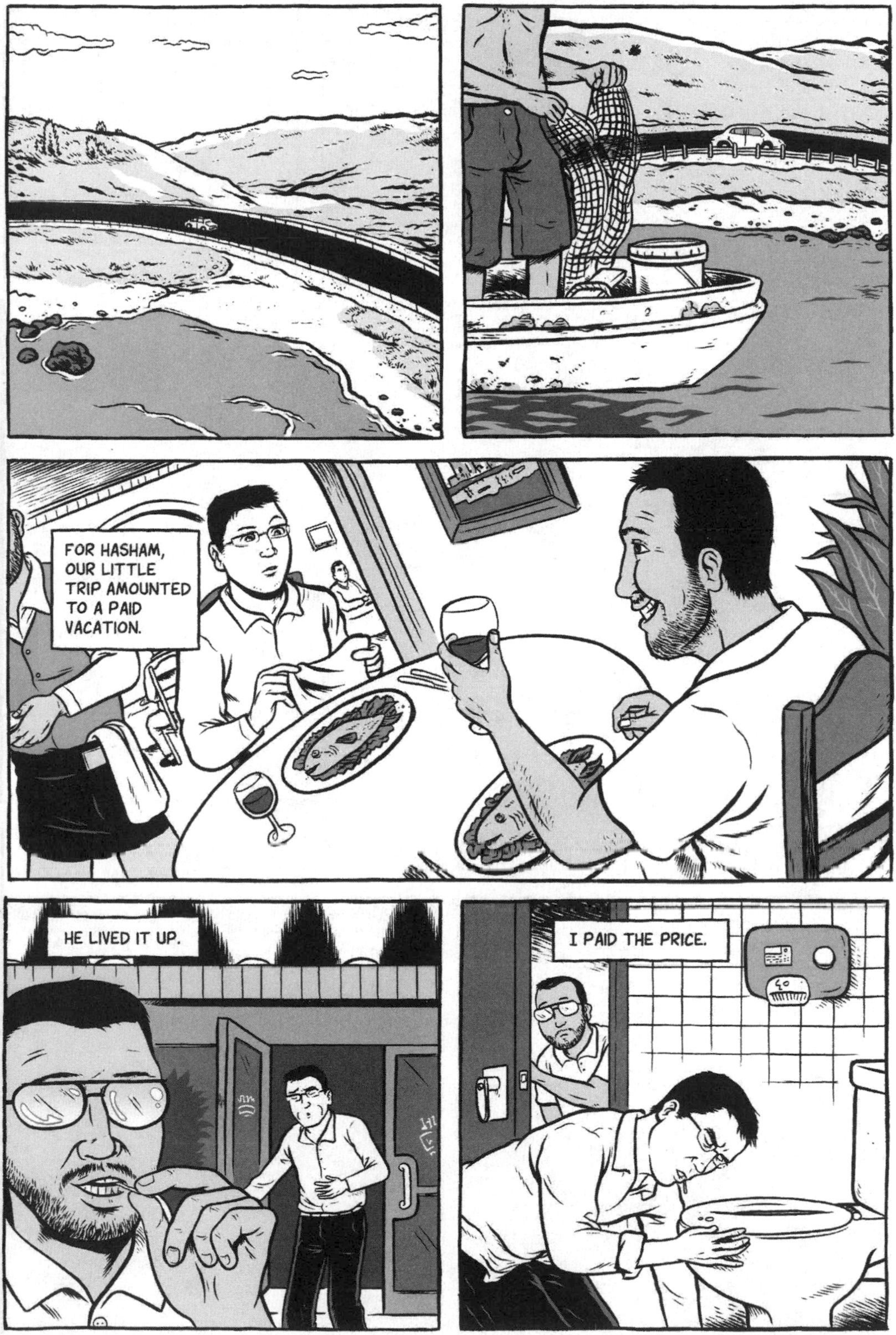
FOR HASHAM, OUR LITTLE TRIP AMOUNTED TO A PAID VACATION.
HE LIVED IT UP.
I PAID THE PRICE.

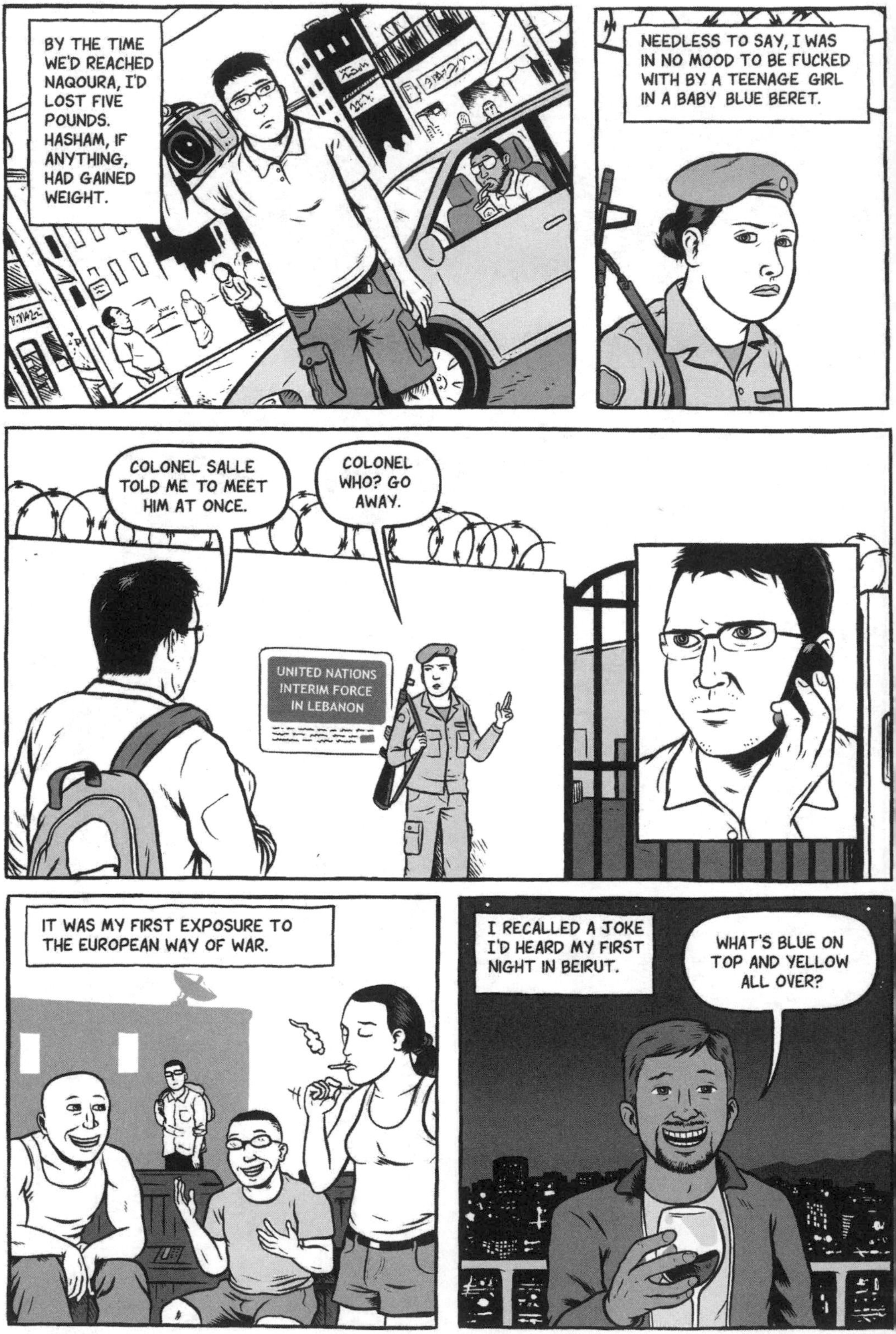

BY THE TIME WE'D REACHED NAQOURA, I'D LOST FIVE POUNDS. HASHAM, IF ANYTHING, HAD GAINED WEIGHT.
NEEDLESS TO SAY, I WAS IN NO MOOD TO BE FUCKED WITH BY A TEENAGE GIRL IN A BABY BLUE BERET.
COLONEL SALLE TOLD ME TO MEET HIM AT ONCE.
COLONEL WHO? GO AWAY.
UNITED NATIONS INTERIM FORCE IN LEBANON
IT WAS MY FIRST EXPOSURE TO THE EUROPEAN WAY OF WAR.
I RECALLED A JOKE I'D HEARD MY FIRST NIGHT IN BEIRUT.
WHAT'S BLUE ON TOP AND YELLOW ALL OVER?

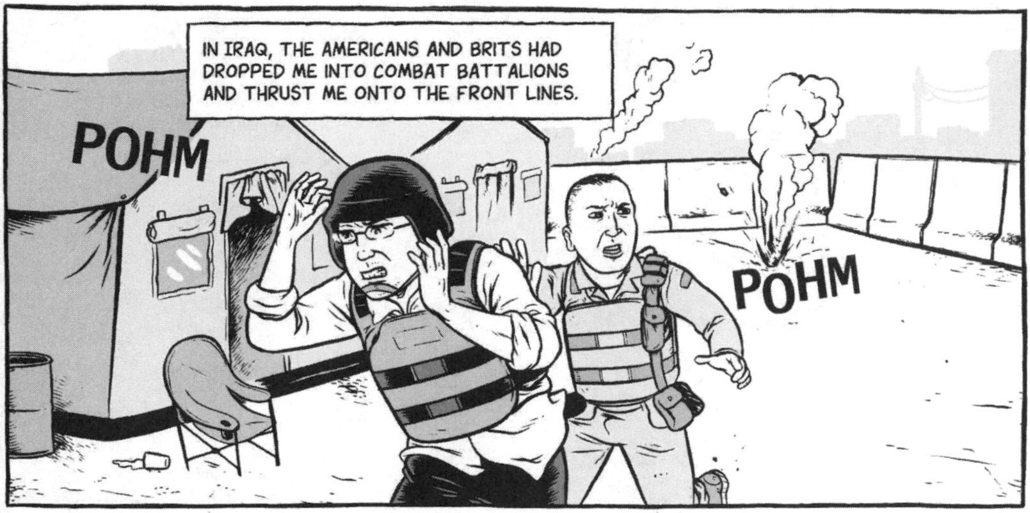
IN IRAQ, THE AMERICANS AND BRITS HAD DROPPED ME INTO COMBAT BATTALIONS AND THRUST ME ONTO THE FRONT LINES.
POHM
POHM

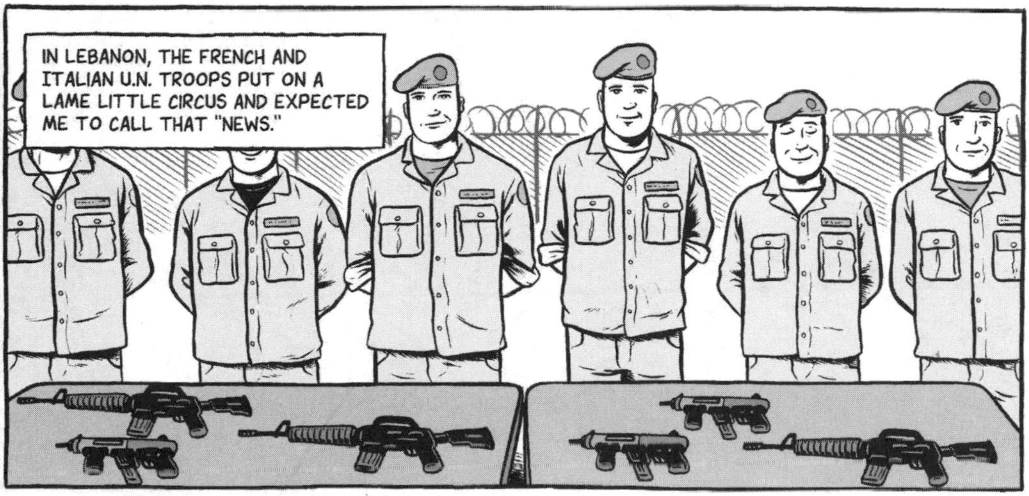
IN LEBANON, THE FRENCH AND ITALIAN U.N. TROOPS PUT ON A LAME LITTLE CIRCUS AND EXPECTED ME TO CALL THAT "NEWS."

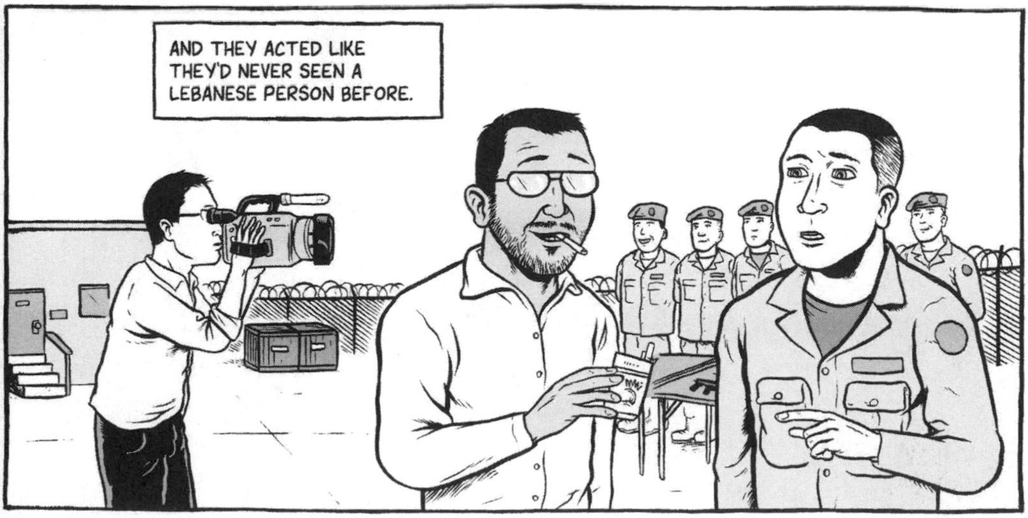
AND THEY ACTED LIKE THEY'D NEVER SEEN A LEBANESE PERSON BEFORE.

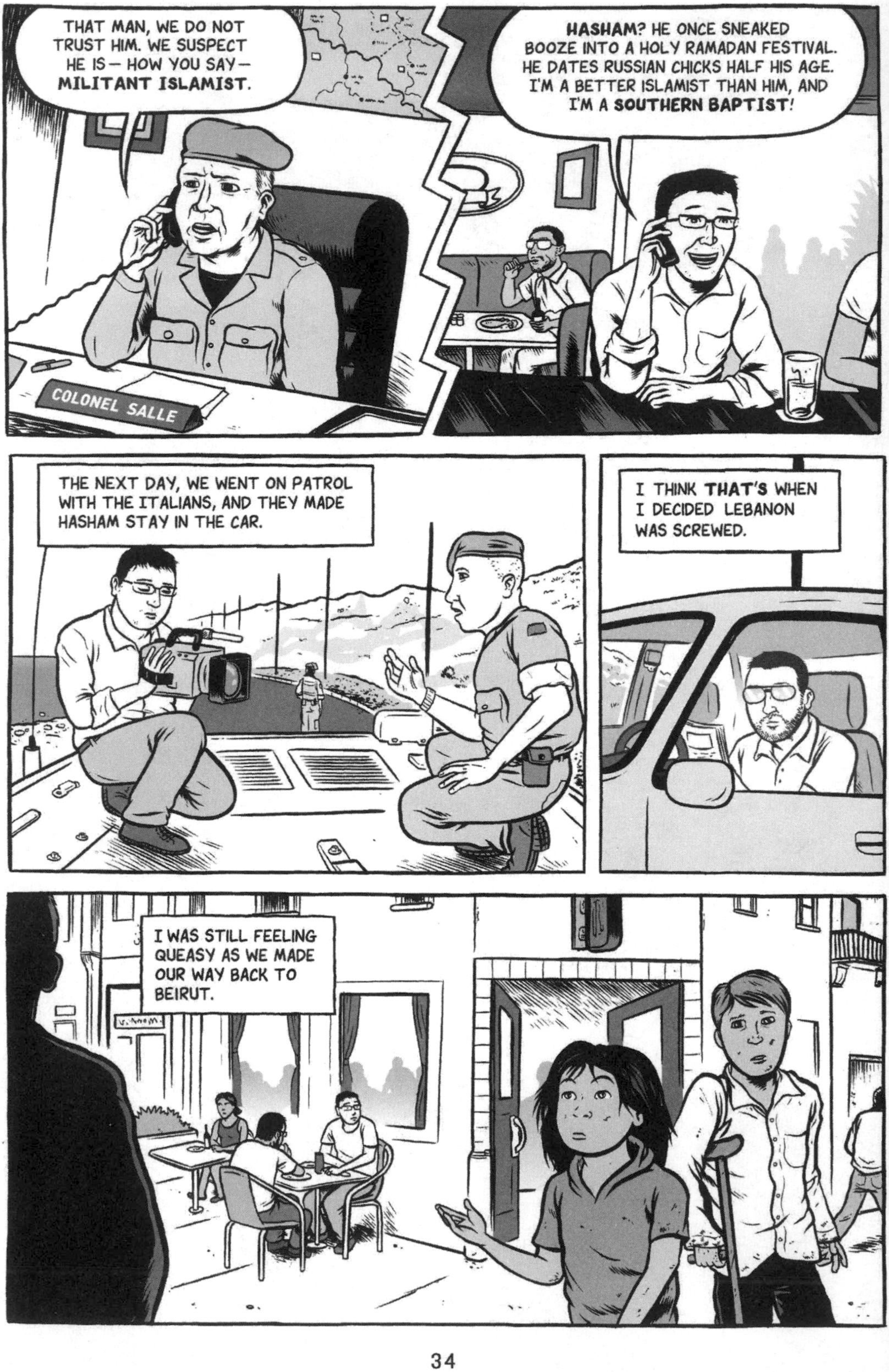
THAT MAN, WE DO NOT TRUST HIM. WE SUSPECT HE IS — HOW YOU SAY — MILITANT ISLAMIST.
COLONEL SALLE
HASHAM? HE ONCE SNEAKED BOOZE INTO A HOLY RAMADAN FESTIVAL. HE DATES RUSSIAN CHICKS HALF HIS AGE. I'M A BETTER ISLAMIST THAN HIM, AND I'M A SOUTHERN BAPTIST!
THE NEXT DAY, WE WENT ON PATROL WITH THE ITALIANS, AND THEY MADE HASHAM STAY IN THE CAR.
I THINK THAT'S WHEN I DECIDED LEBANON WAS SCREWED.
I WAS STILL FEELING QUEASY AS WE MADE OUR WAY BACK TO BEIRUT.

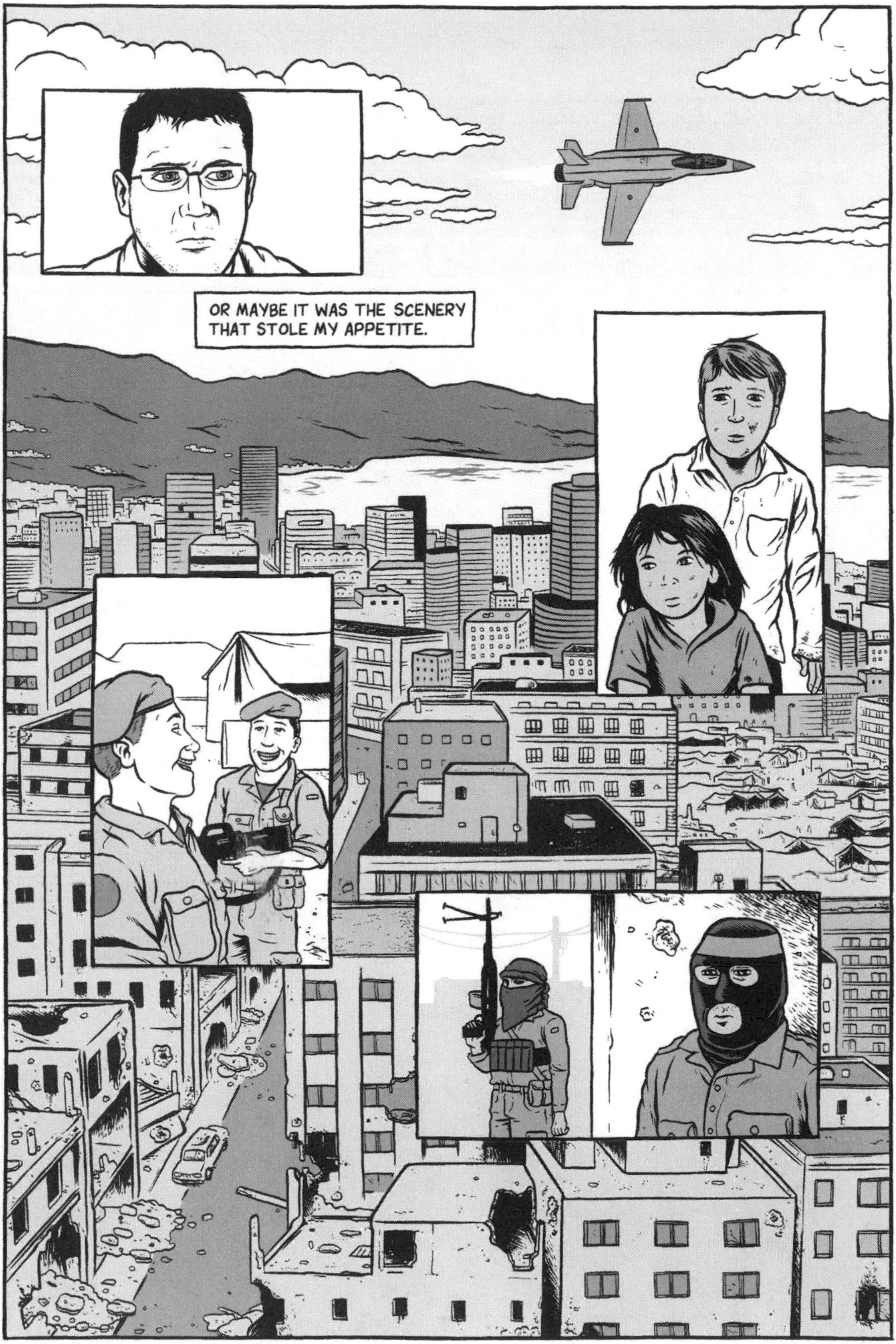
OR MAYBE IT WAS THE SCENERY THAT STOLE MY APPETITE.

WASHINGTON, D.C.

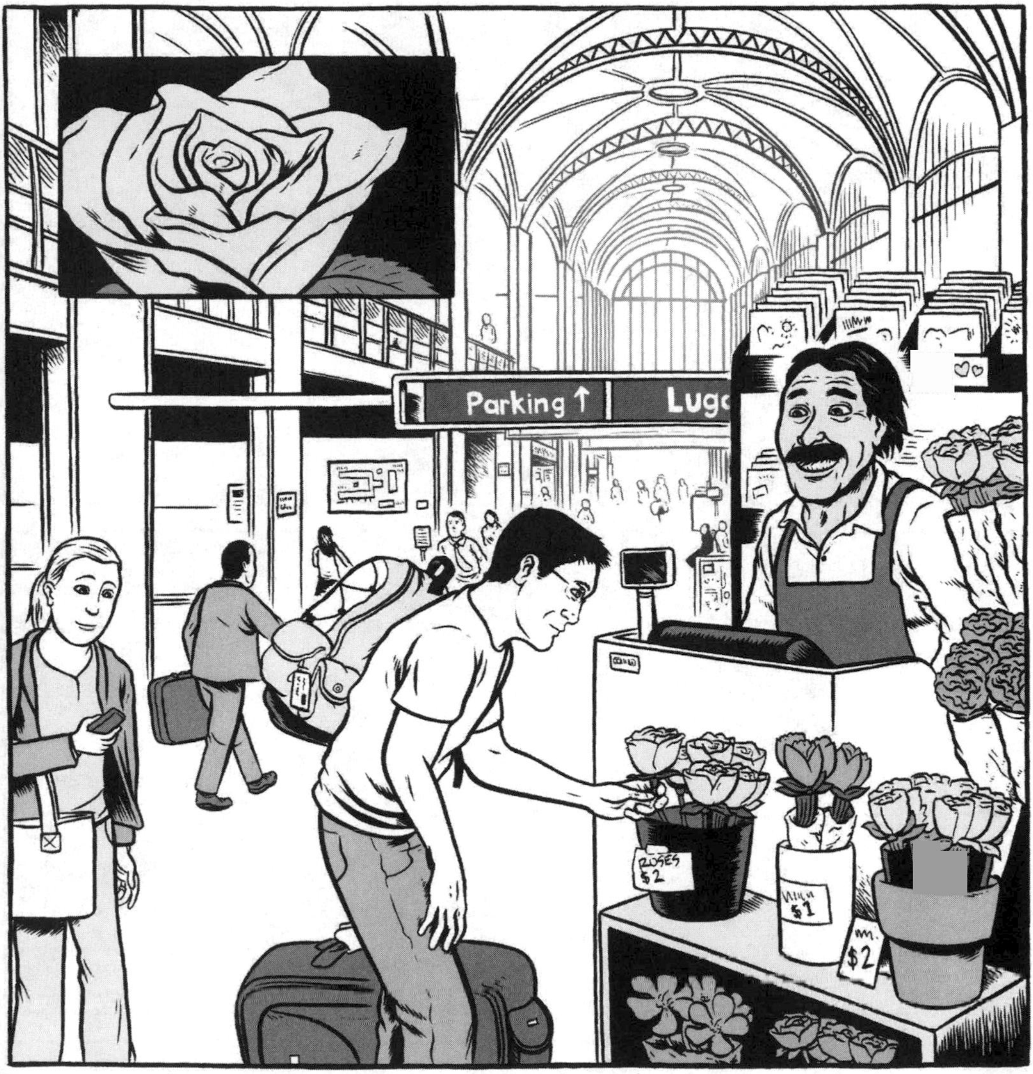
Parking ↑
ROSES $2
$1
$2

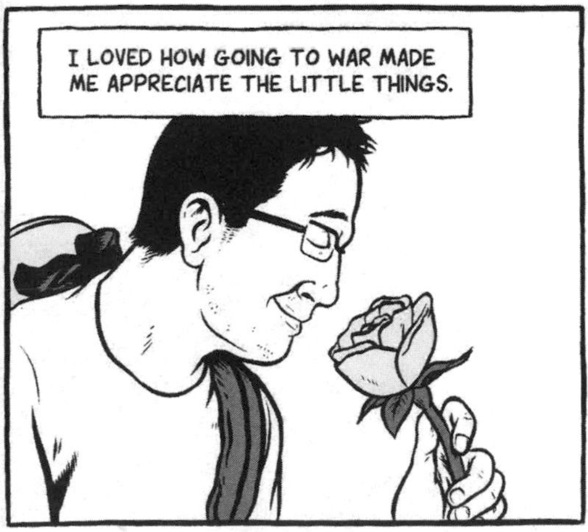
I LOVED HOW GOING TO WAR MADE ME APPRECIATE THE LITTLE THINGS.

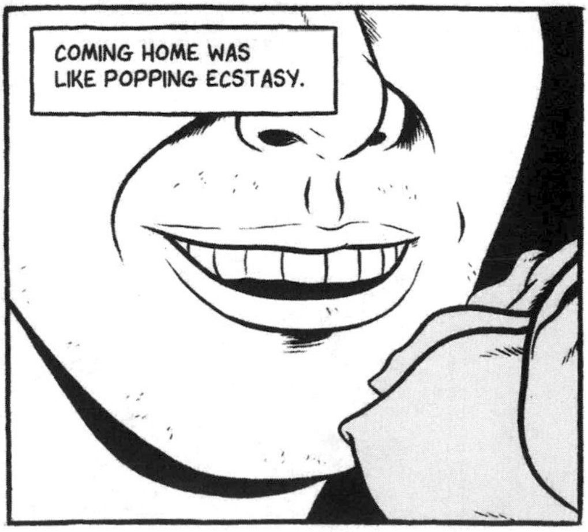
COMING HOME WAS LIKE POPPING ECSTASY.

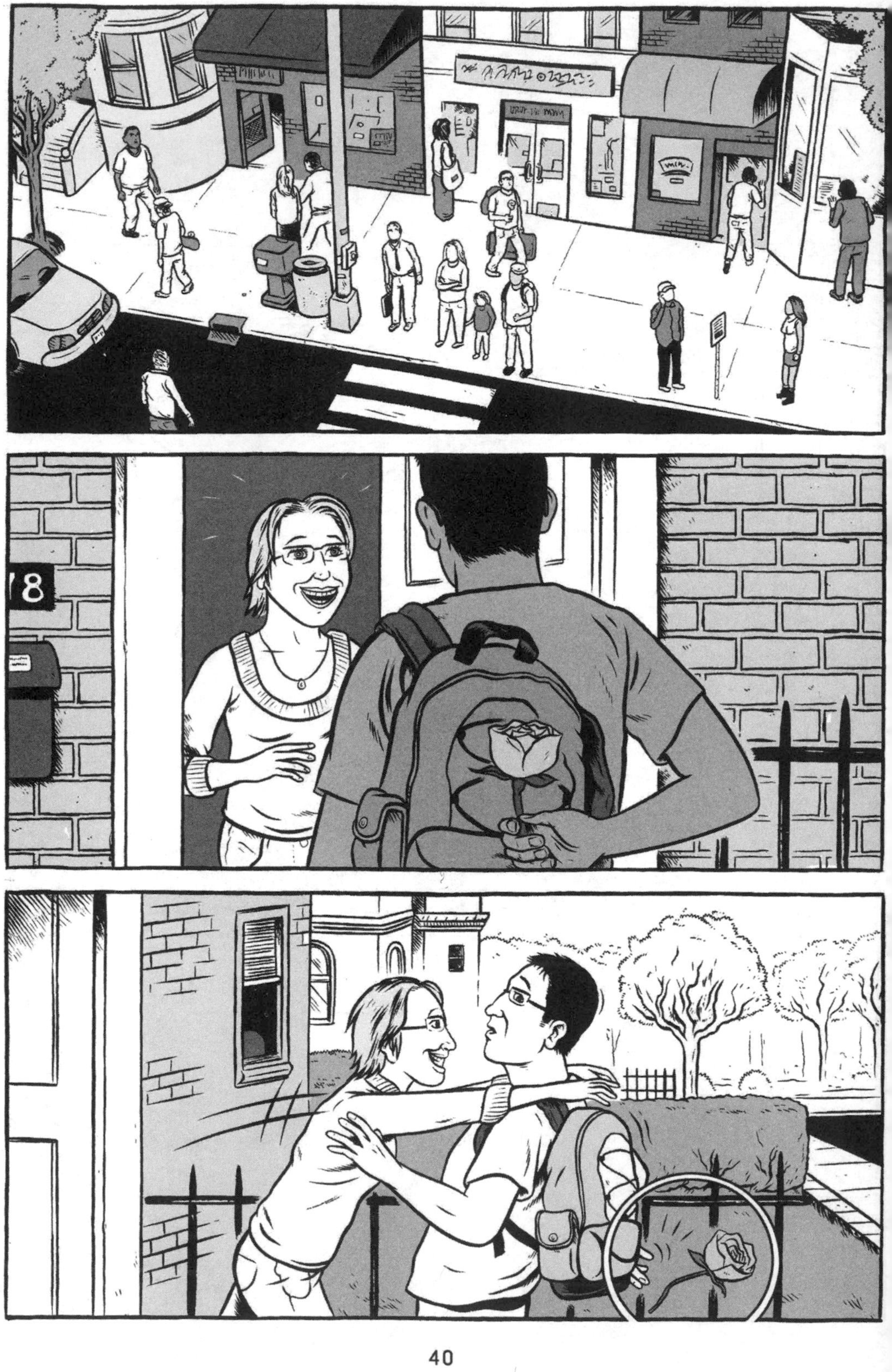

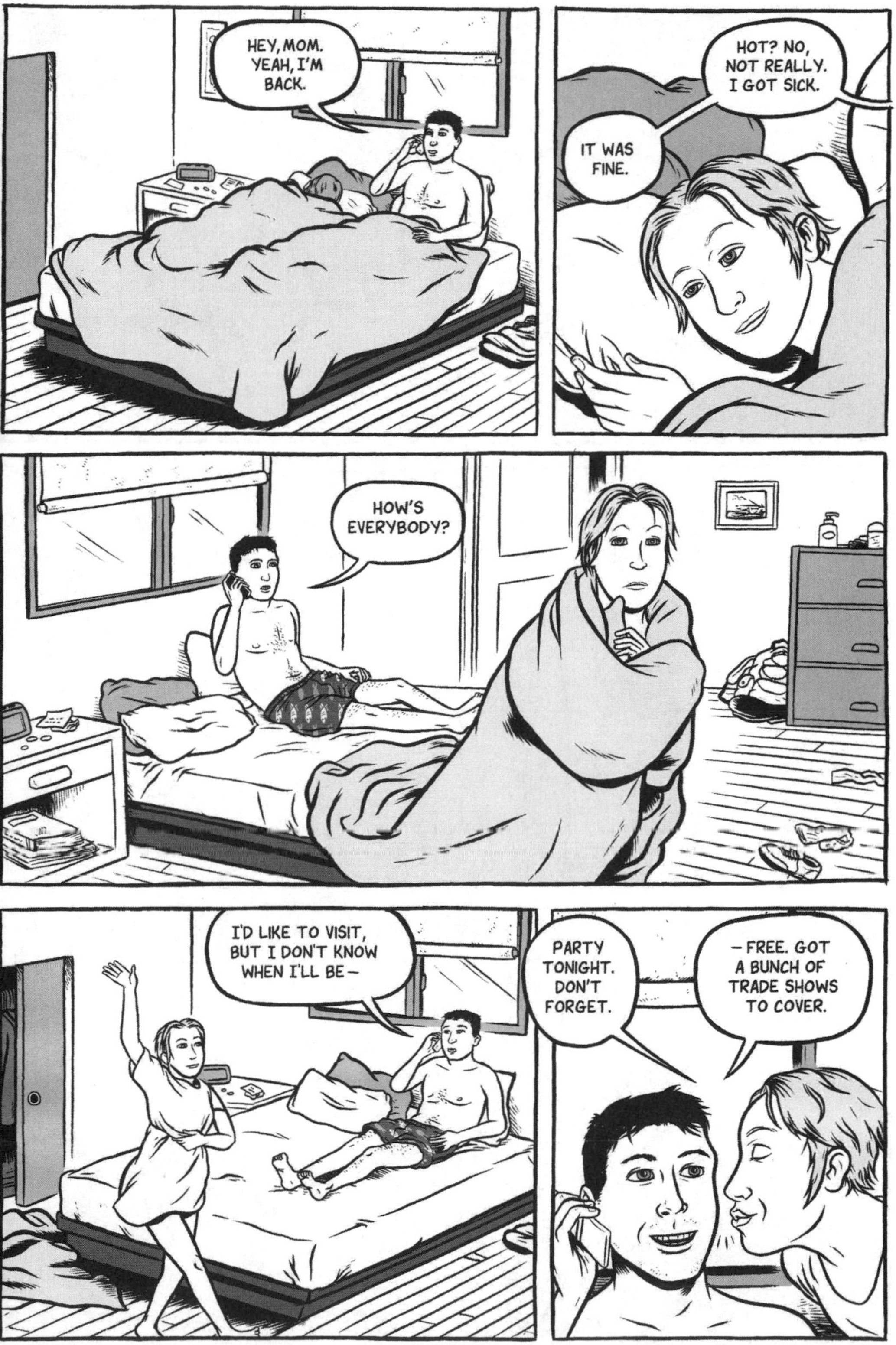
HEY, MOM. YEAH, I'M BACK.
HOT? NO, NOT REALLY. I GOT SICK.
IT WAS FINE.
HOW'S EVERYBODY?
I'D LIKE TO VISIT, BUT I DON'T KNOW WHEN I'LL BE—
PARTY TONIGHT. DON'T FORGET.
—FREE. GOT A BUNCH OF TRADE SHOWS TO COVER.

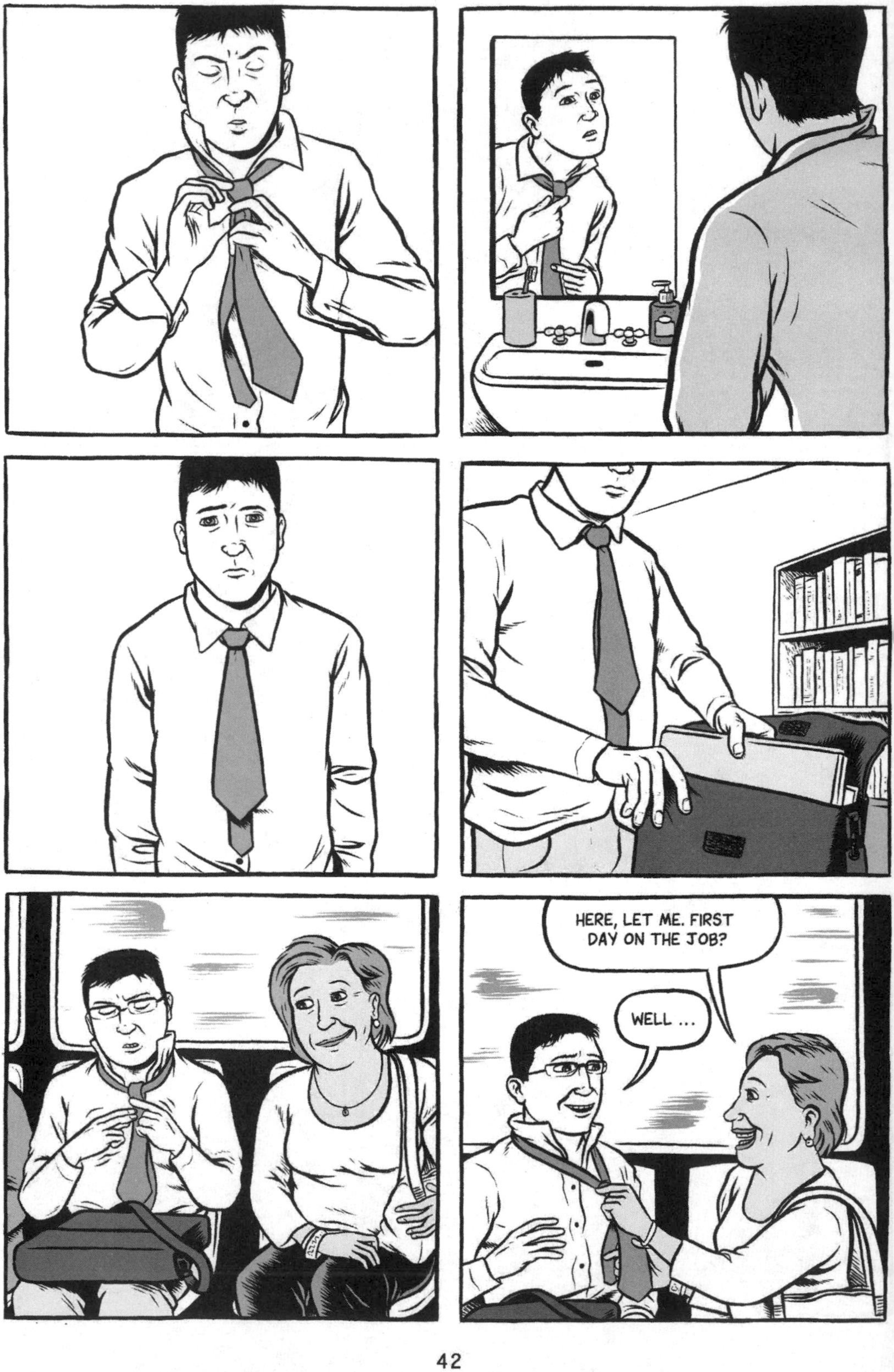
HERE, LET ME. FIRST DAY ON THE JOB?
WELL ...

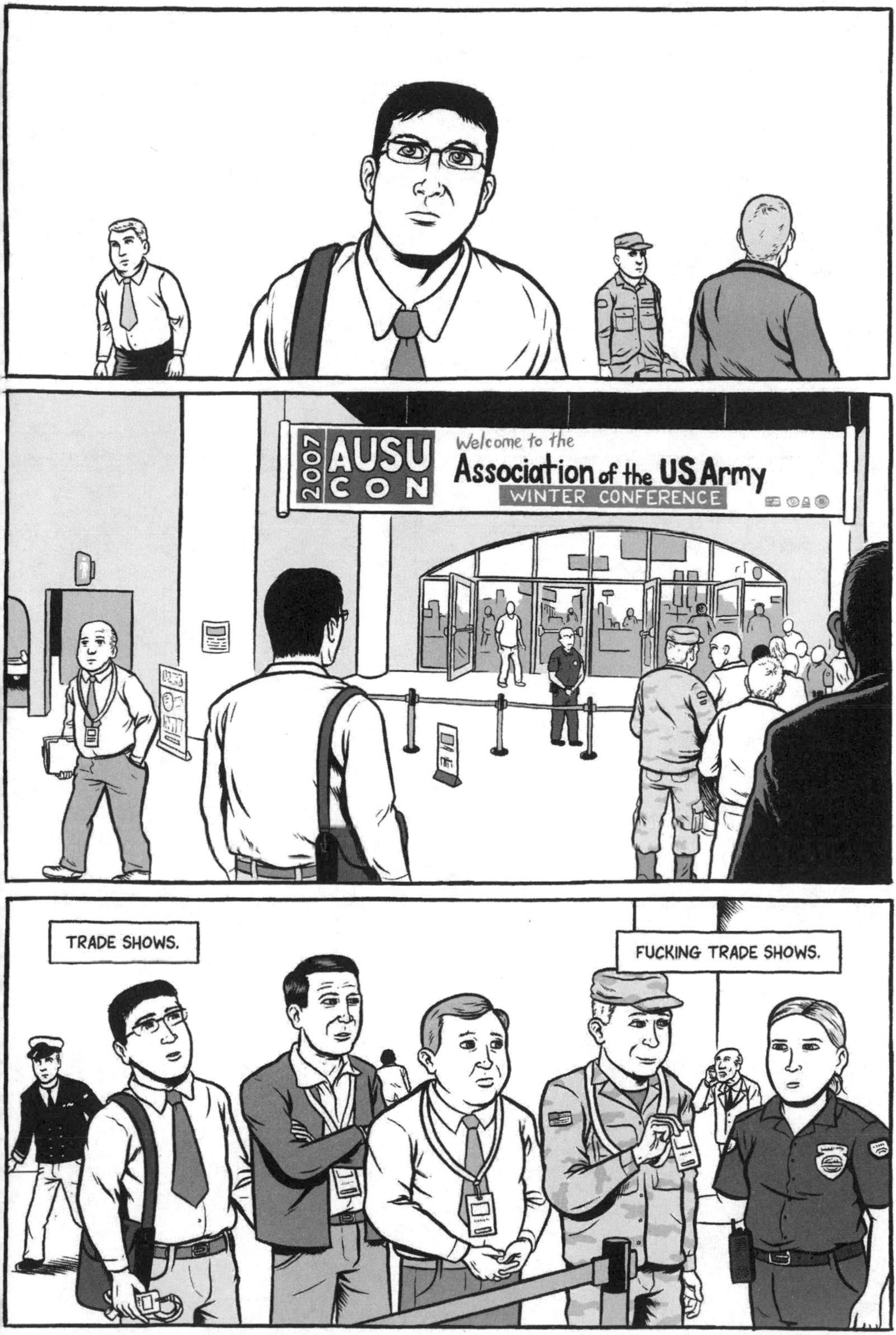
2007
AUSU
CON
Welcome to the
Association of the US Army
WINTER CONFERENCE
TRADE SHOWS.
FUCKING TRADE SHOWS.

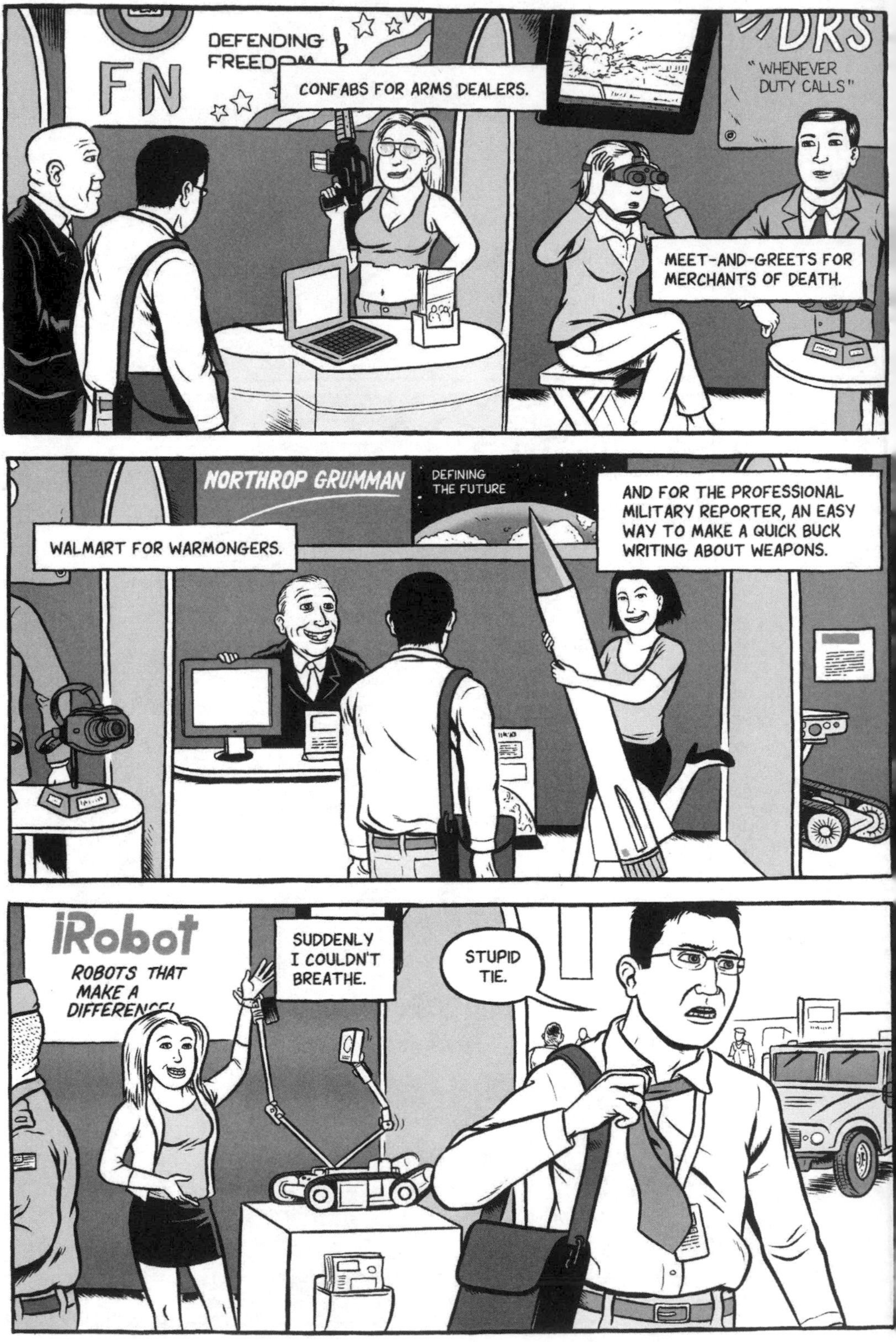
DEFENDING FREEDOM
FN
CONFABS FOR ARMS DEALERS.
DRS
"WHENEVER DUTY CALLS"
MEET-AND-GREETS FOR MERCHANTS OF DEATH.
NORTHROP GRUMMAN
DEFINING THE FUTURE
WALMART FOR WARMONGERS.
AND FOR THE PROFESSIONAL MILITARY REPORTER, AN EASY WAY TO MAKE A QUICK BUCK WRITING ABOUT WEAPONS.
iRobot
ROBOTS THAT MAKE A DIFFERENCE!
SUDDENLY I COULDN'T BREATHE.
STUPID TIE.

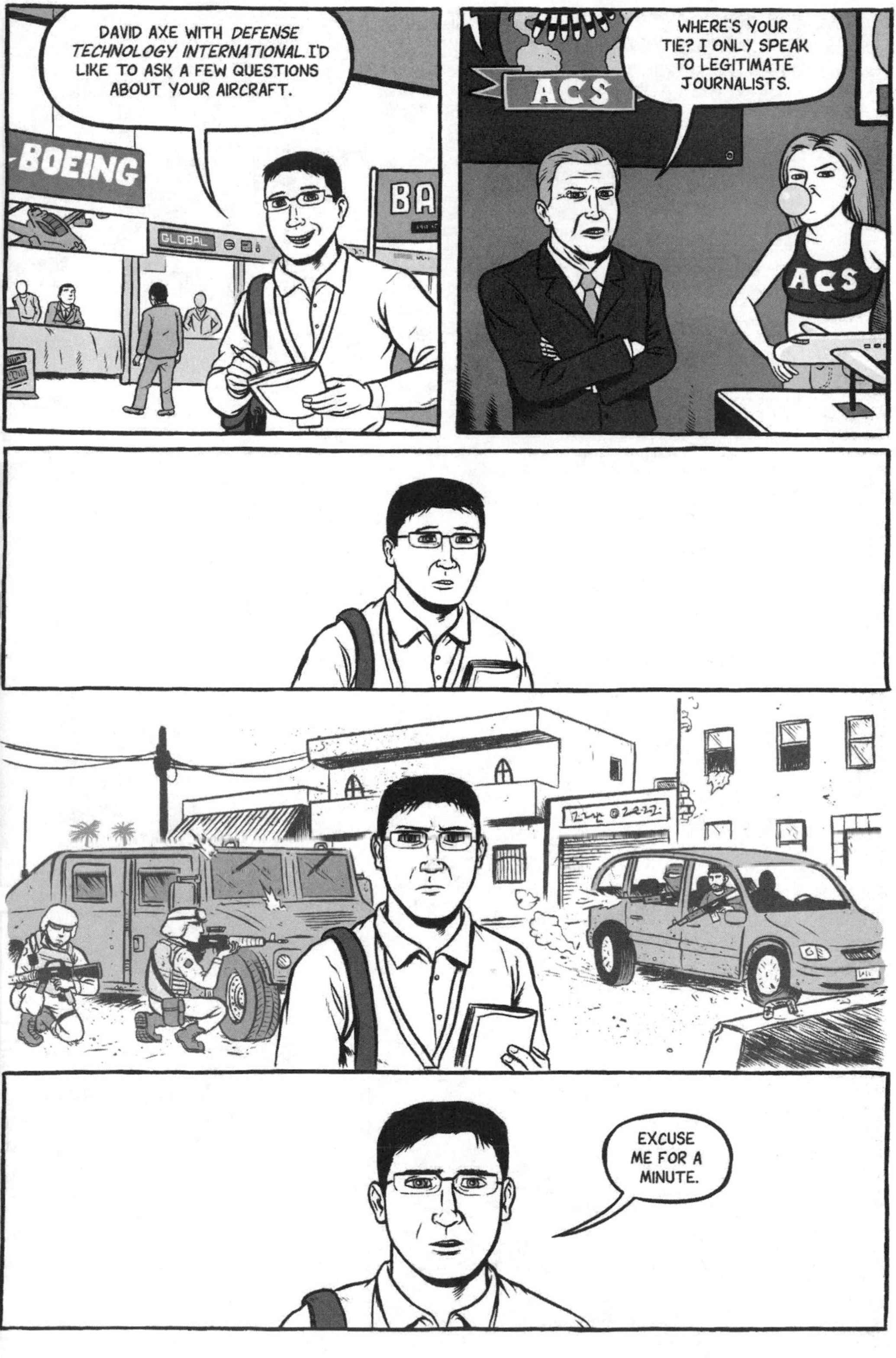
DAVID AXE WITH *DEFENSE TECHNOLOGY INTERNATIONAL.* I'D LIKE TO ASK A FEW QUESTIONS ABOUT YOUR AIRCRAFT.
BOEING
GLOBAL
BA
ACS
WHERE'S YOUR TIE? I ONLY SPEAK TO LEGITIMATE JOURNALISTS.
ACS
EXCUSE ME FOR A MINUTE.

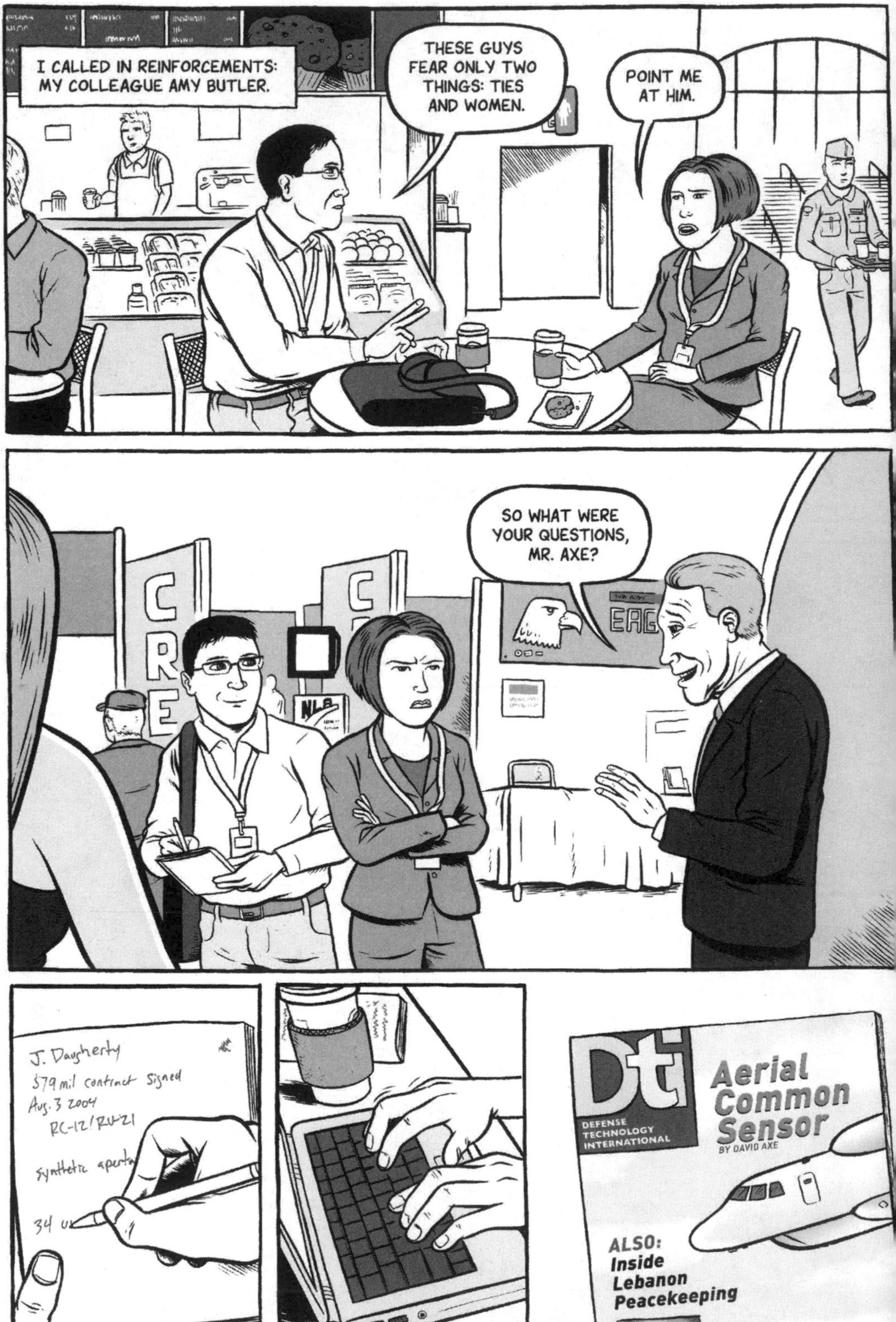
I CALLED IN REINFORCEMENTS: MY COLLEAGUE AMY BUTLER.
THESE GUYS FEAR ONLY TWO THINGS: TIES AND WOMEN.
POINT ME AT HIM.
SO WHAT WERE YOUR QUESTIONS, MR. AXE?
J. Daugherty
$79 mil contract signed
Aug. 3 2004
RC-12/RU-21
DEFENSE TECHNOLOGY INTERNATIONAL
Aerial Common Sensor
BY DAVID AXE
ALSO:
Inside Lebanon Peacekeeping

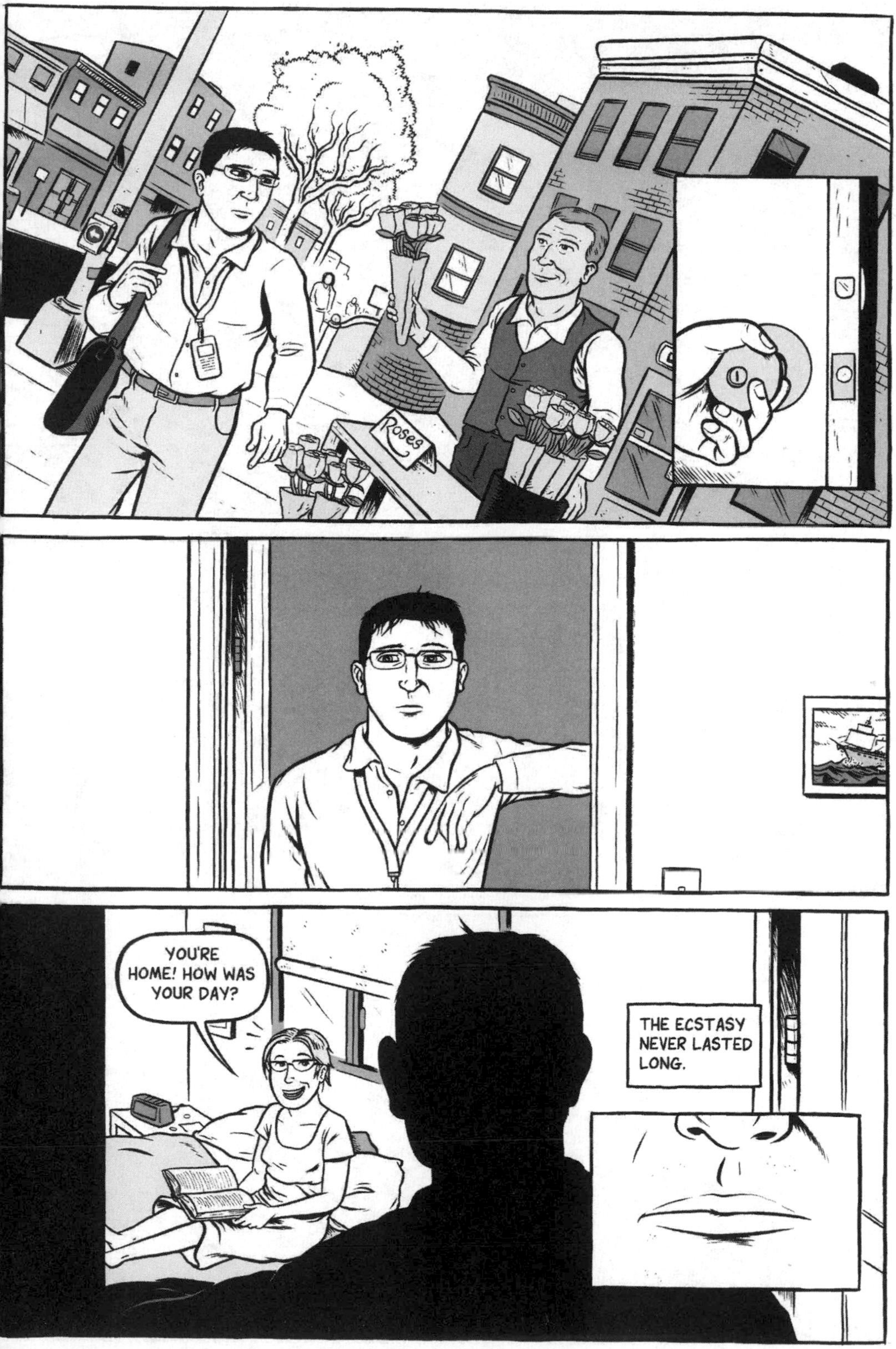
Roses
YOU'RE HOME! HOW WAS YOUR DAY?
THE ECSTASY NEVER LASTED LONG.

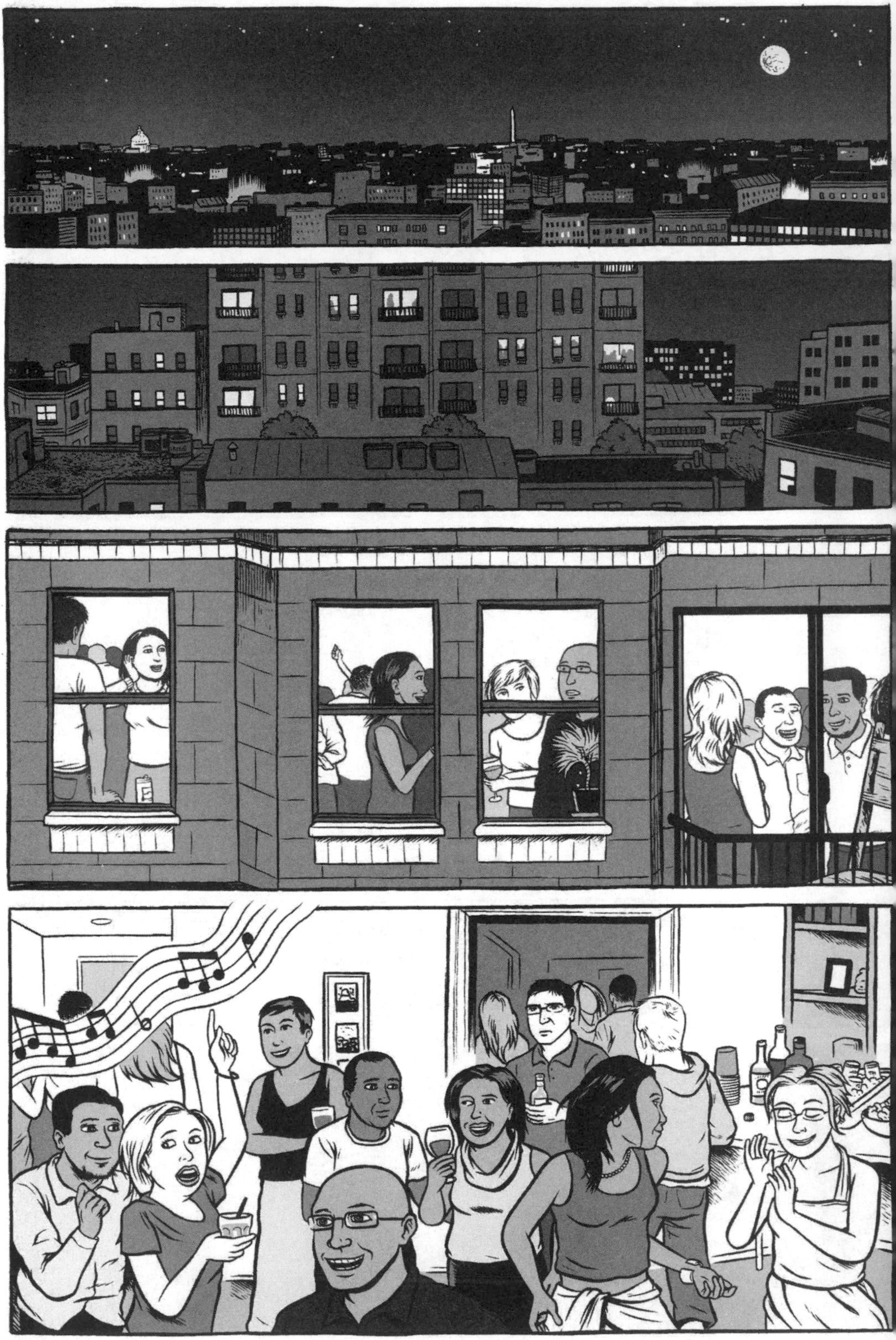

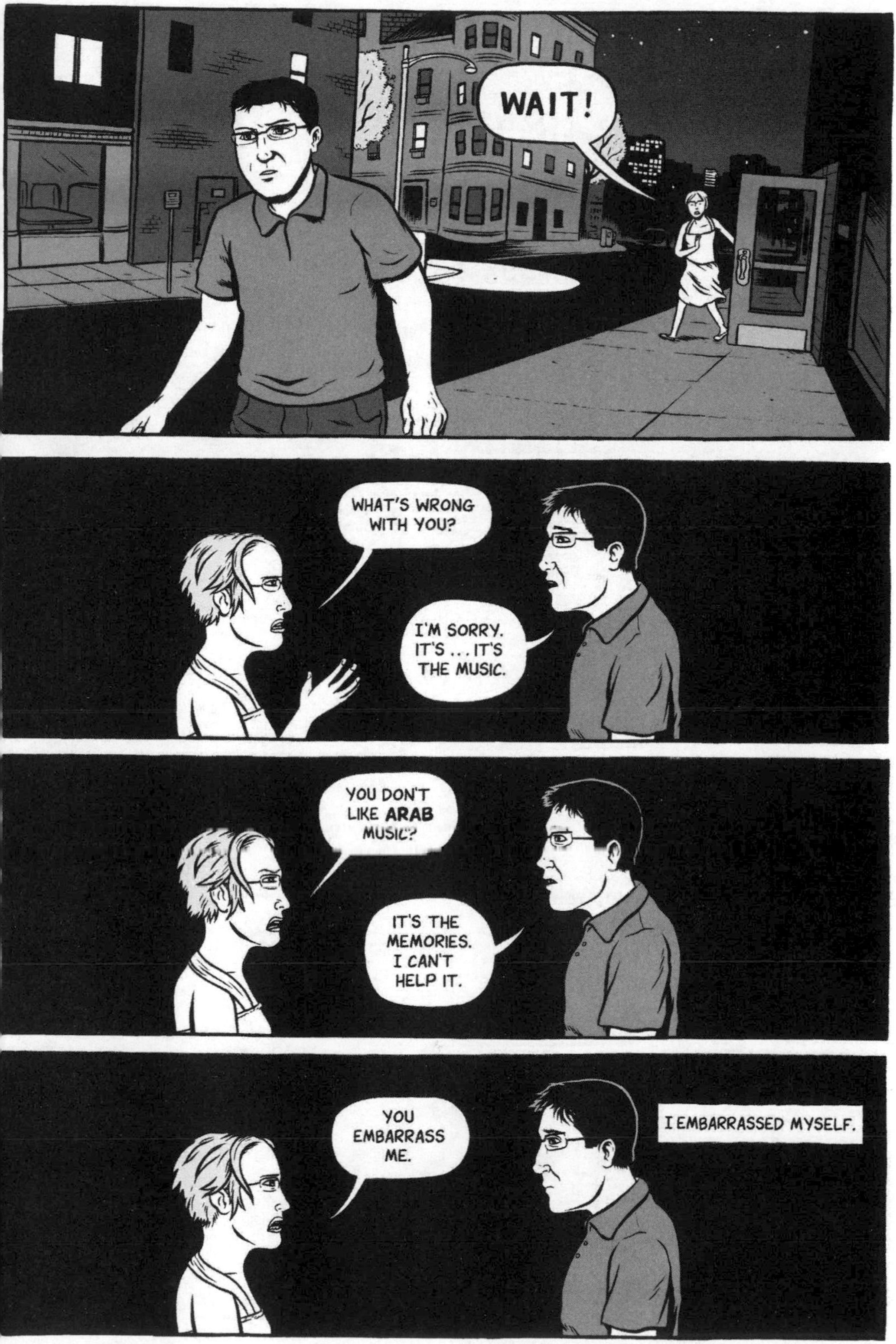
WAIT!
WHAT'S WRONG WITH YOU?
I'M SORRY. IT'S ... IT'S THE MUSIC.
YOU DON'T LIKE ARAB MUSIC?
IT'S THE MEMORIES. I CAN'T HELP IT.
YOU EMBARRASS ME.
I EMBARRASSED MYSELF.

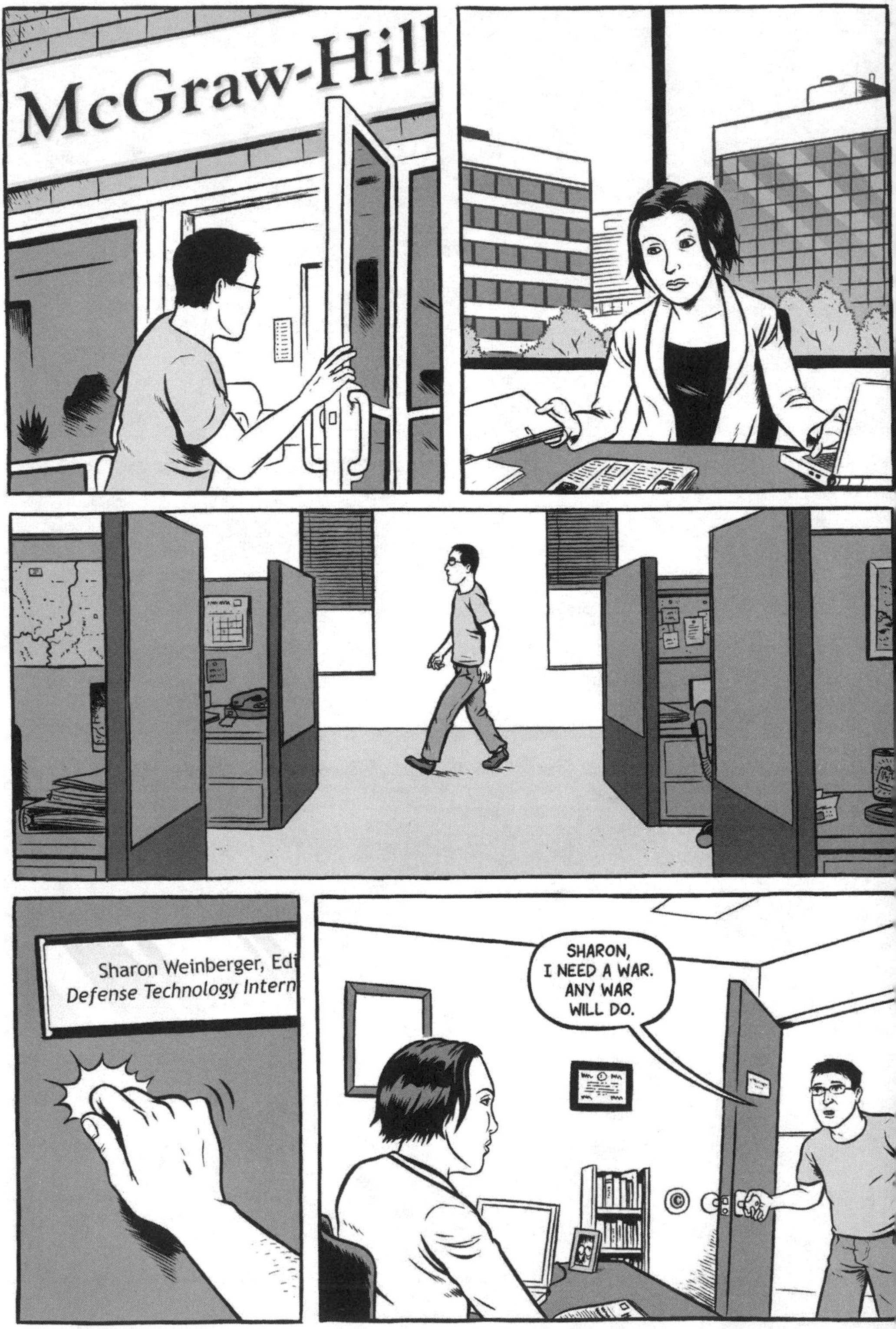
McGraw-Hill
Sharon Weinberger, Edi
Defense Technology Intern
SHARON, I NEED A WAR. ANY WAR WILL DO.

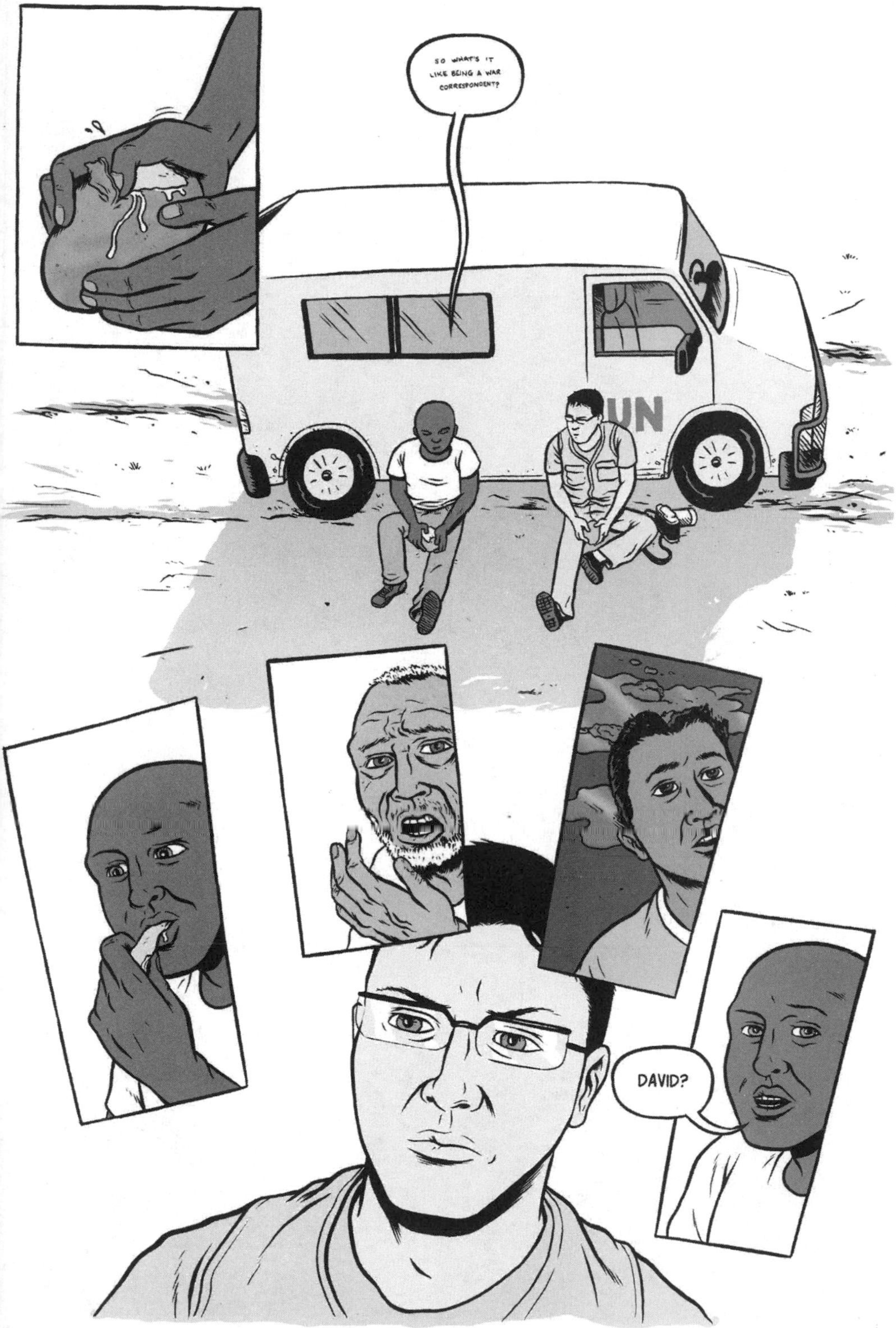
SO WHAT'S IT LIKE BEING A WAR CORRESPONDENT?
UN
DAVID?

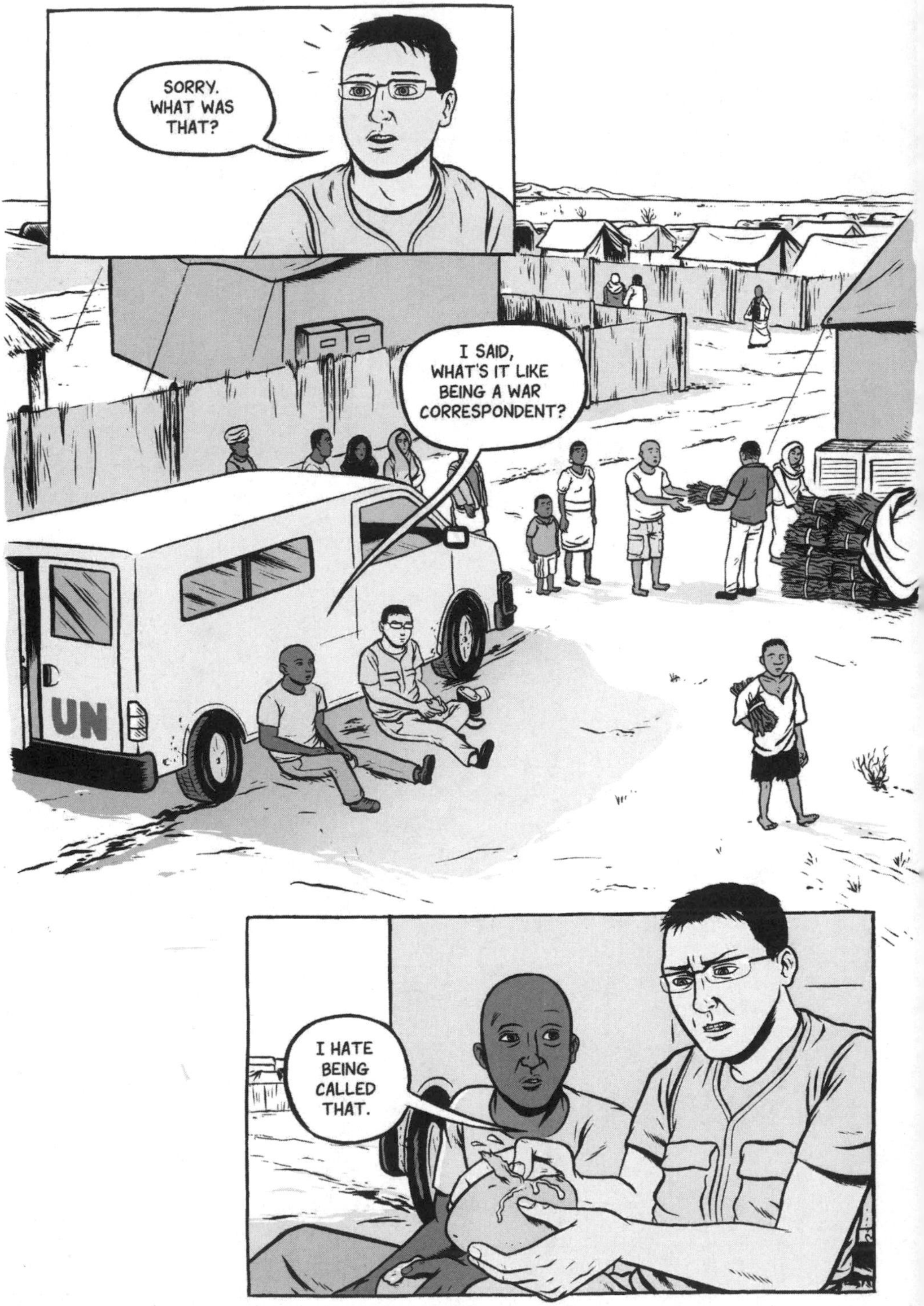
SORRY. WHAT WAS THAT?
I SAID, WHAT'S IT LIKE BEING A WAR CORRESPONDENT?
UN
I HATE BEING CALLED THAT.

EAST TIMOR

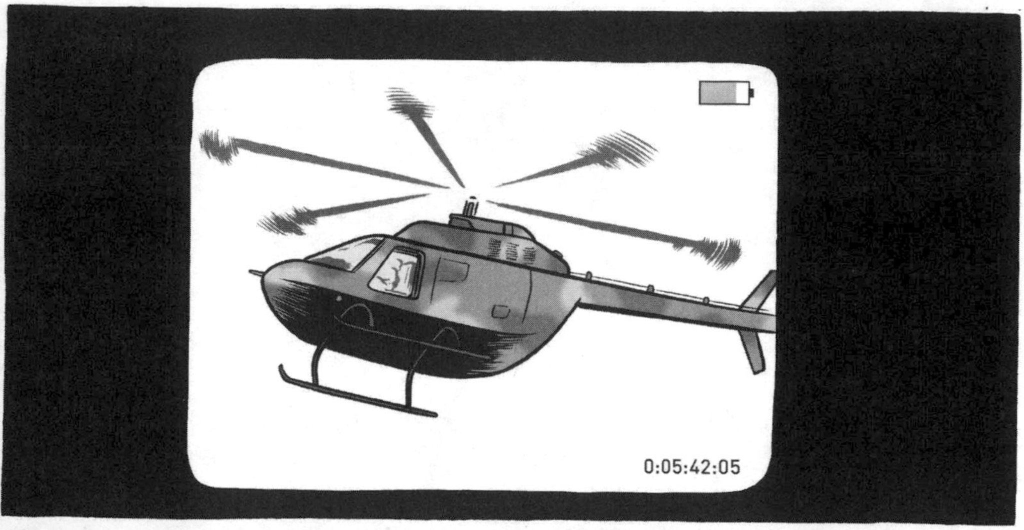
0:05:42:05

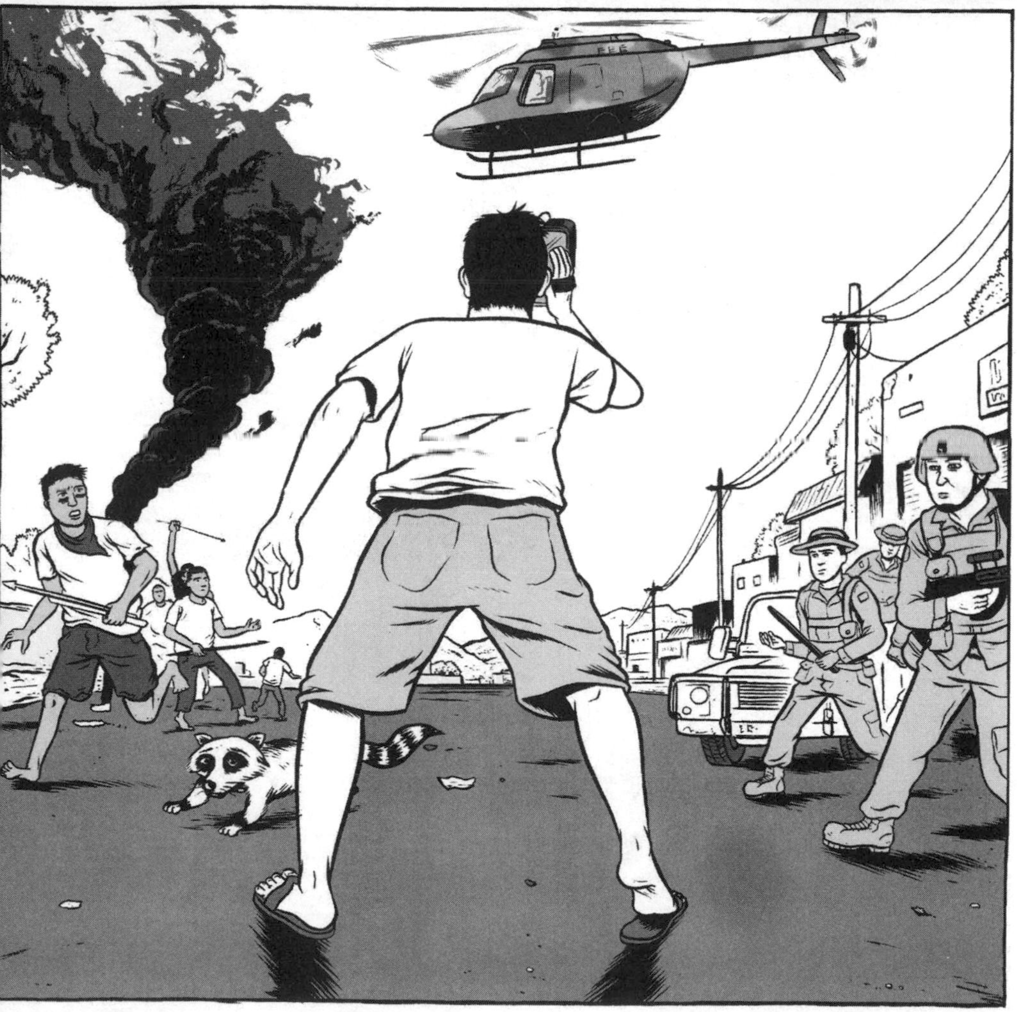

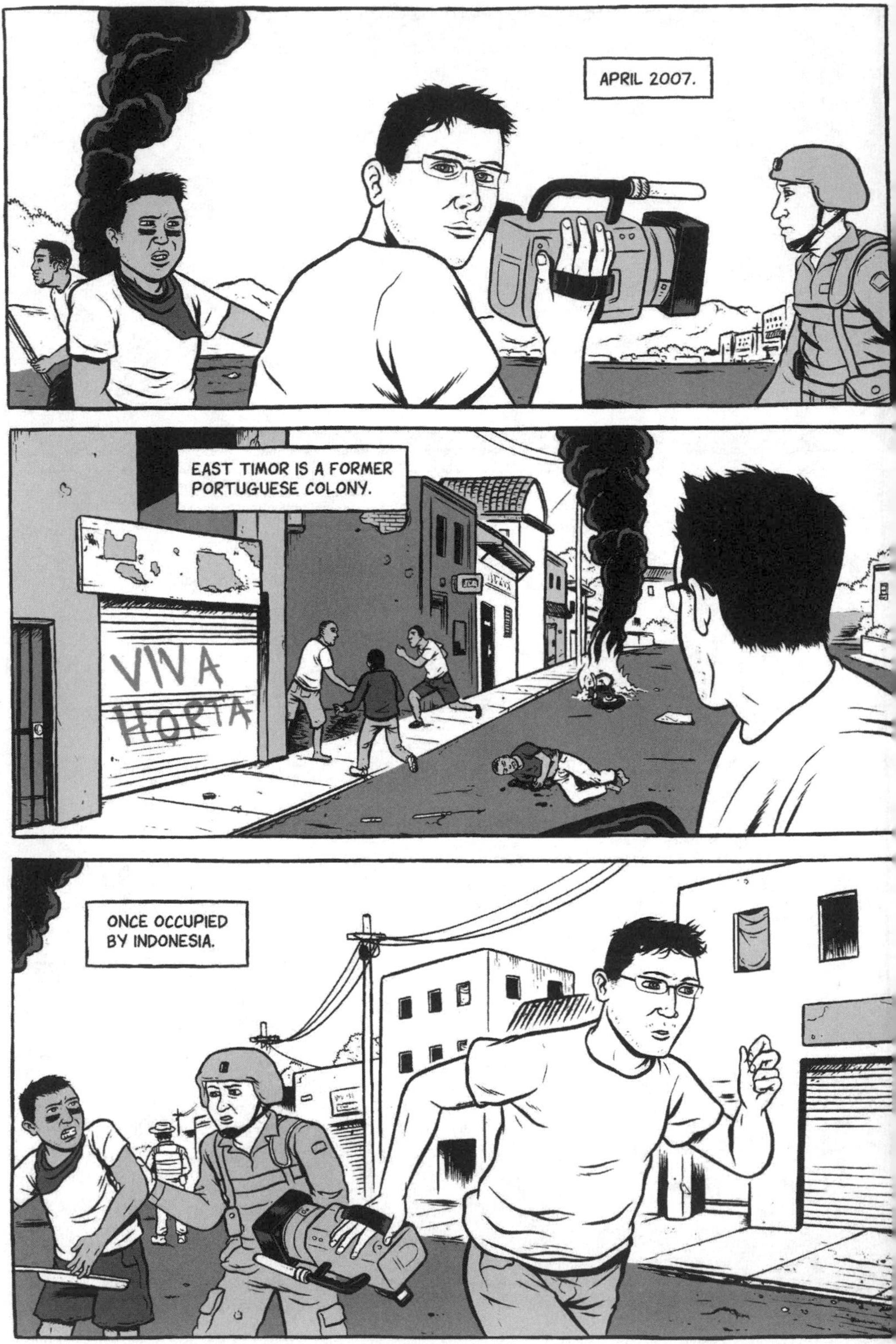
APRIL 2007.
EAST TIMOR IS A FORMER PORTUGUESE COLONY.
VIVA HORTA
ONCE OCCUPIED BY INDONESIA.

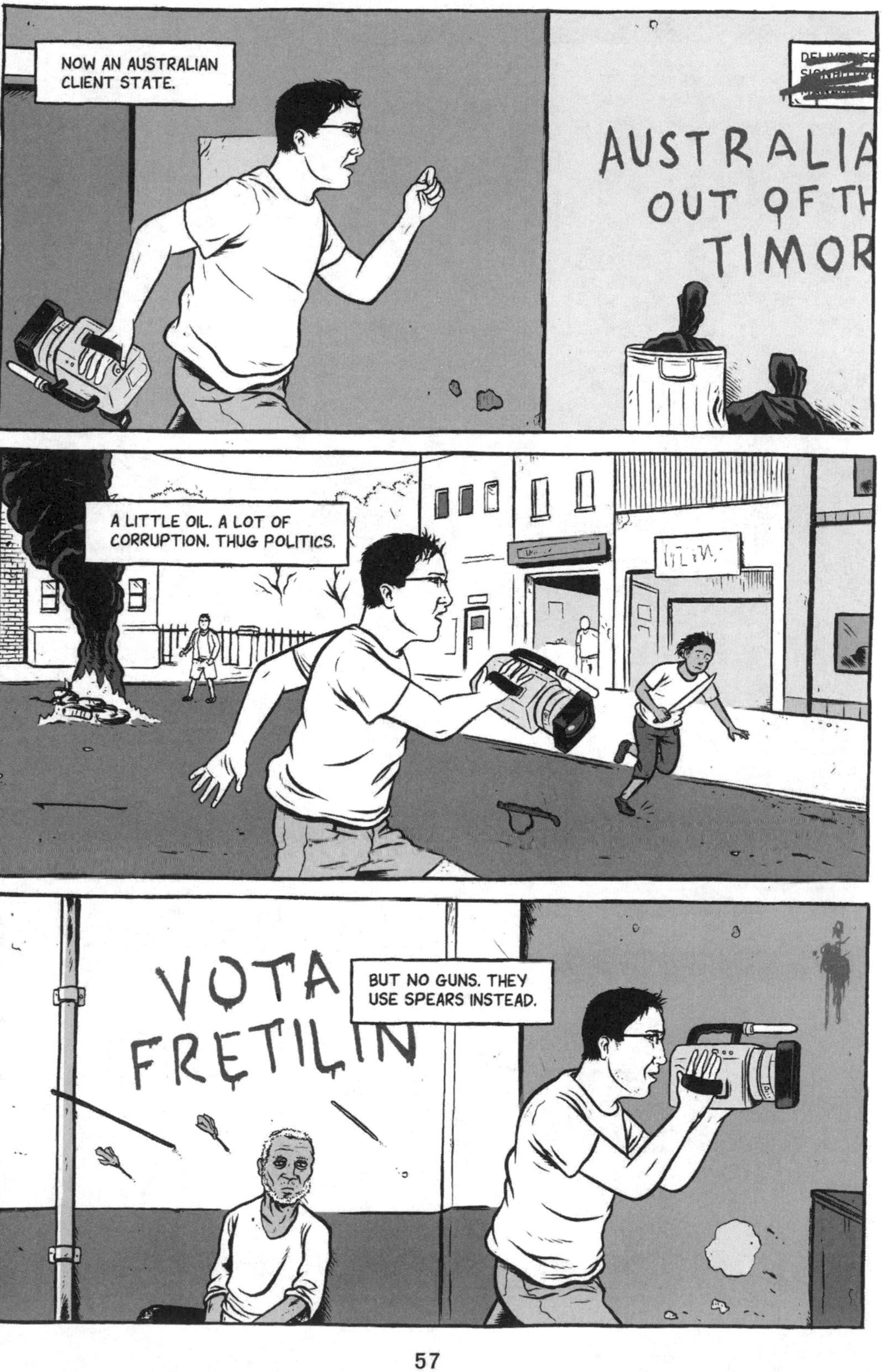
NOW AN AUSTRALIAN CLIENT STATE.
AUSTRALIA
OUT OF TH
TIMOR
A LITTLE OIL. A LOT OF CORRUPTION. THUG POLITICS.
VOTA
FRETILIN
BUT NO GUNS. THEY USE SPEARS INSTEAD.

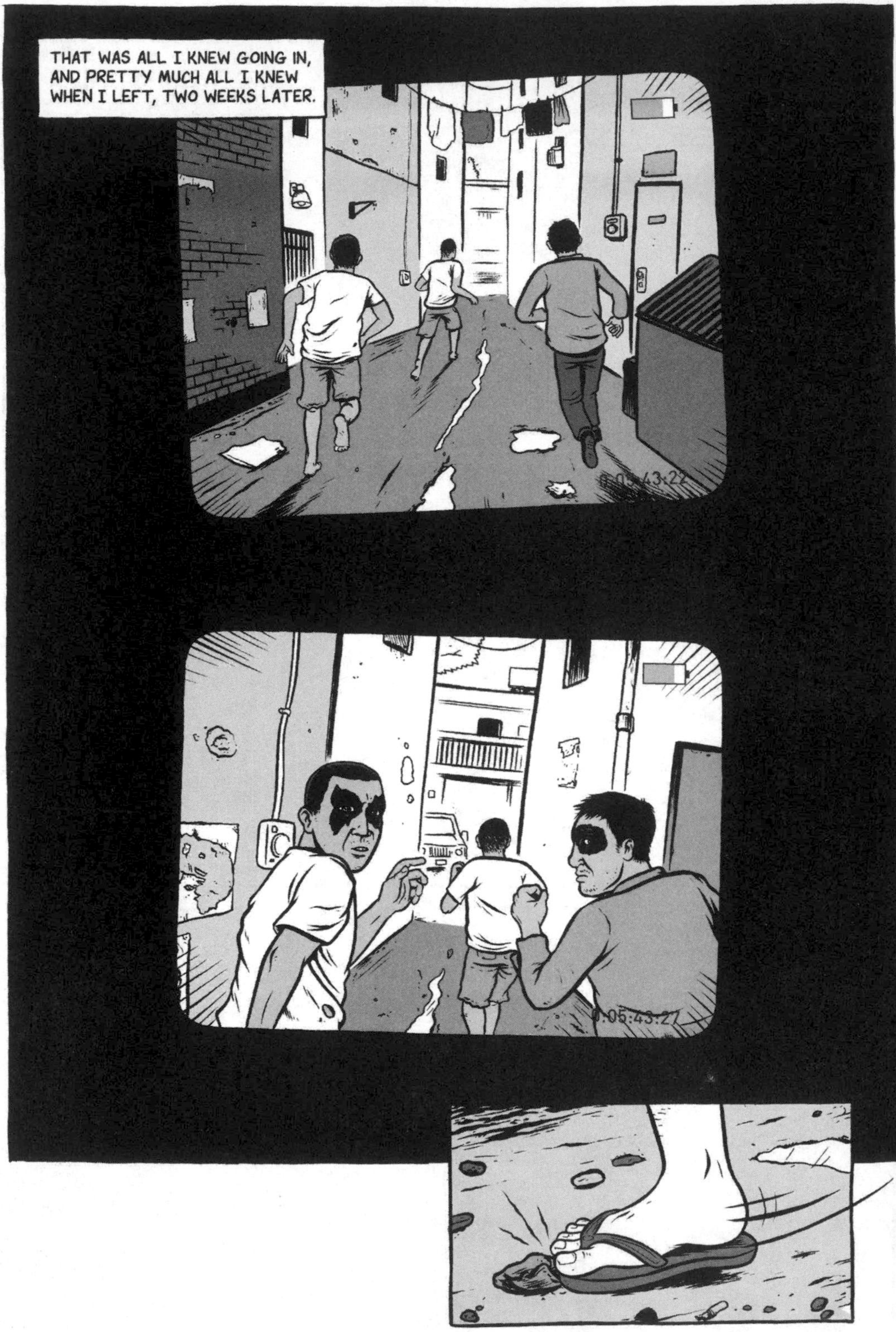
THAT WAS ALL I KNEW GOING IN, AND PRETTY MUCH ALL I KNEW WHEN I LEFT, TWO WEEKS LATER.

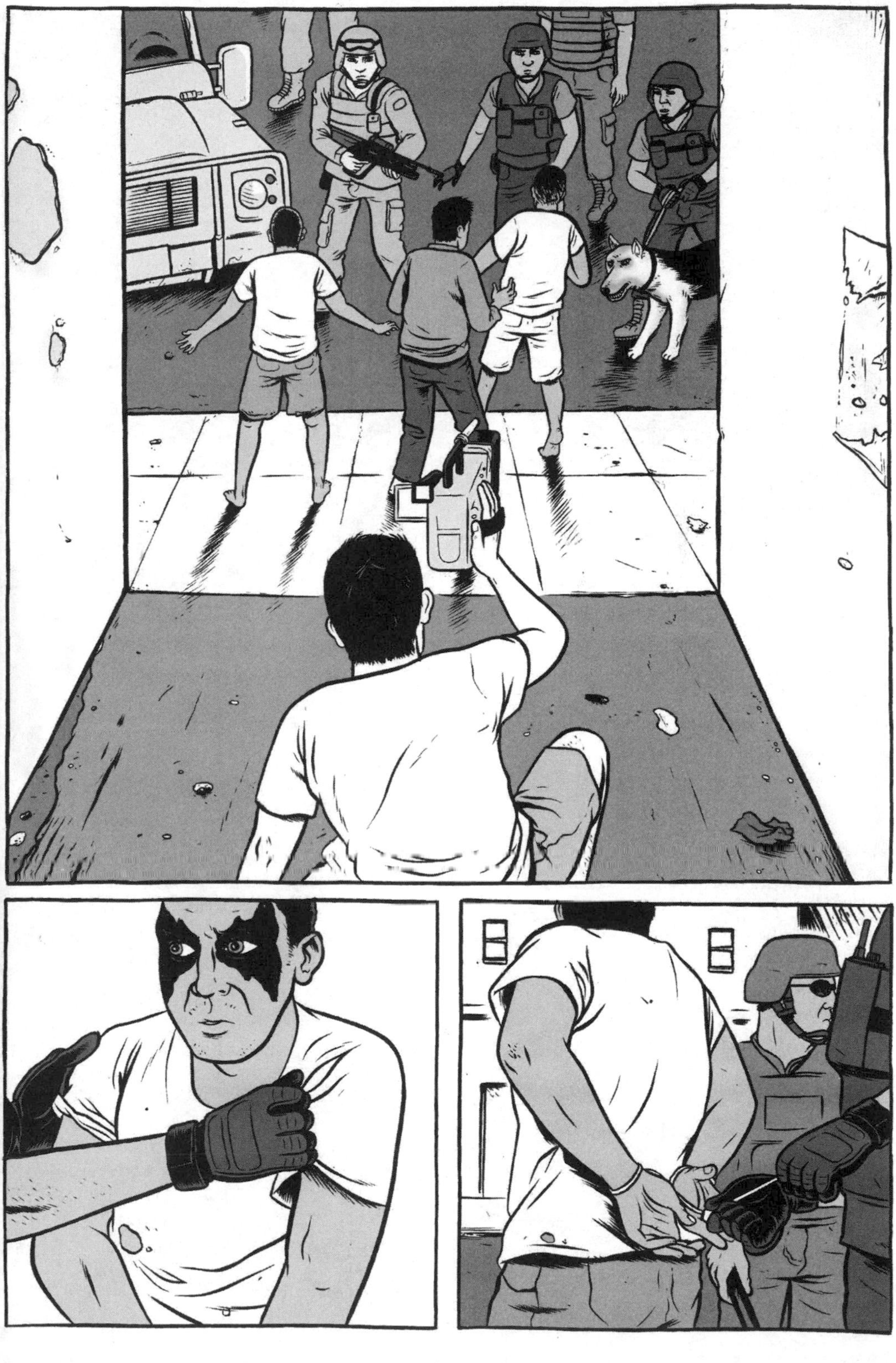

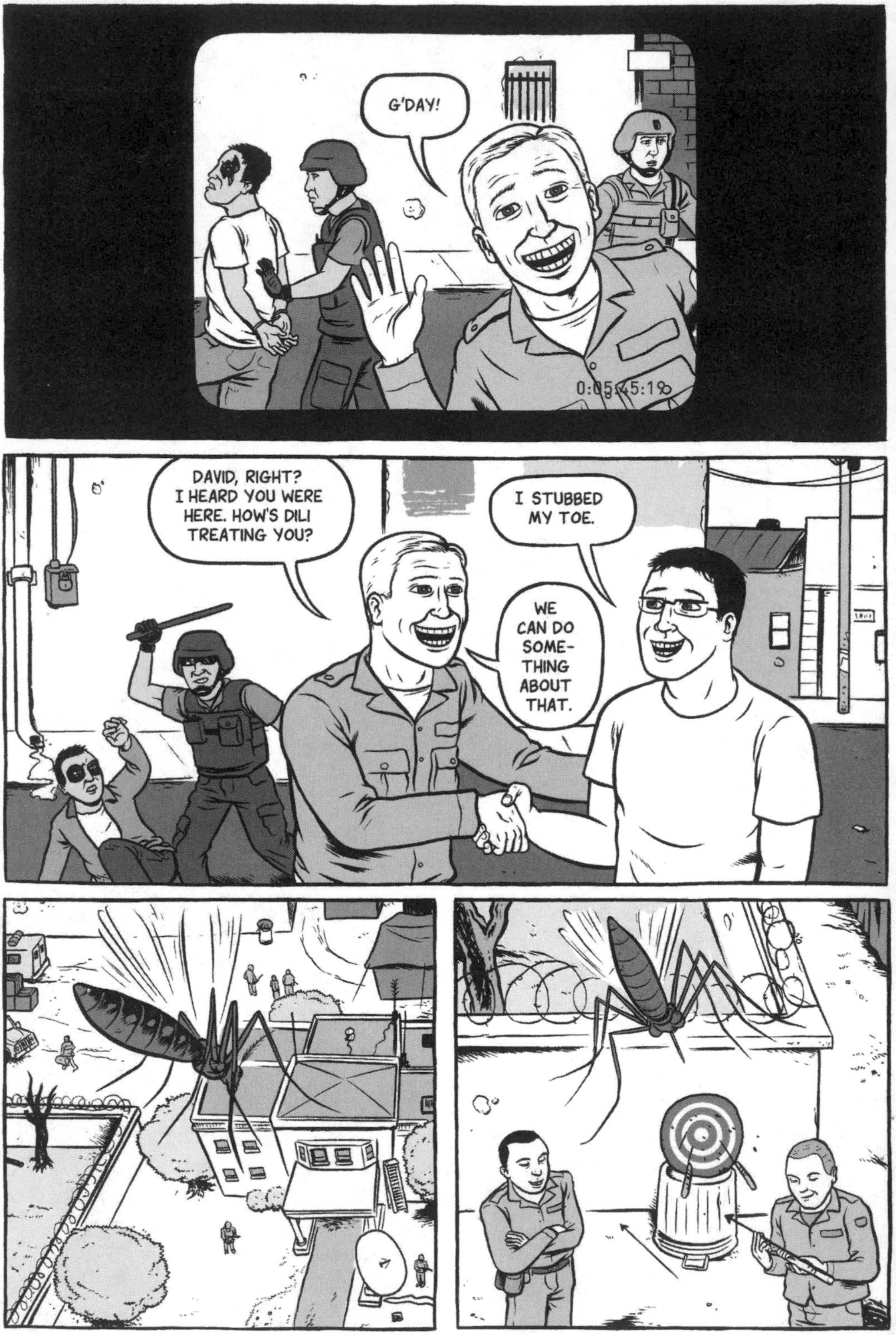
G'DAY!
0:05:45:19
DAVID, RIGHT? I HEARD YOU WERE HERE. HOW'S DILI TREATING YOU?
I STUBBED MY TOE.
WE CAN DO SOME-THING ABOUT THAT.

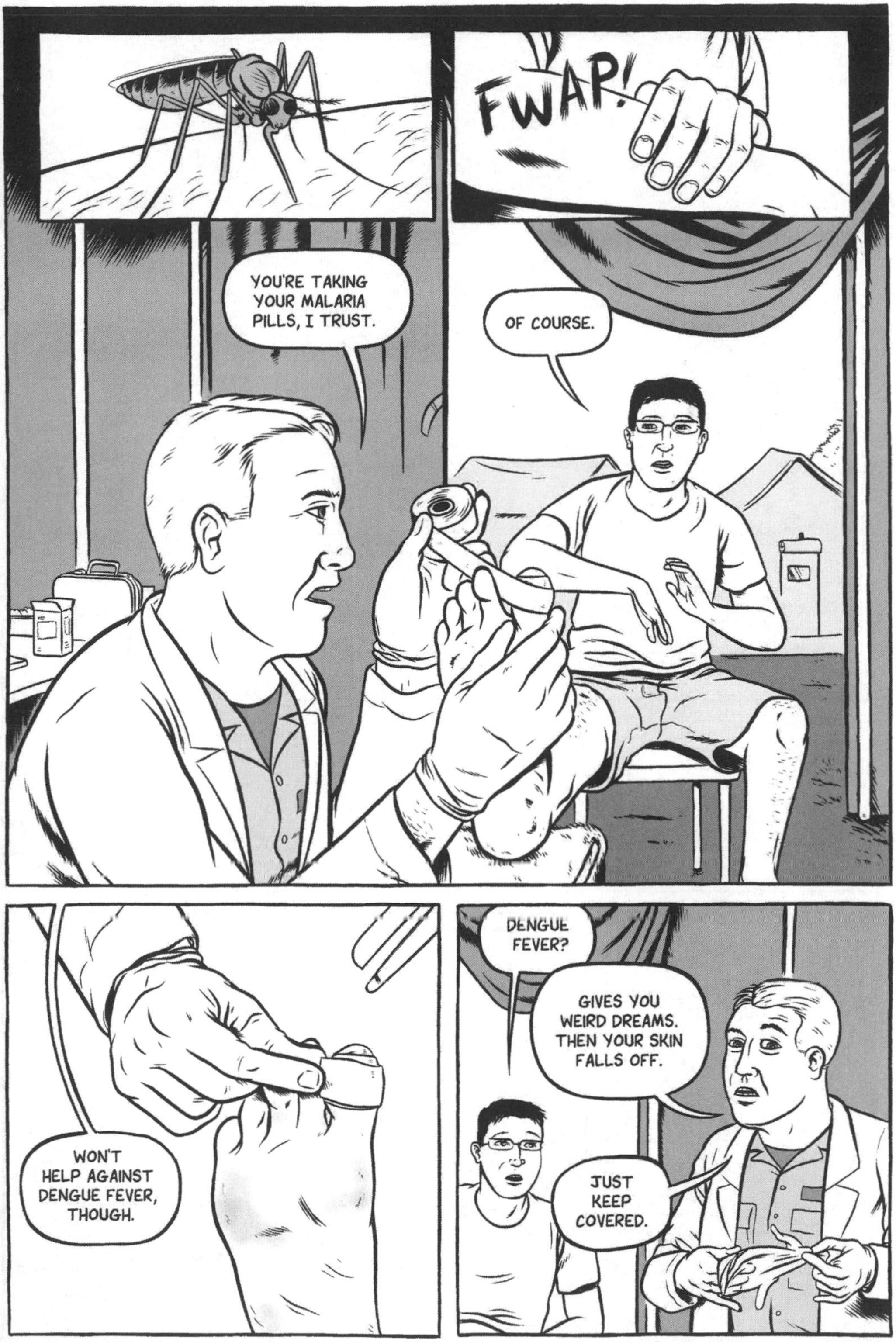
FWAP!
YOU'RE TAKING YOUR MALARIA PILLS, I TRUST.
OF COURSE.
WON'T HELP AGAINST DENGUE FEVER, THOUGH.
DENGUE FEVER?
GIVES YOU WEIRD DREAMS. THEN YOUR SKIN FALLS OFF.
JUST KEEP COVERED.

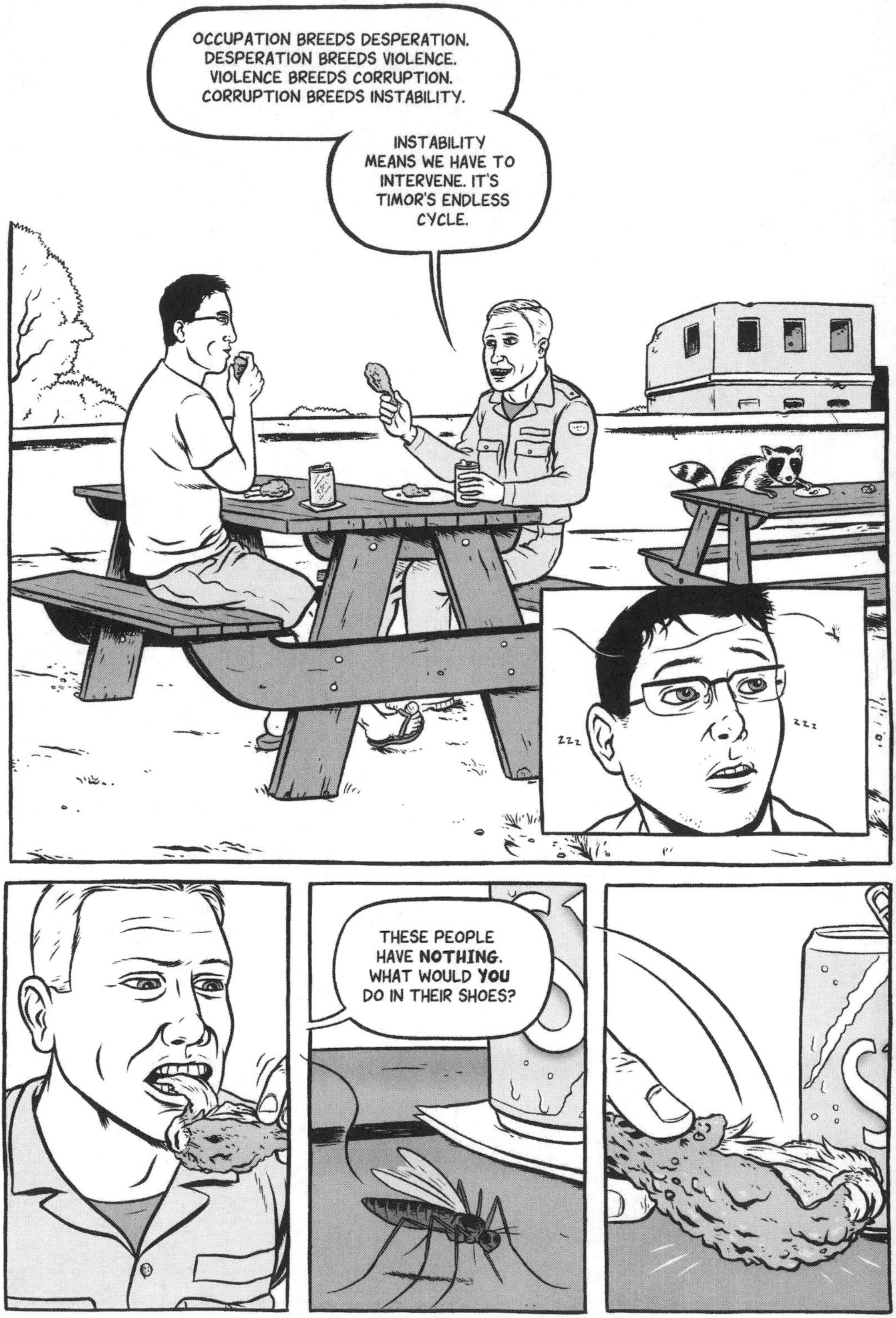
OCCUPATION BREEDS DESPERATION. DESPERATION BREEDS VIOLENCE. VIOLENCE BREEDS CORRUPTION. CORRUPTION BREEDS INSTABILITY.
INSTABILITY MEANS WE HAVE TO INTERVENE. IT'S TIMOR'S ENDLESS CYCLE.
ZZZ
ZZZ
THESE PEOPLE HAVE **NOTHING**. WHAT WOULD **YOU** DO IN THEIR SHOES?

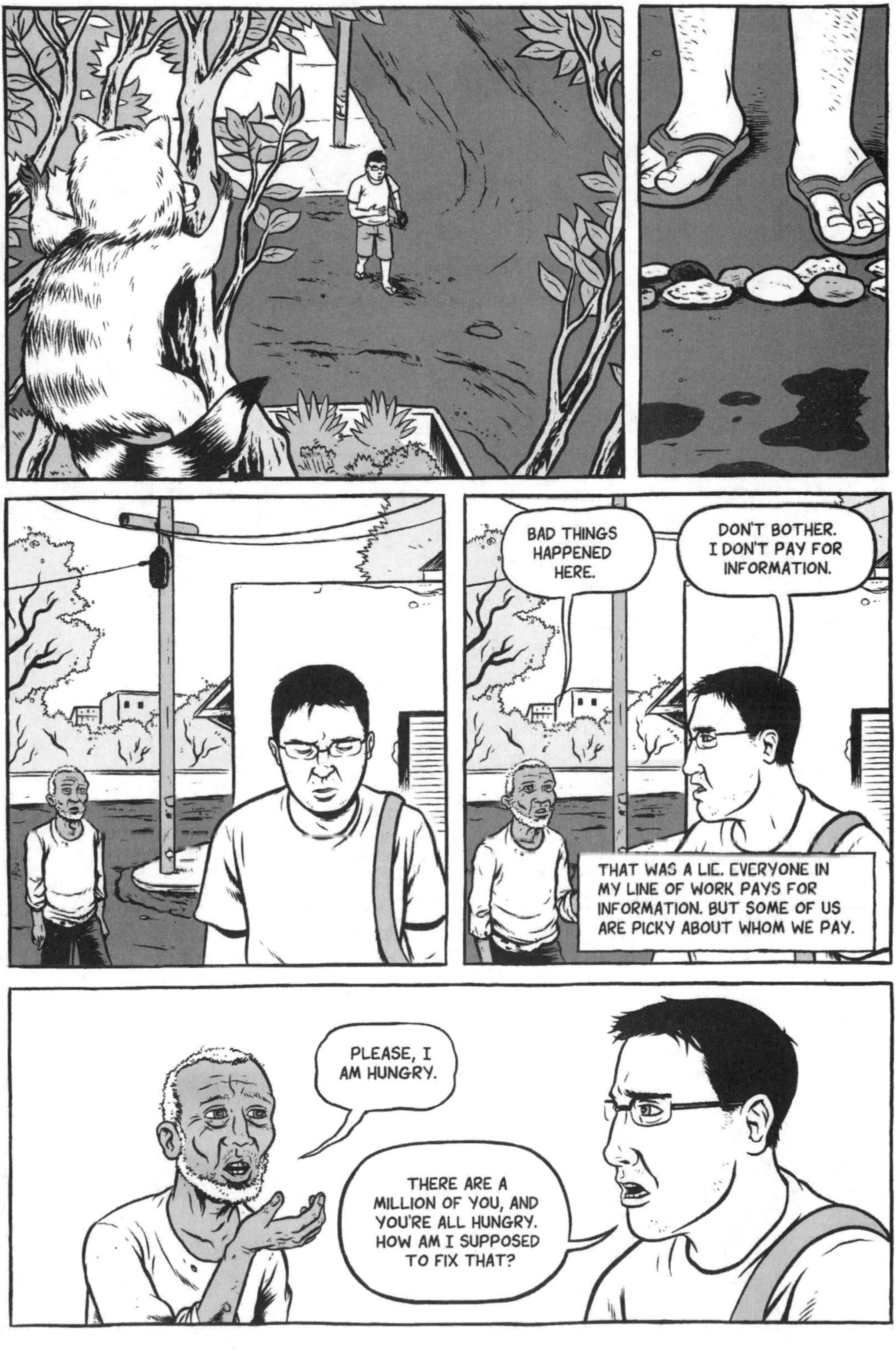
BAD THINGS HAPPENED HERE.
DON'T BOTHER. I DON'T PAY FOR INFORMATION.
THAT WAS A LIE. EVERYONE IN MY LINE OF WORK PAYS FOR INFORMATION. BUT SOME OF US ARE PICKY ABOUT WHOM WE PAY.
PLEASE, I AM HUNGRY.
THERE ARE A MILLION OF YOU, AND YOU'RE ALL HUNGRY. HOW AM I SUPPOSED TO FIX THAT?

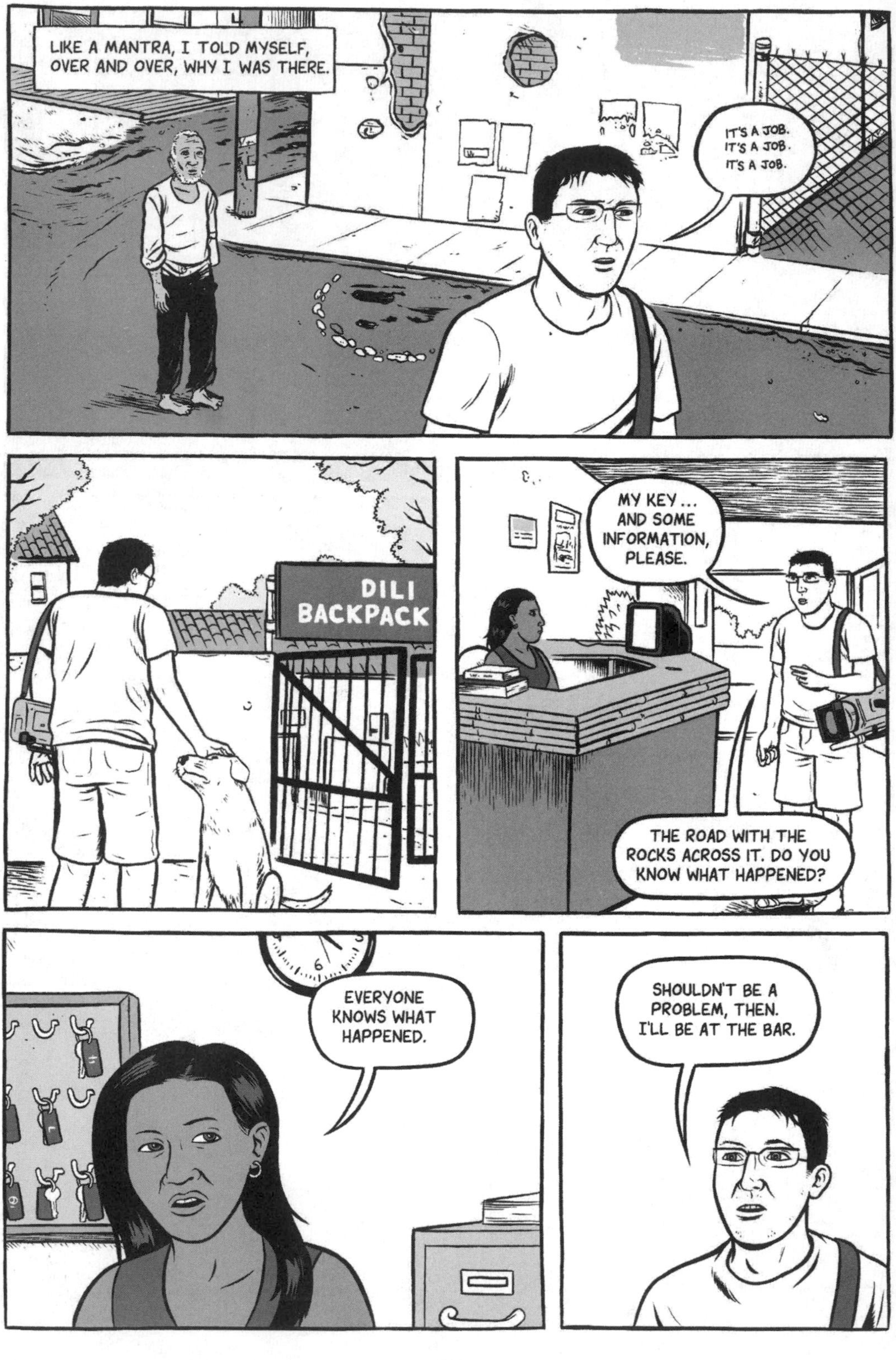
LIKE A MANTRA, I TOLD MYSELF, OVER AND OVER, WHY I WAS THERE.
IT'S A JOB. IT'S A JOB. IT'S A JOB.
DILI BACKPACK
MY KEY ... AND SOME INFORMATION, PLEASE.
THE ROAD WITH THE ROCKS ACROSS IT. DO YOU KNOW WHAT HAPPENED?
EVERYONE KNOWS WHAT HAPPENED.
SHOULDN'T BE A PROBLEM, THEN. I'LL BE AT THE BAR.

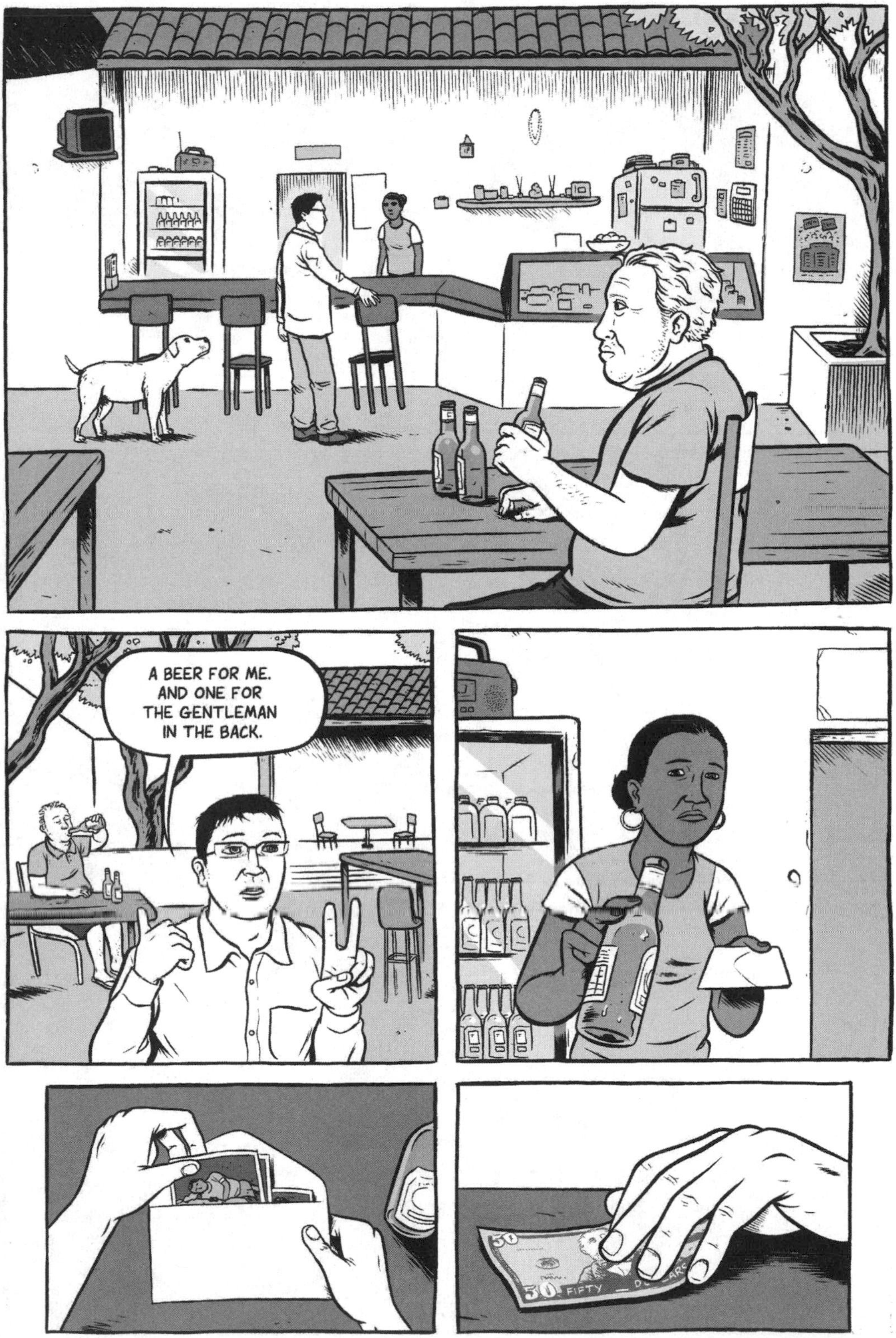
A BEER FOR ME. AND ONE FOR THE GENTLEMAN IN THE BACK.
FIFTY

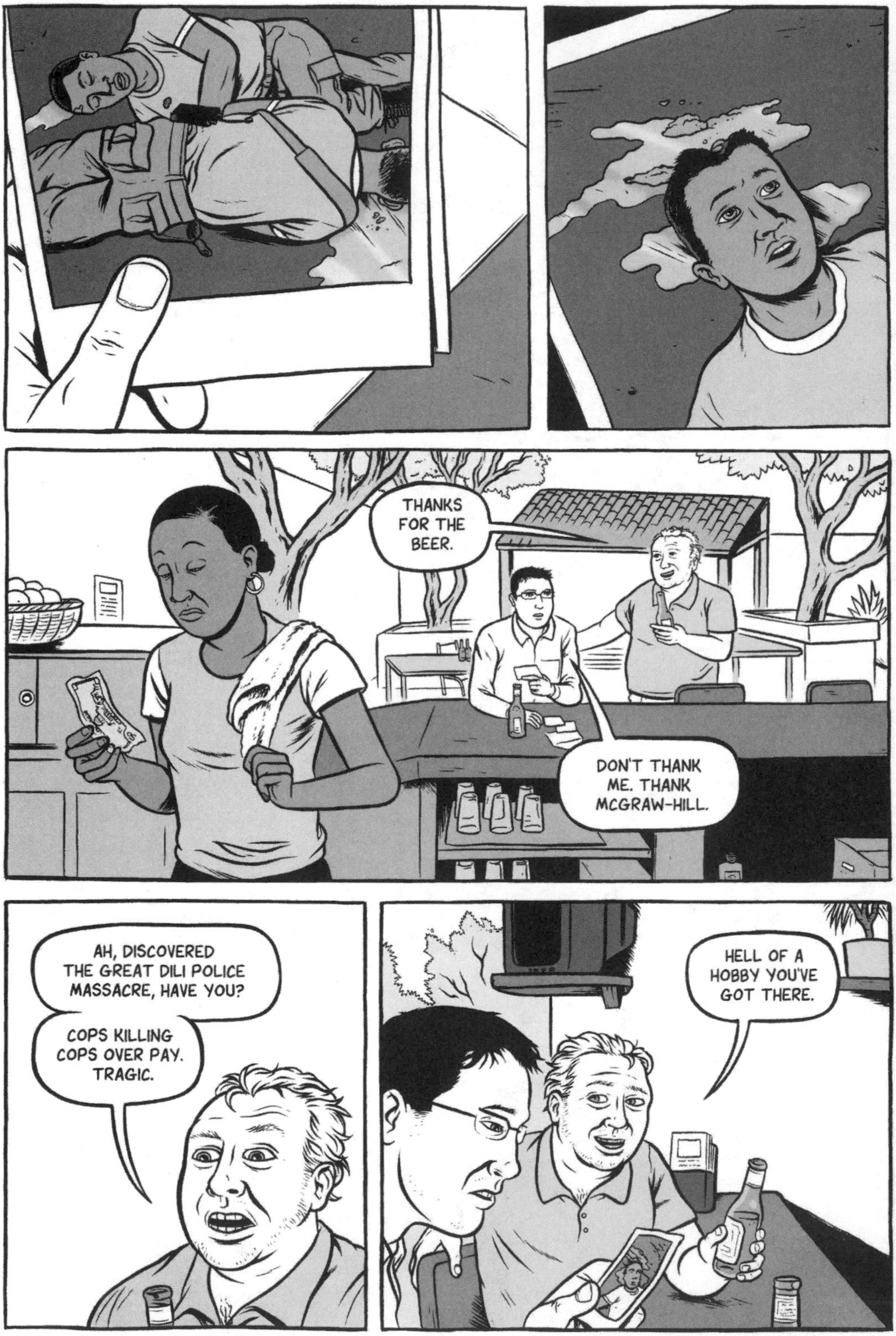
THANKS FOR THE BEER.
DON'T THANK ME. THANK MCGRAW-HILL.
AH, DISCOVERED THE GREAT DILI POLICE MASSACRE, HAVE YOU?
COPS KILLING COPS OVER PAY. TRAGIC.
HELL OF A HOBBY YOU'VE GOT THERE.

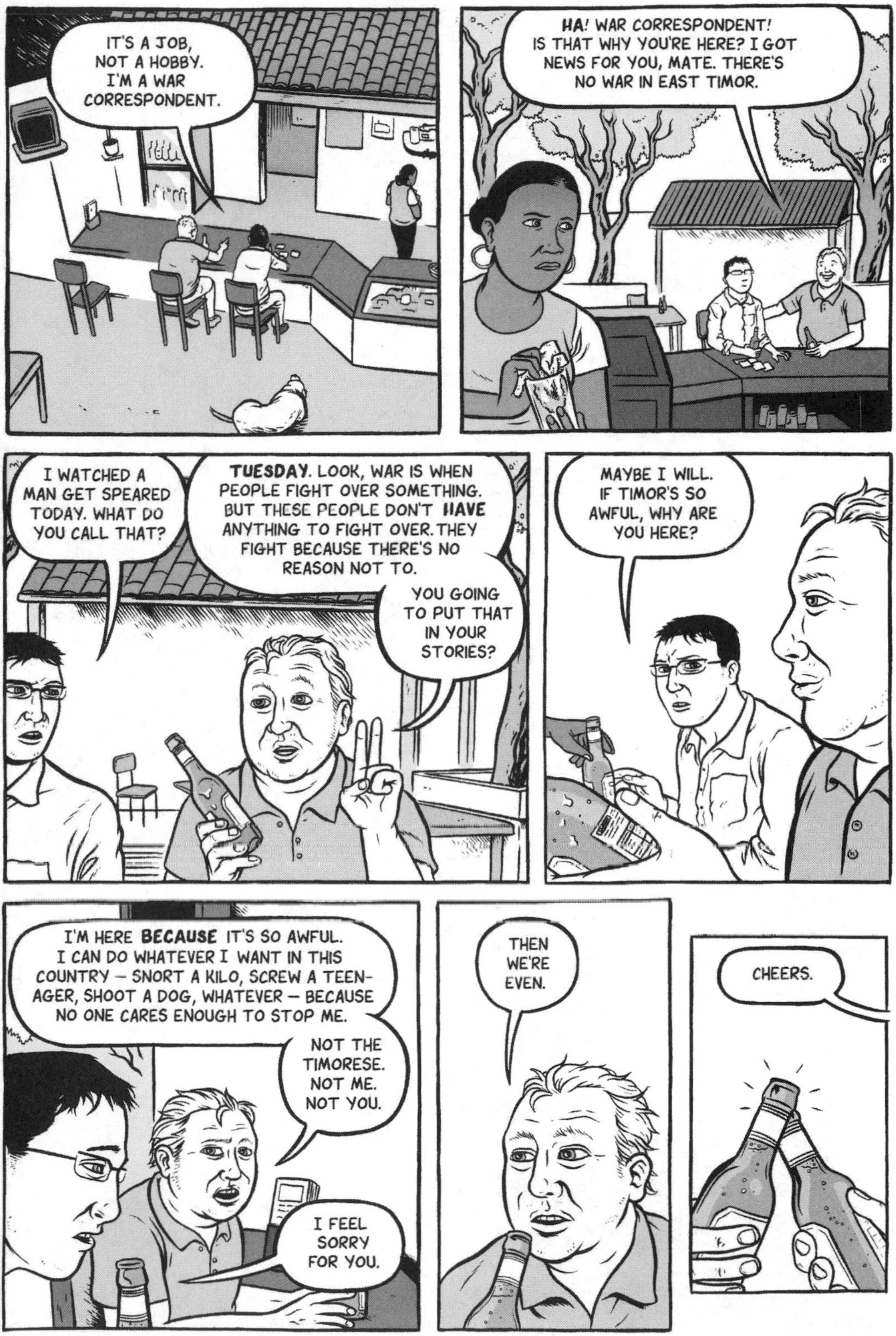
IT'S A JOB, NOT A HOBBY. I'M A WAR CORRESPONDENT.
HA! WAR CORRESPONDENT! IS THAT WHY YOU'RE HERE? I GOT NEWS FOR YOU, MATE. THERE'S NO WAR IN EAST TIMOR.
I WATCHED A MAN GET SPEARED TODAY. WHAT DO YOU CALL THAT?
TUESDAY. LOOK, WAR IS WHEN PEOPLE FIGHT OVER SOMETHING. BUT THESE PEOPLE DON'T HAVE ANYTHING TO FIGHT OVER. THEY FIGHT BECAUSE THERE'S NO REASON NOT TO.
YOU GOING TO PUT THAT IN YOUR STORIES?
MAYBE I WILL. IF TIMOR'S SO AWFUL, WHY ARE YOU HERE?
I'M HERE BECAUSE IT'S SO AWFUL. I CAN DO WHATEVER I WANT IN THIS COUNTRY — SNORT A KILO, SCREW A TEEN-AGER, SHOOT A DOG, WHATEVER — BECAUSE NO ONE CARES ENOUGH TO STOP ME.
NOT THE TIMORESE. NOT ME. NOT YOU.
I FEEL SORRY FOR YOU.
THEN WE'RE EVEN.
CHEERS.

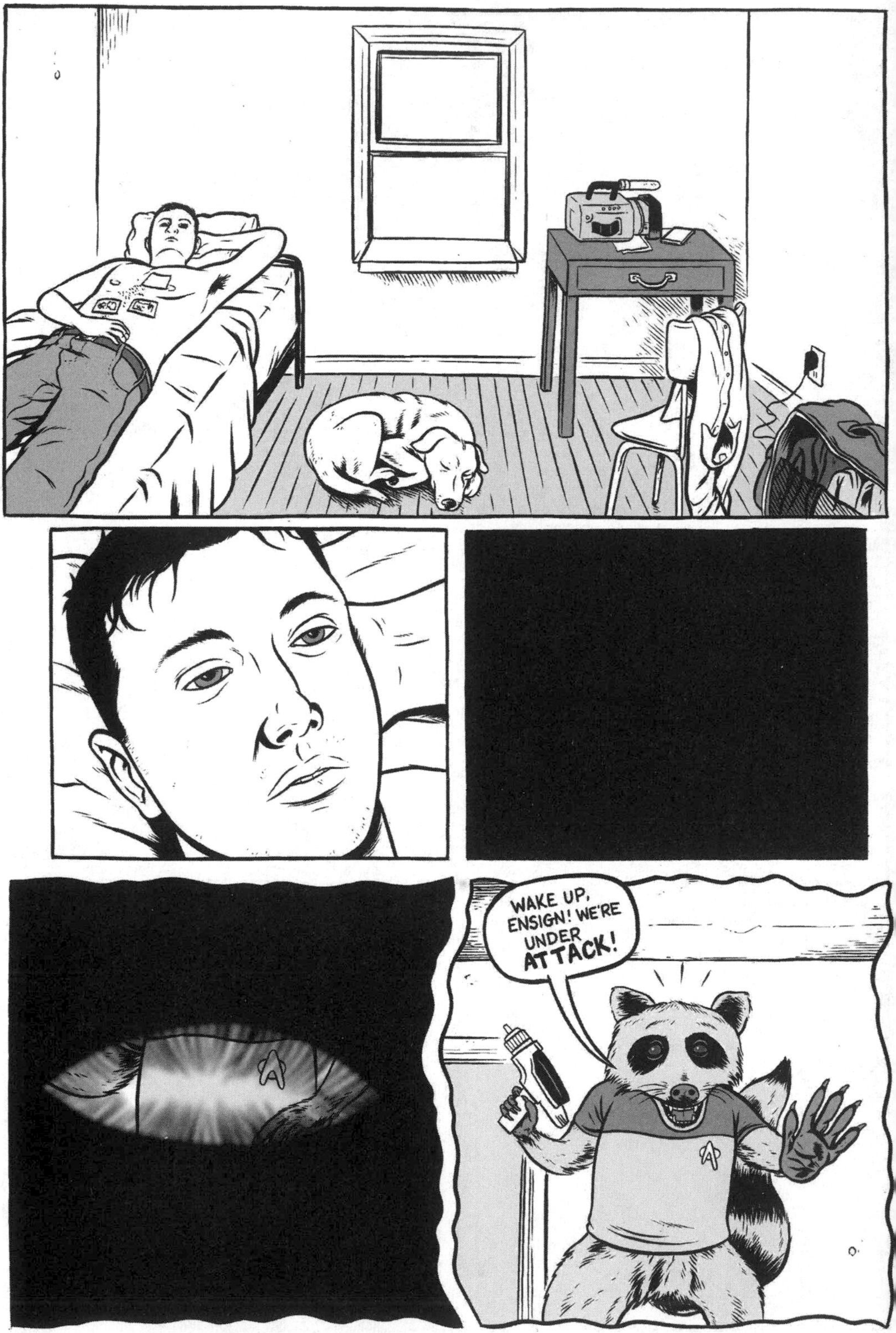
WAKE UP, ENSIGN! WE'RE UNDER ATTACK!

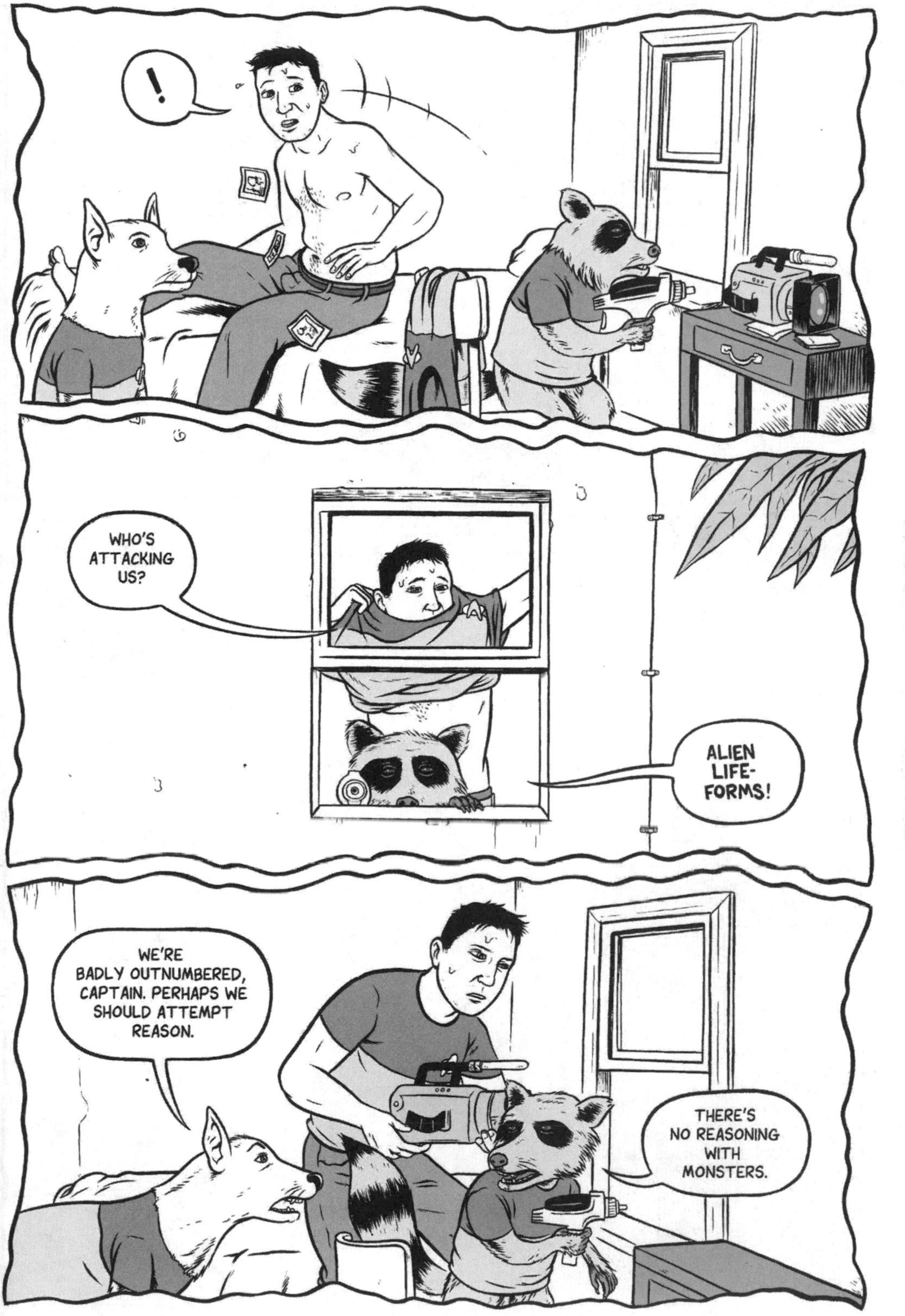
!
WHO'S ATTACKING US?
ALIEN LIFE-FORMS!
WE'RE BADLY OUTNUMBERED, CAPTAIN. PERHAPS WE SHOULD ATTEMPT REASON.
THERE'S NO REASONING WITH MONSTERS.

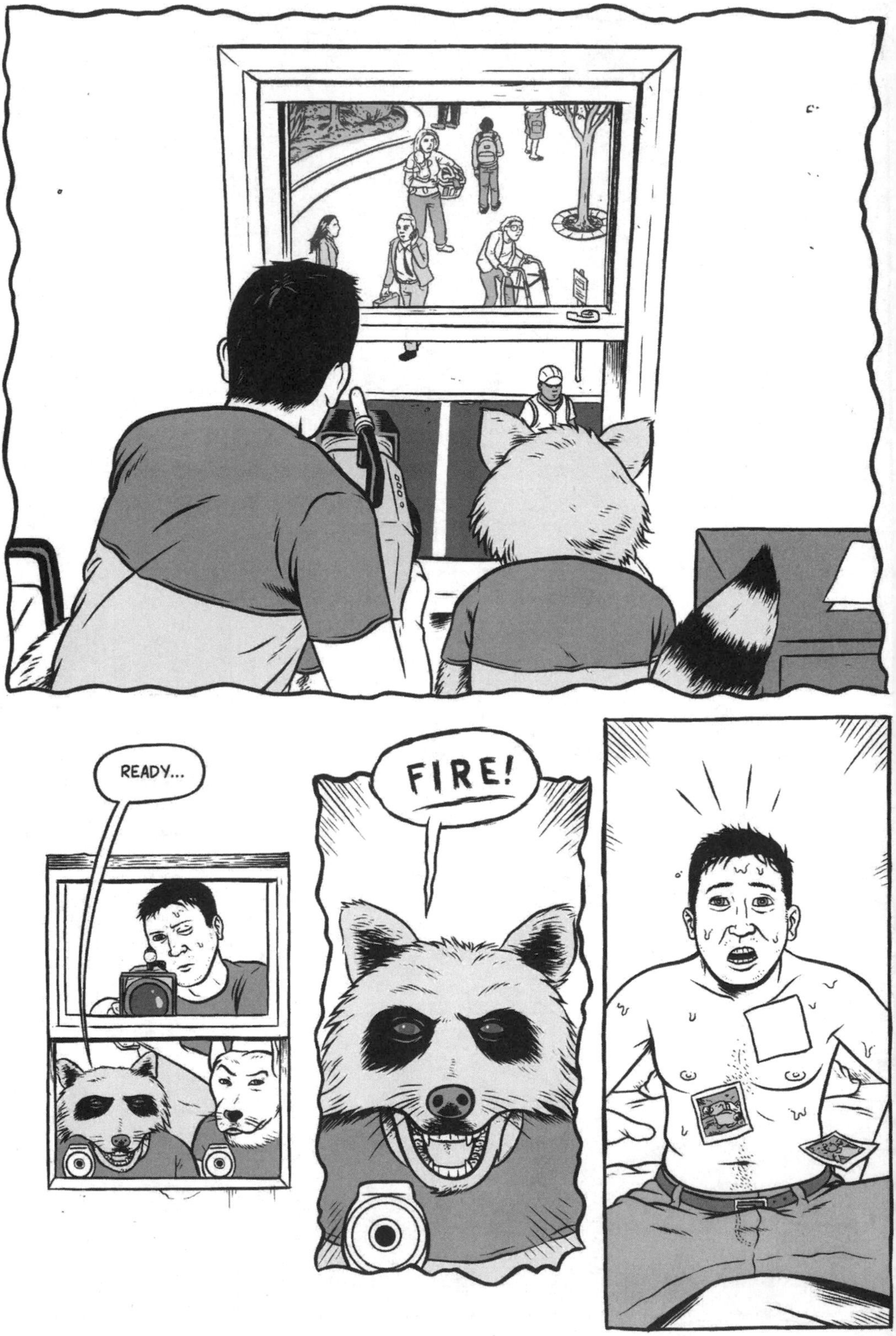
READY...
FIRE!

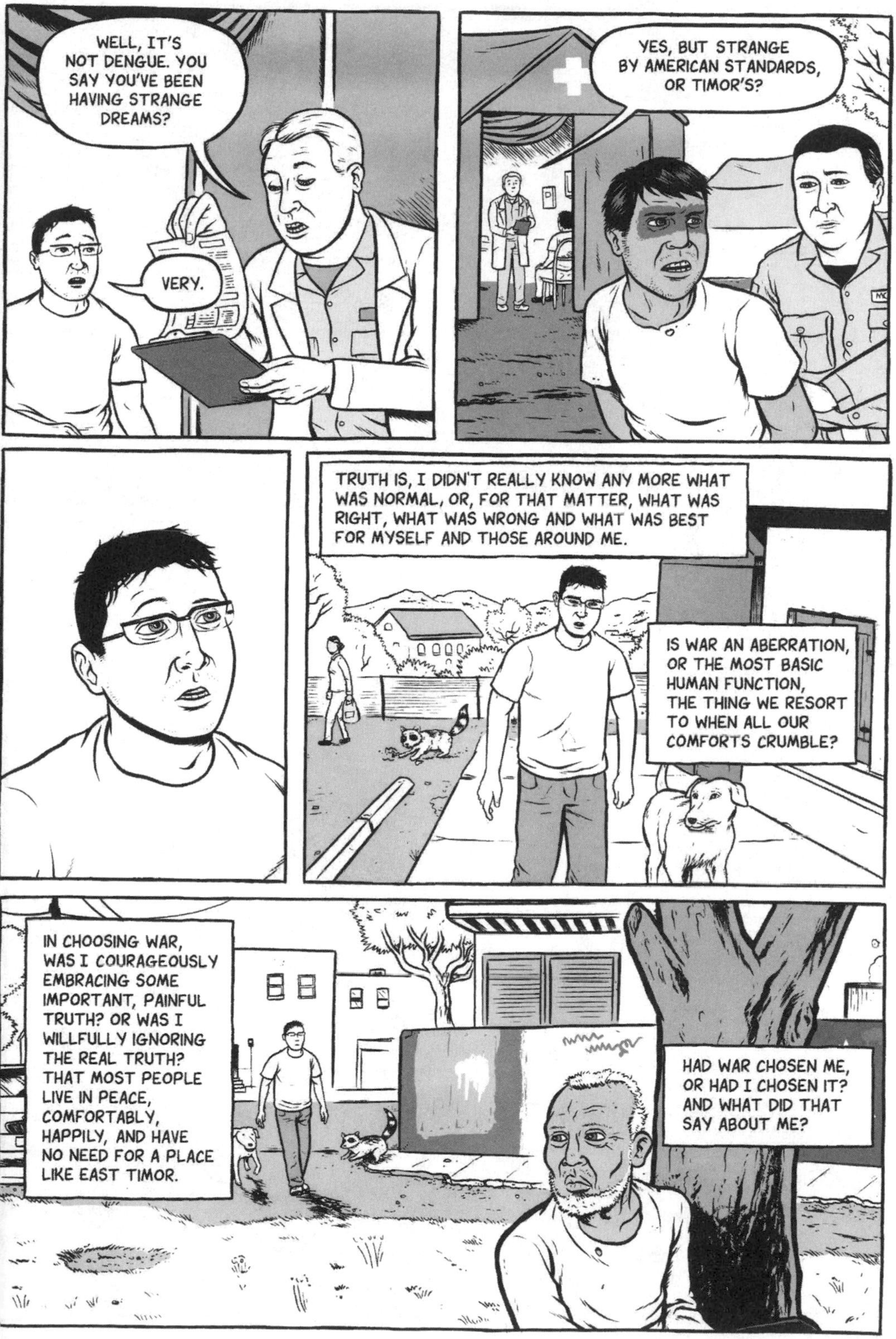
WELL, IT'S NOT DENGUE. YOU SAY YOU'VE BEEN HAVING STRANGE DREAMS?
VERY.
YES, BUT STRANGE BY AMERICAN STANDARDS, OR TIMOR'S?
TRUTH IS, I DIDN'T REALLY KNOW ANY MORE WHAT WAS NORMAL, OR, FOR THAT MATTER, WHAT WAS RIGHT, WHAT WAS WRONG AND WHAT WAS BEST FOR MYSELF AND THOSE AROUND ME.
IS WAR AN ABERRATION, OR THE MOST BASIC HUMAN FUNCTION, THE THING WE RESORT TO WHEN ALL OUR COMFORTS CRUMBLE?
IN CHOOSING WAR, WAS I COURAGEOUSLY EMBRACING SOME IMPORTANT, PAINFUL TRUTH? OR WAS I WILLFULLY IGNORING THE REAL TRUTH? THAT MOST PEOPLE LIVE IN PEACE, COMFORTABLY, HAPPILY, AND HAVE NO NEED FOR A PLACE LIKE EAST TIMOR.
HAD WAR CHOSEN ME, OR HAD I CHOSEN IT? AND WHAT DID THAT SAY ABOUT ME?

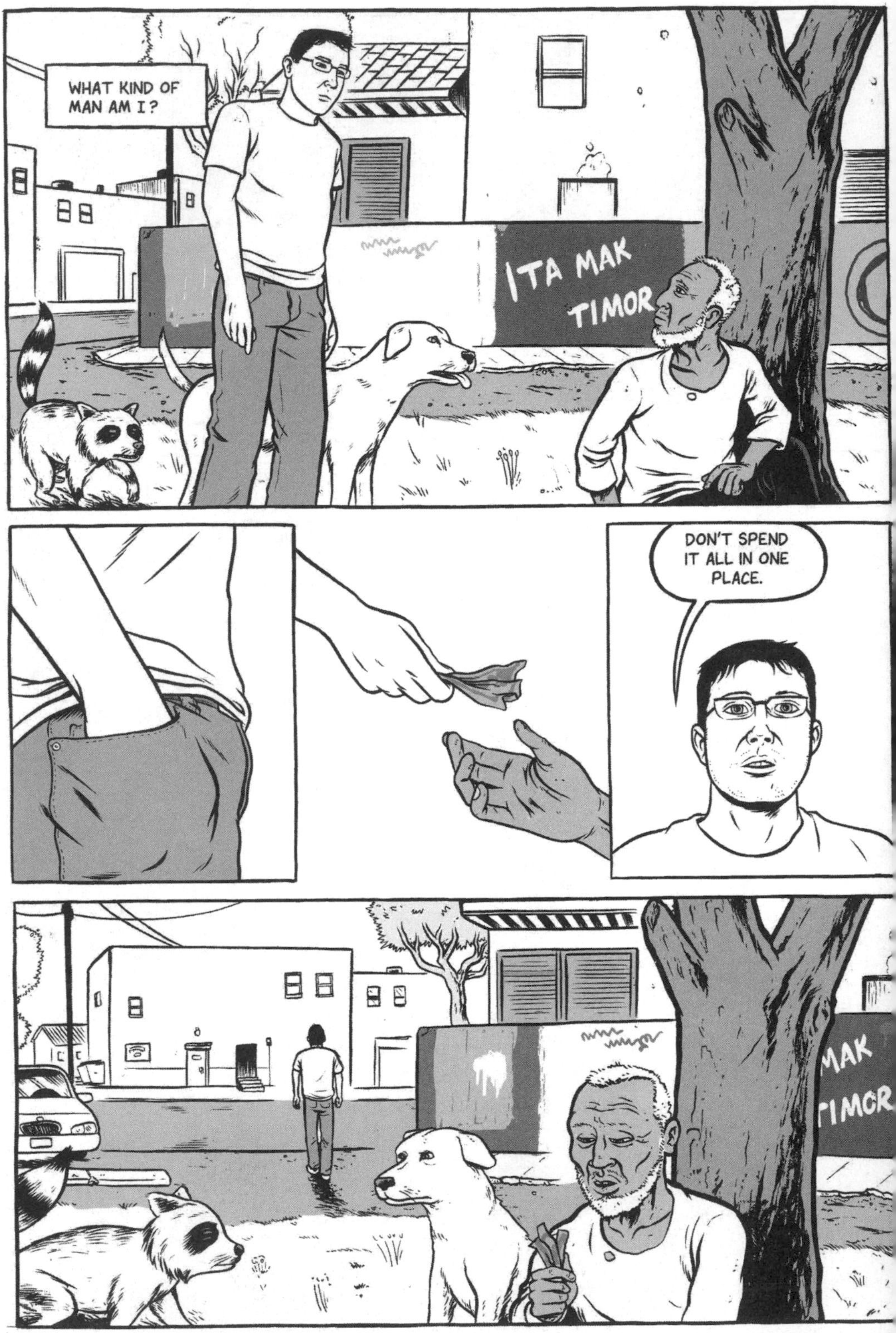
WHAT KIND OF MAN AM I?
ITA MAK TIMOR
DON'T SPEND IT ALL IN ONE PLACE.
MAK TIMOR

AFGHANISTAN

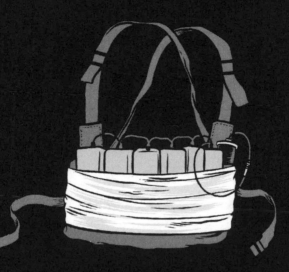

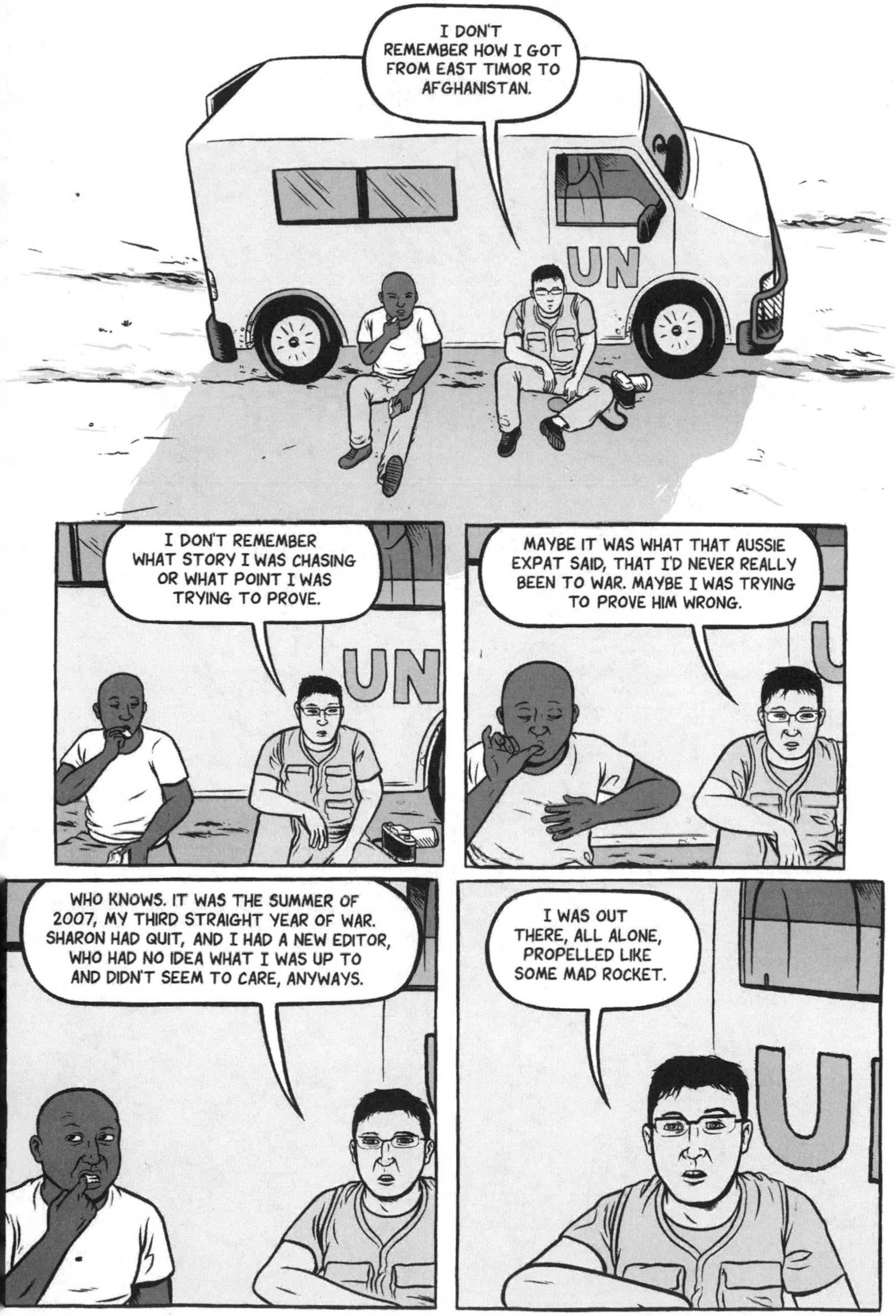
I DON'T REMEMBER HOW I GOT FROM EAST TIMOR TO AFGHANISTAN.
UN
I DON'T REMEMBER WHAT STORY I WAS CHASING OR WHAT POINT I WAS TRYING TO PROVE.
UN
MAYBE IT WAS WHAT THAT AUSSIE EXPAT SAID, THAT I'D NEVER REALLY BEEN TO WAR. MAYBE I WAS TRYING TO PROVE HIM WRONG.
WHO KNOWS. IT WAS THE SUMMER OF 2007, MY THIRD STRAIGHT YEAR OF WAR. SHARON HAD QUIT, AND I HAD A NEW EDITOR, WHO HAD NO IDEA WHAT I WAS UP TO AND DIDN'T SEEM TO CARE, ANYWAYS.
I WAS OUT THERE, ALL ALONE, PROPELLED LIKE SOME MAD ROCKET.

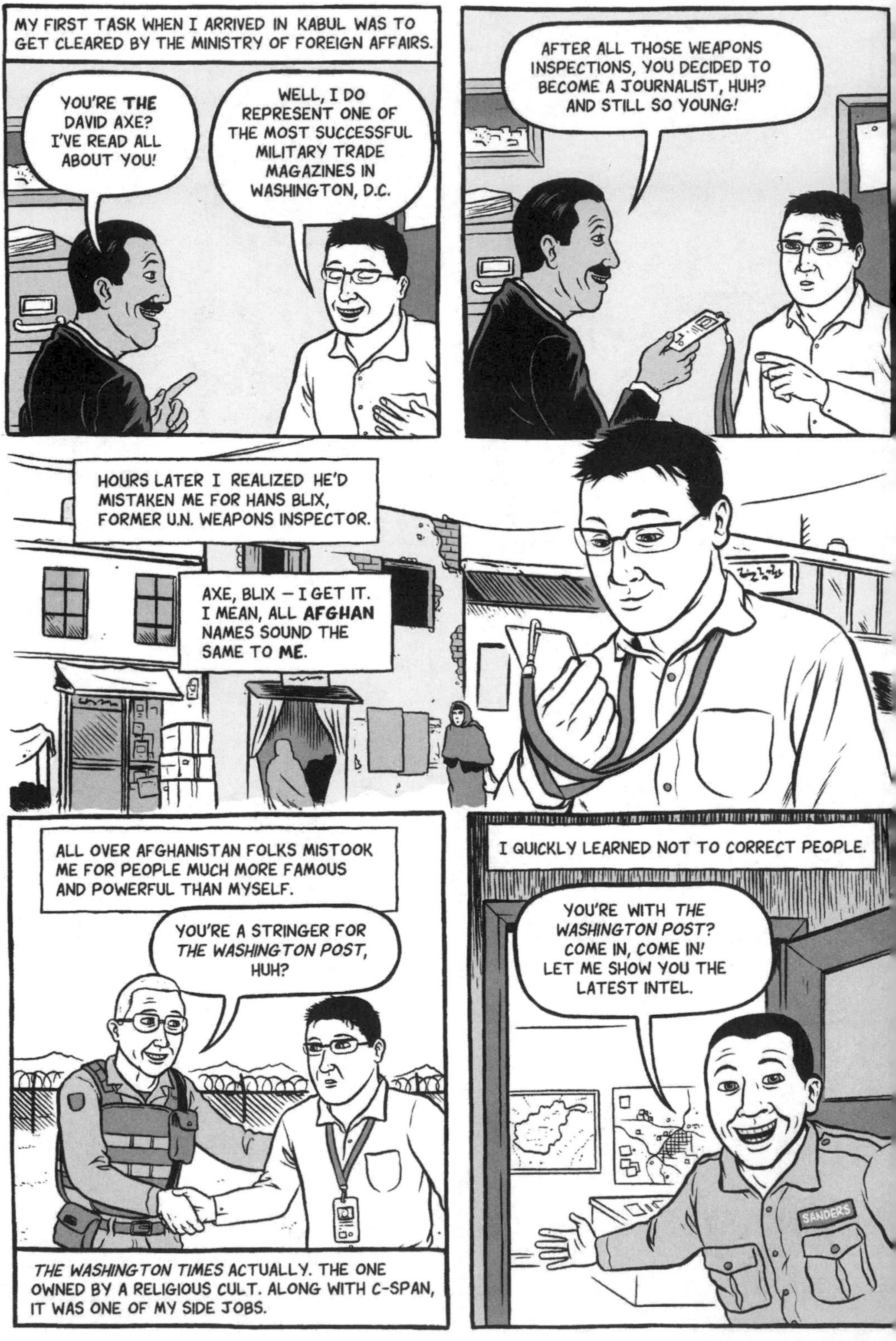
MY FIRST TASK WHEN I ARRIVED IN KABUL WAS TO GET CLEARED BY THE MINISTRY OF FOREIGN AFFAIRS.
YOU'RE **THE** DAVID AXE? I'VE READ ALL ABOUT YOU!
WELL, I DO REPRESENT ONE OF THE MOST SUCCESSFUL MILITARY TRADE MAGAZINES IN WASHINGTON, D.C.
AFTER ALL THOSE WEAPONS INSPECTIONS, YOU DECIDED TO BECOME A JOURNALIST, HUH? AND STILL SO YOUNG!
HOURS LATER I REALIZED HE'D MISTAKEN ME FOR HANS BLIX, FORMER U.N. WEAPONS INSPECTOR.
AXE, BLIX — I GET IT. I MEAN, ALL **AFGHAN** NAMES SOUND THE SAME TO **ME**.
ALL OVER AFGHANISTAN FOLKS MISTOOK ME FOR PEOPLE MUCH MORE FAMOUS AND POWERFUL THAN MYSELF.
YOU'RE A STRINGER FOR *THE WASHINGTON POST*, HUH?
THE WASHINGTON TIMES ACTUALLY. THE ONE OWNED BY A RELIGIOUS CULT. ALONG WITH C-SPAN, IT WAS ONE OF MY SIDE JOBS.
I QUICKLY LEARNED NOT TO CORRECT PEOPLE.
YOU'RE WITH *THE WASHINGTON POST*? COME IN, COME IN! LET ME SHOW YOU THE LATEST INTEL.
SANDERS

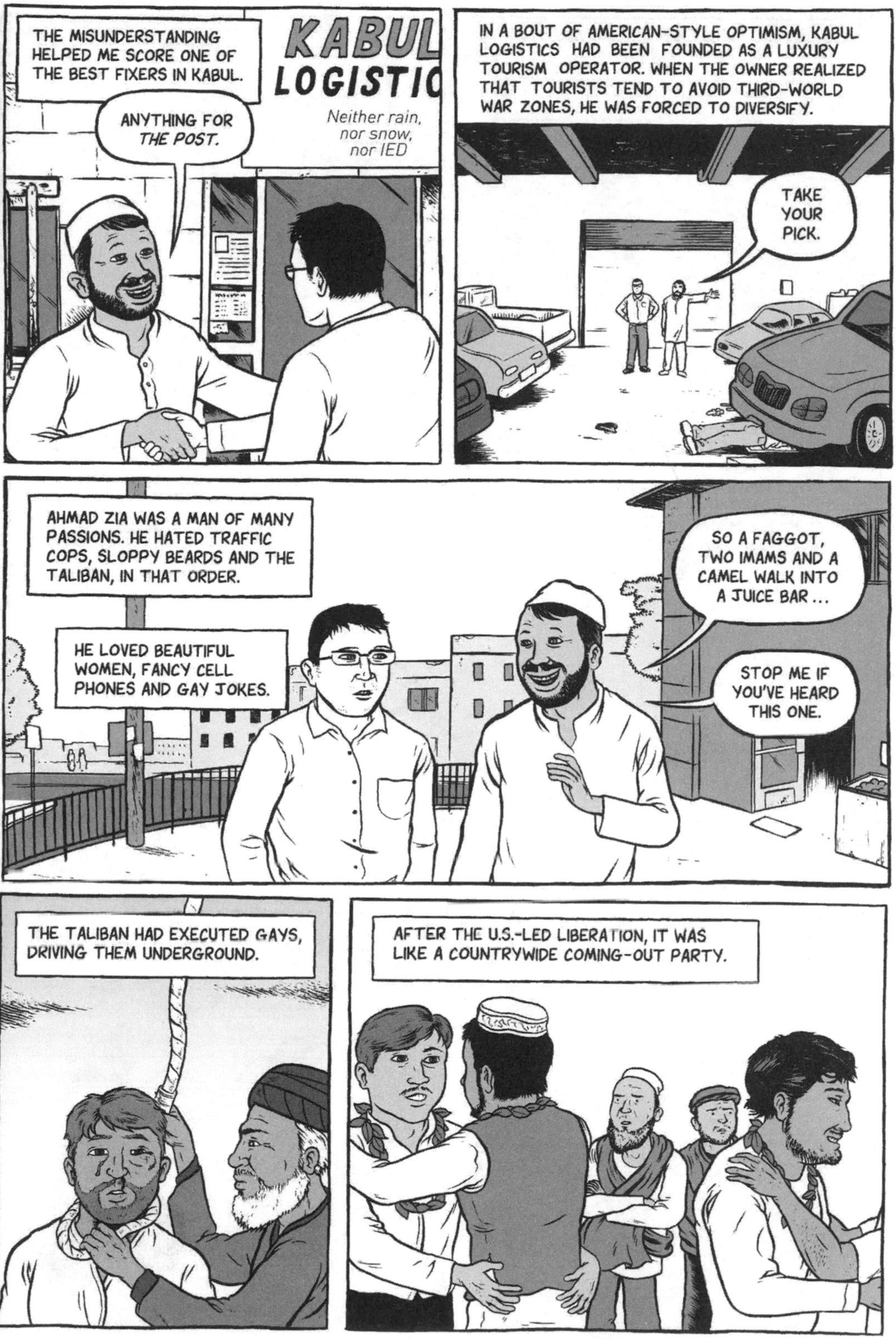
THE MISUNDERSTANDING HELPED ME SCORE ONE OF THE BEST FIXERS IN KABUL.
KABUL LOGISTIC
Neither rain, nor snow, nor IED
ANYTHING FOR THE POST.
IN A BOUT OF AMERICAN-STYLE OPTIMISM, KABUL LOGISTICS HAD BEEN FOUNDED AS A LUXURY TOURISM OPERATOR. WHEN THE OWNER REALIZED THAT TOURISTS TEND TO AVOID THIRD-WORLD WAR ZONES, HE WAS FORCED TO DIVERSIFY.
TAKE YOUR PICK.
AHMAD ZIA WAS A MAN OF MANY PASSIONS. HE HATED TRAFFIC COPS, SLOPPY BEARDS AND THE TALIBAN, IN THAT ORDER.
HE LOVED BEAUTIFUL WOMEN, FANCY CELL PHONES AND GAY JOKES.
SO A FAGGOT, TWO IMAMS AND A CAMEL WALK INTO A JUICE BAR...
STOP ME IF YOU'VE HEARD THIS ONE.
THE TALIBAN HAD EXECUTED GAYS, DRIVING THEM UNDERGROUND.
AFTER THE U.S.-LED LIBERATION, IT WAS LIKE A COUNTRYWIDE COMING-OUT PARTY.

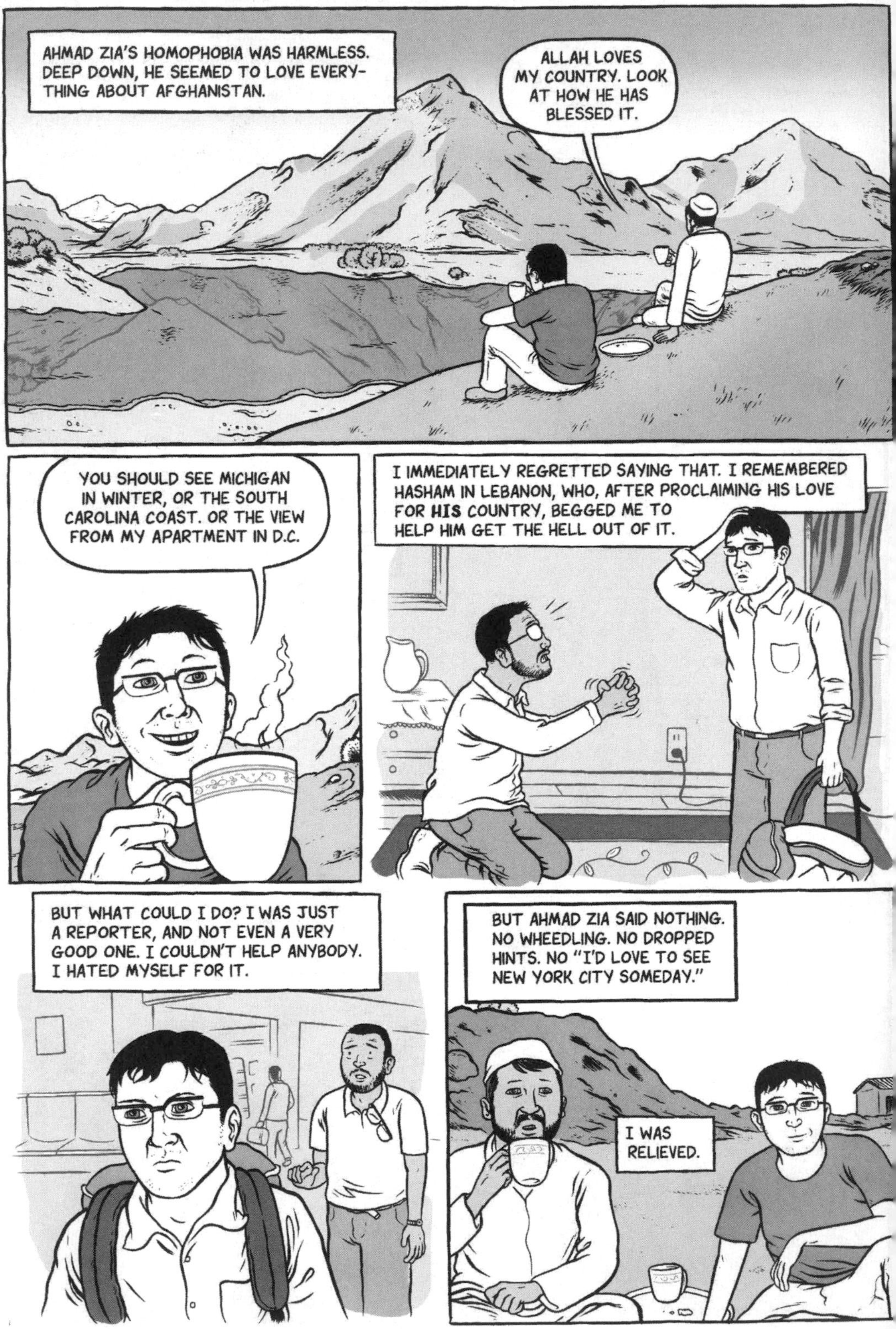
AHMAD ZIA'S HOMOPHOBIA WAS HARMLESS. DEEP DOWN, HE SEEMED TO LOVE EVERY-THING ABOUT AFGHANISTAN.
ALLAH LOVES MY COUNTRY. LOOK AT HOW HE HAS BLESSED IT.
YOU SHOULD SEE MICHIGAN IN WINTER, OR THE SOUTH CAROLINA COAST. OR THE VIEW FROM MY APARTMENT IN D.C.
I IMMEDIATELY REGRETTED SAYING THAT. I REMEMBERED HASHAM IN LEBANON, WHO, AFTER PROCLAIMING HIS LOVE FOR HIS COUNTRY, BEGGED ME TO HELP HIM GET THE HELL OUT OF IT.
BUT WHAT COULD I DO? I WAS JUST A REPORTER, AND NOT EVEN A VERY GOOD ONE. I COULDN'T HELP ANYBODY. I HATED MYSELF FOR IT.
BUT AHMAD ZIA SAID NOTHING. NO WHEEDLING. NO DROPPED HINTS. NO "I'D LOVE TO SEE NEW YORK CITY SOMEDAY."
I WAS RELIEVED.

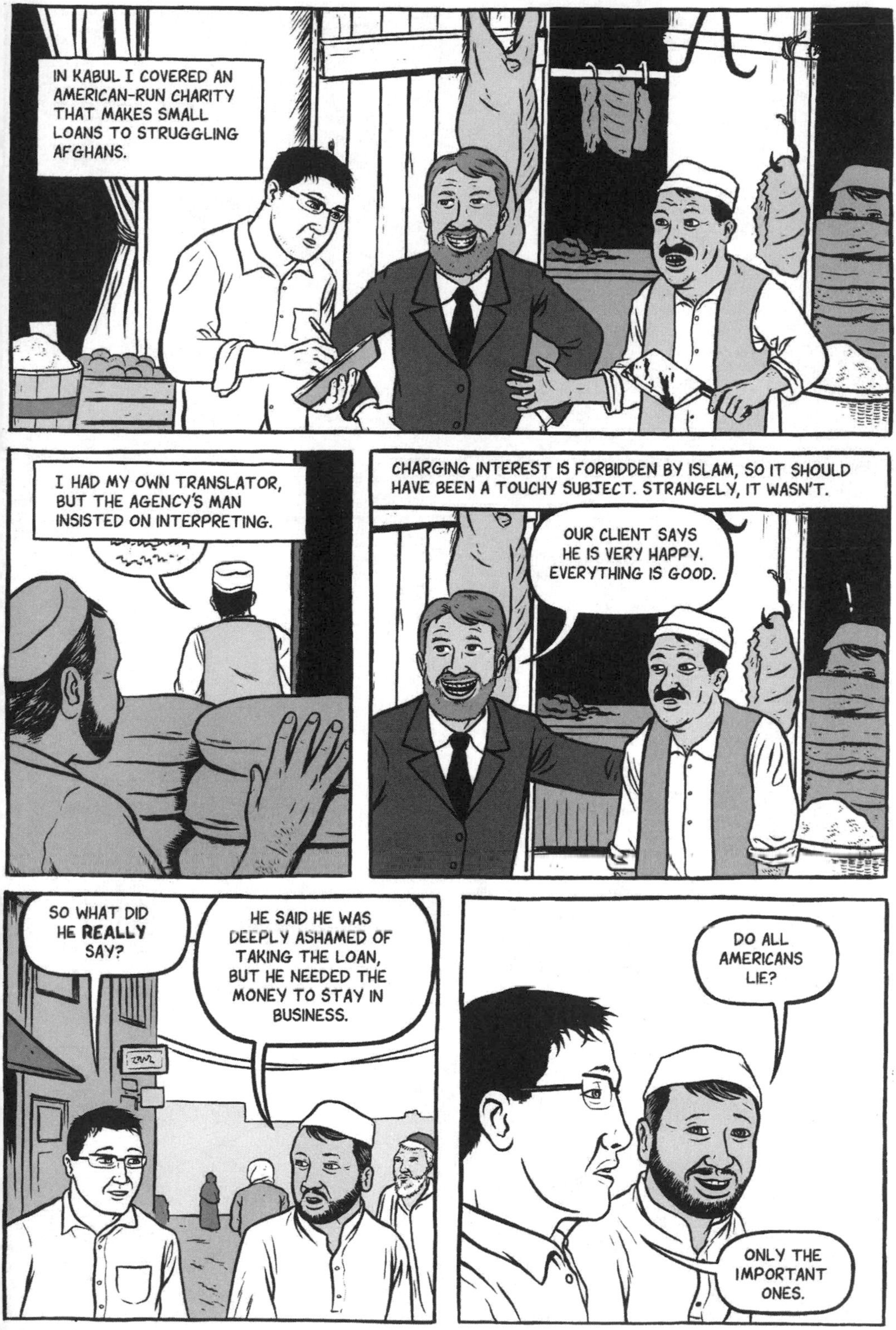
IN KABUL I COVERED AN AMERICAN-RUN CHARITY THAT MAKES SMALL LOANS TO STRUGGLING AFGHANS.
I HAD MY OWN TRANSLATOR, BUT THE AGENCY'S MAN INSISTED ON INTERPRETING.
CHARGING INTEREST IS FORBIDDEN BY ISLAM, SO IT SHOULD HAVE BEEN A TOUCHY SUBJECT. STRANGELY, IT WASN'T.
OUR CLIENT SAYS HE IS VERY HAPPY. EVERYTHING IS GOOD.
SO WHAT DID HE **REALLY** SAY?
HE SAID HE WAS DEEPLY ASHAMED OF TAKING THE LOAN, BUT HE NEEDED THE MONEY TO STAY IN BUSINESS.
DO ALL AMERICANS LIE?
ONLY THE IMPORTANT ONES.

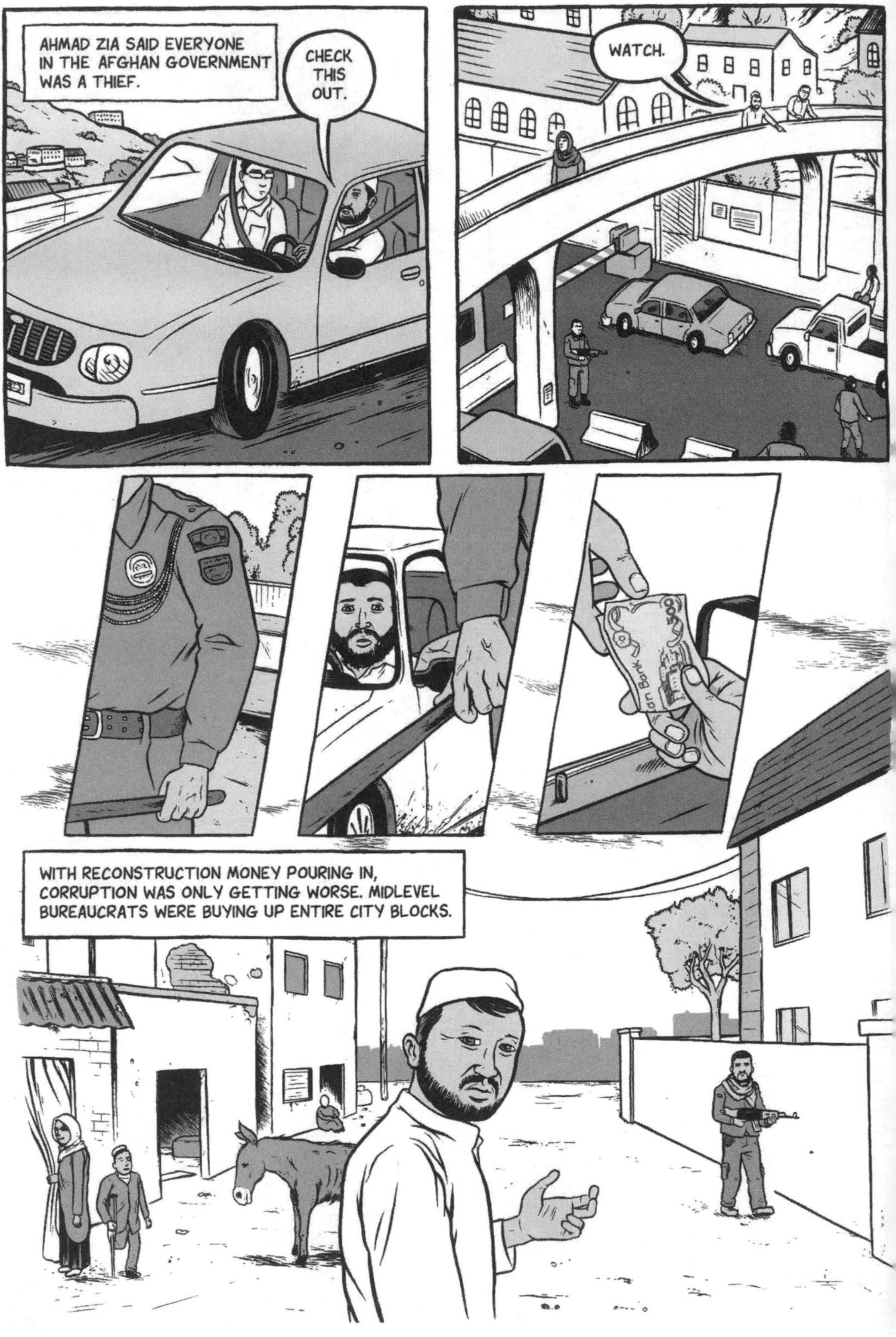
AHMAD ZIA SAID EVERYONE IN THE AFGHAN GOVERNMENT WAS A THIEF.
CHECK THIS OUT.
WATCH.
WITH RECONSTRUCTION MONEY POURING IN, CORRUPTION WAS ONLY GETTING WORSE. MIDLEVEL BUREAUCRATS WERE BUYING UP ENTIRE CITY BLOCKS.

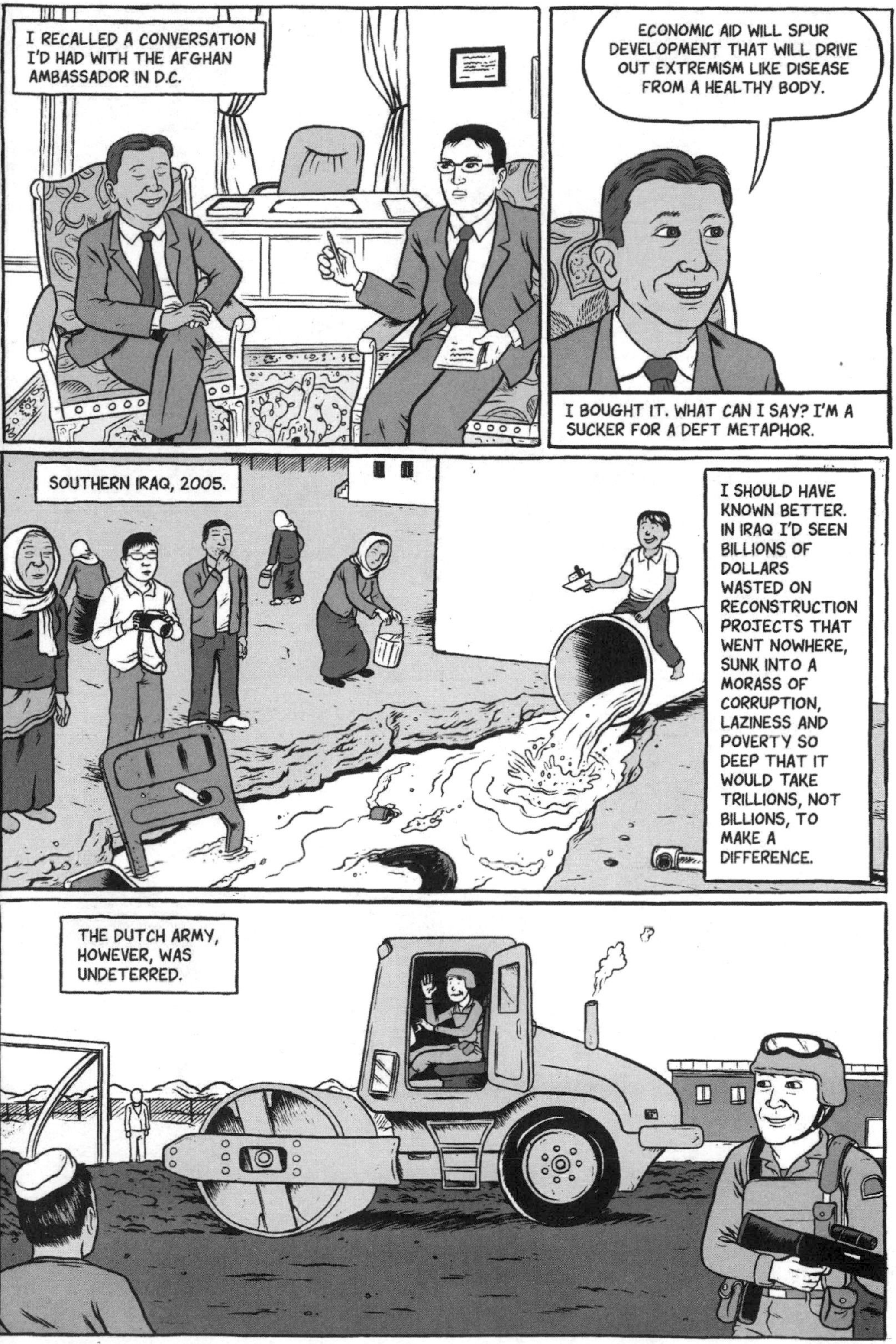
I RECALLED A CONVERSATION I'D HAD WITH THE AFGHAN AMBASSADOR IN D.C.
ECONOMIC AID WILL SPUR DEVELOPMENT THAT WILL DRIVE OUT EXTREMISM LIKE DISEASE FROM A HEALTHY BODY.
I BOUGHT IT. WHAT CAN I SAY? I'M A SUCKER FOR A DEFT METAPHOR.
SOUTHERN IRAQ, 2005.
I SHOULD HAVE KNOWN BETTER. IN IRAQ I'D SEEN BILLIONS OF DOLLARS WASTED ON RECONSTRUCTION PROJECTS THAT WENT NOWHERE, SUNK INTO A MORASS OF CORRUPTION, LAZINESS AND POVERTY SO DEEP THAT IT WOULD TAKE TRILLIONS, NOT BILLIONS, TO MAKE A DIFFERENCE.
THE DUTCH ARMY, HOWEVER, WAS UNDETERRED.

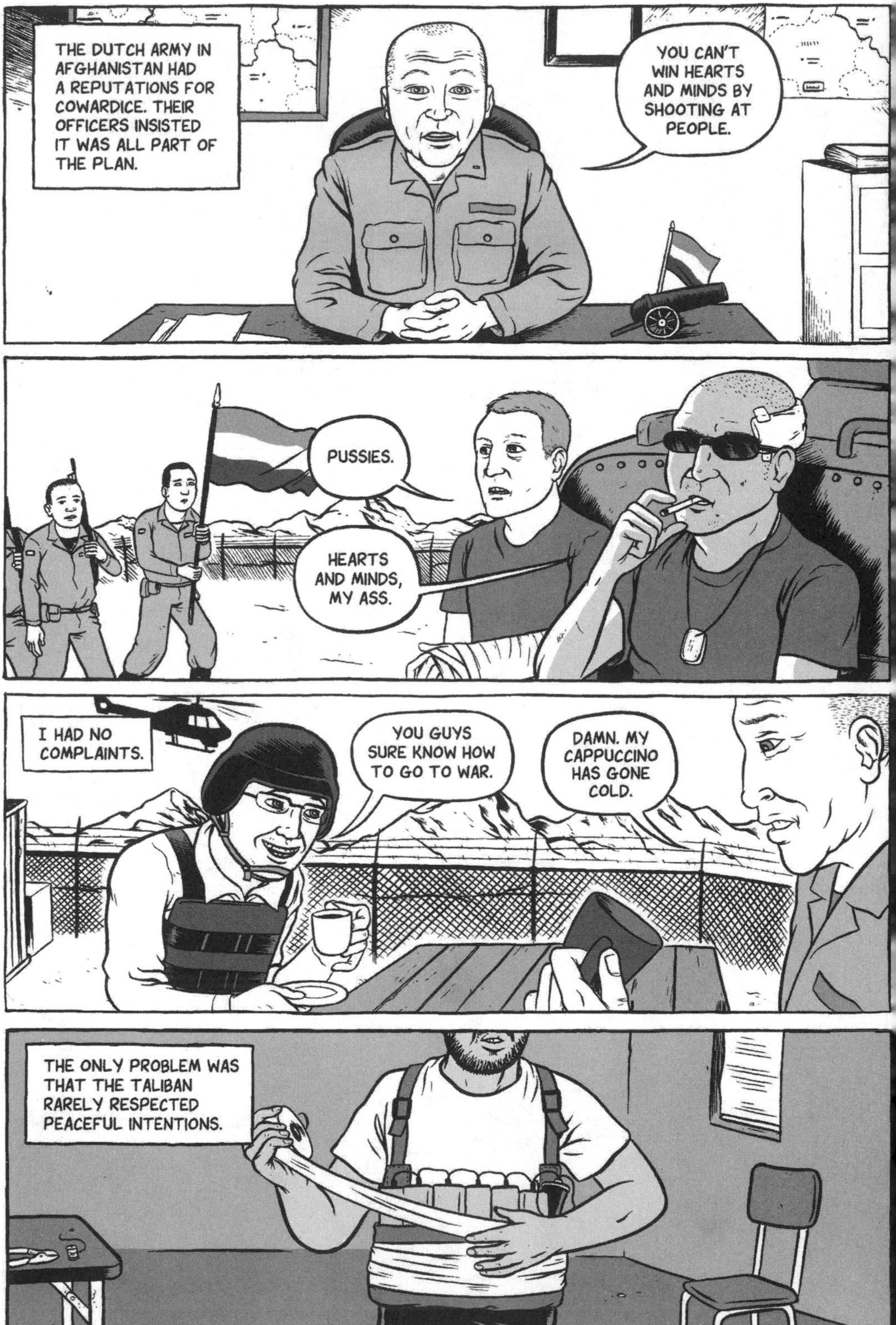
THE DUTCH ARMY IN AFGHANISTAN HAD A REPUTATIONS FOR COWARDICE. THEIR OFFICERS INSISTED IT WAS ALL PART OF THE PLAN.
YOU CAN'T WIN HEARTS AND MINDS BY SHOOTING AT PEOPLE.
PUSSIES.
HEARTS AND MINDS, MY ASS.
I HAD NO COMPLAINTS.
YOU GUYS SURE KNOW HOW TO GO TO WAR.
DAMN. MY CAPPUCCINO HAS GONE COLD.
THE ONLY PROBLEM WAS THAT THE TALIBAN RARELY RESPECTED PEACEFUL INTENTIONS.

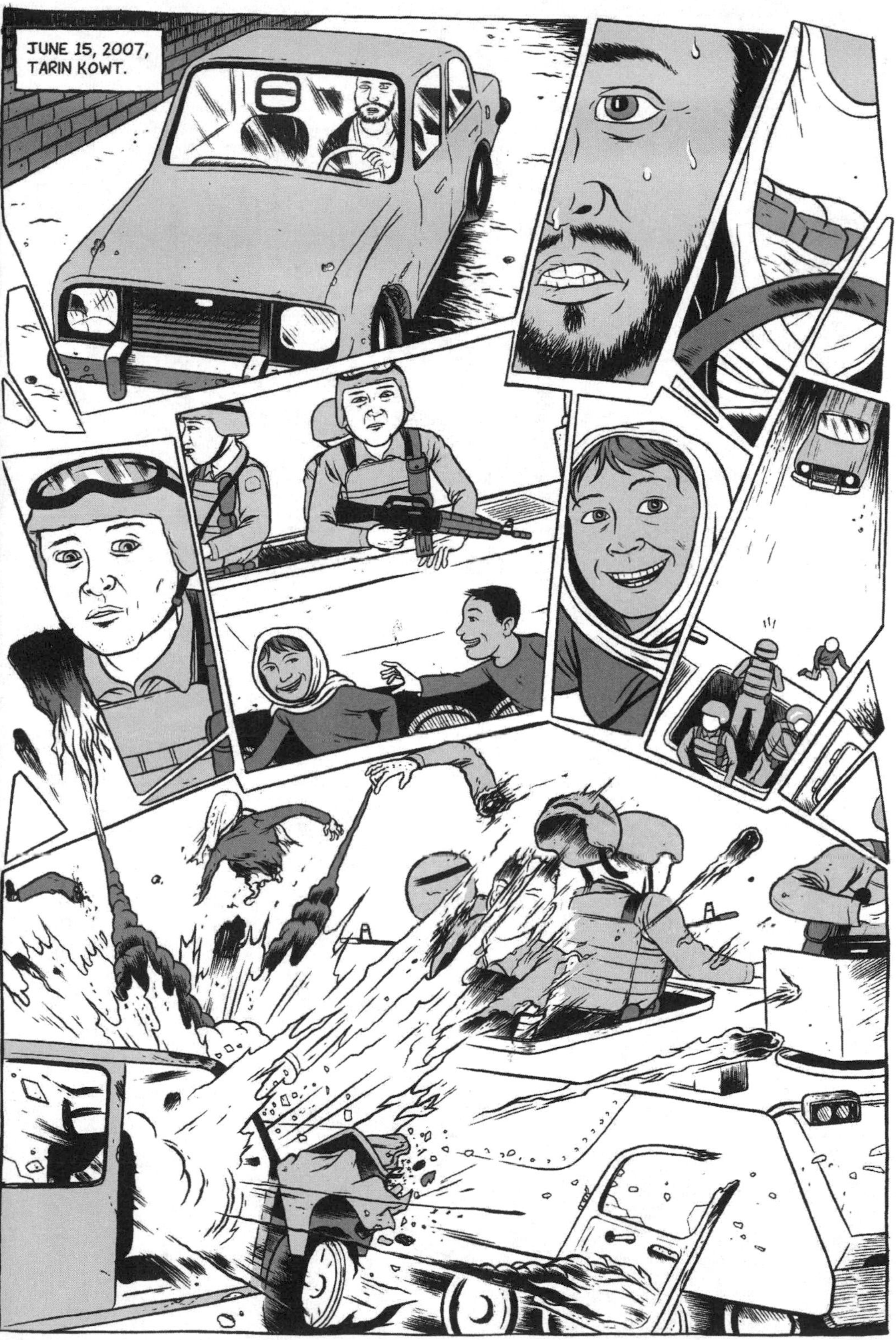
JUNE 15, 2007,
TARIN KOWT.

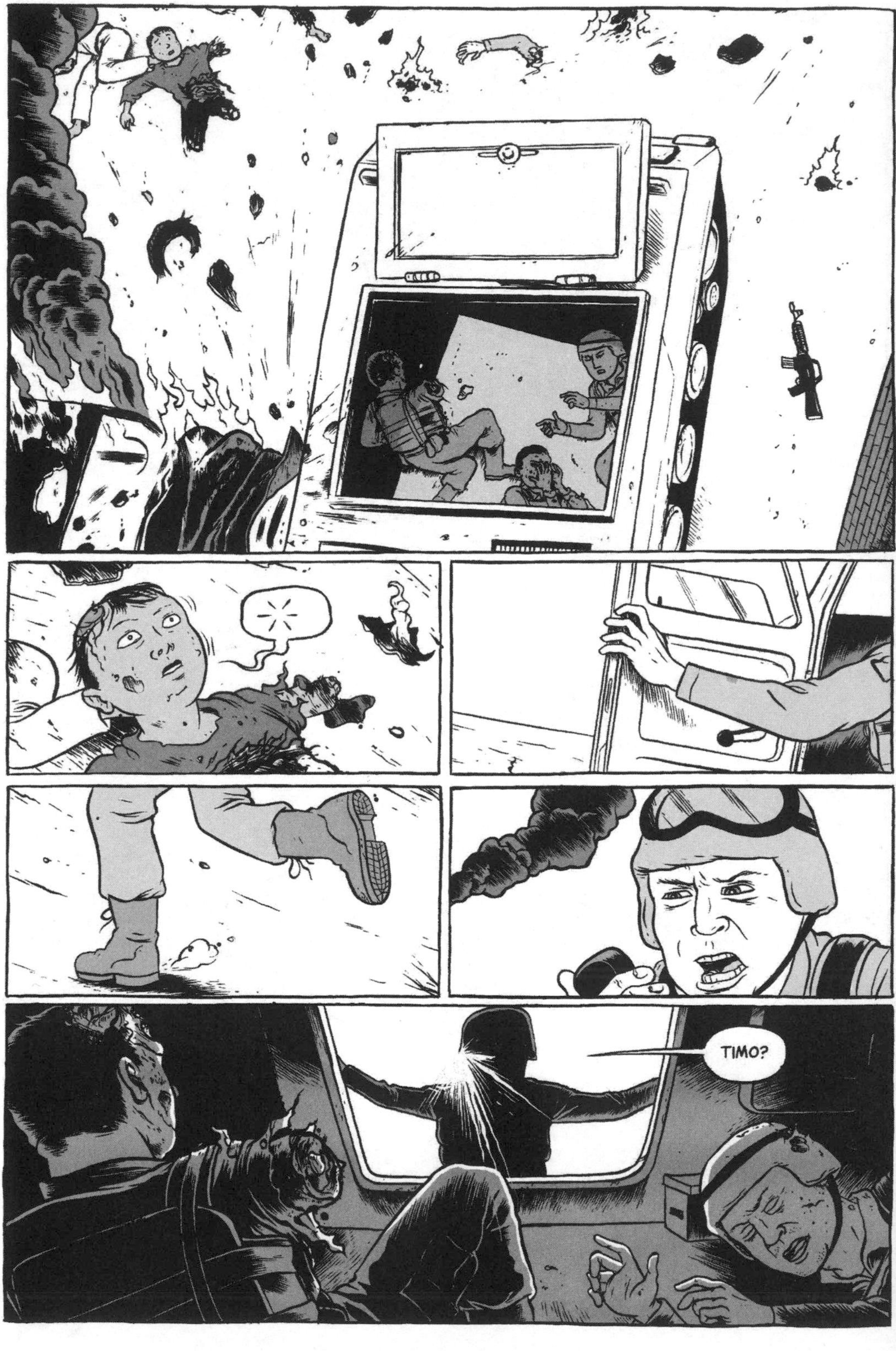
TIMO?

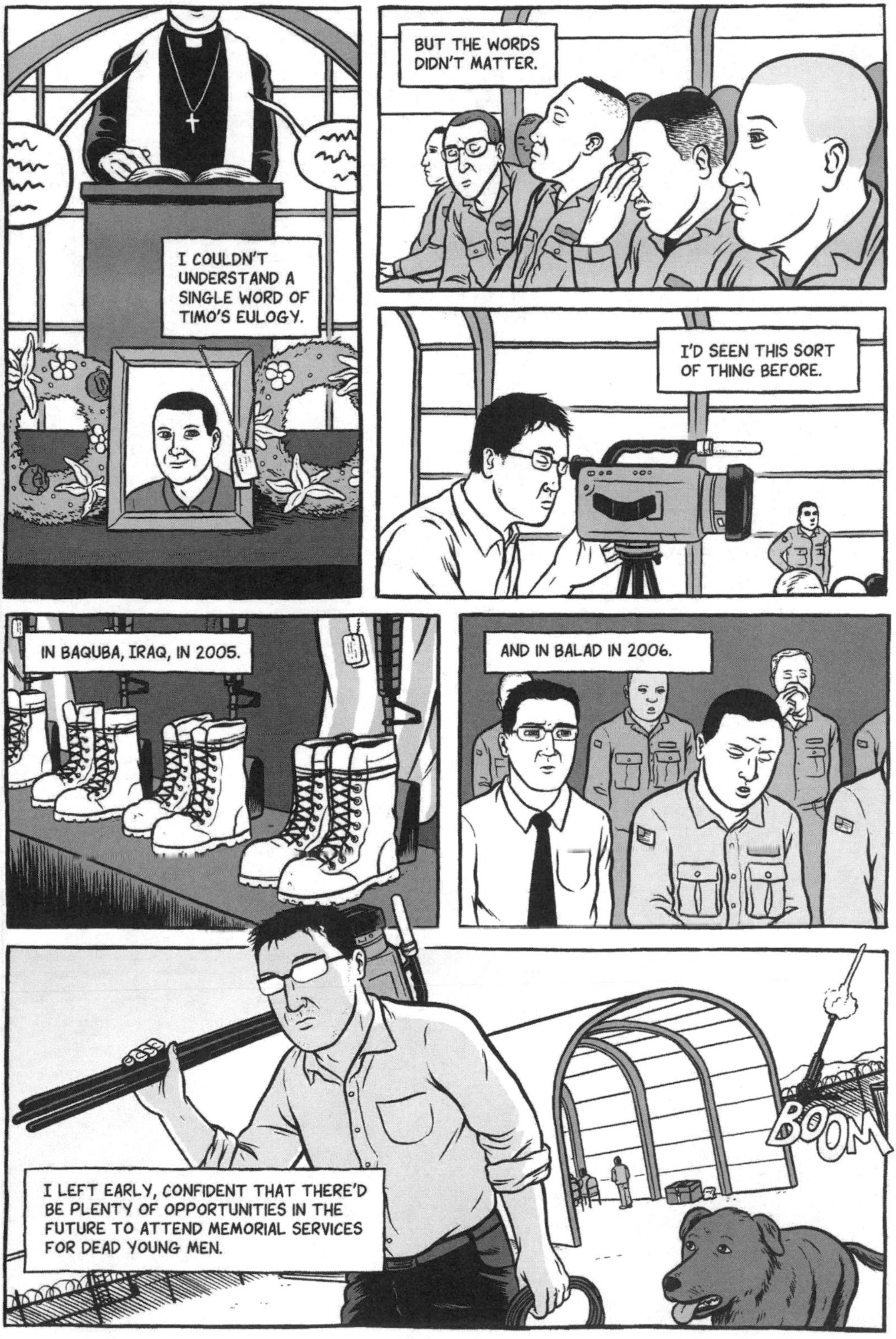
I COULDN'T UNDERSTAND A SINGLE WORD OF TIMO'S EULOGY.
BUT THE WORDS DIDN'T MATTER.
I'D SEEN THIS SORT OF THING BEFORE.
IN BAQUBA, IRAQ, IN 2005.
AND IN BALAD IN 2006.
I LEFT EARLY, CONFIDENT THAT THERE'D BE PLENTY OF OPPORTUNITIES IN THE FUTURE TO ATTEND MEMORIAL SERVICES FOR DEAD YOUNG MEN.
BOOM

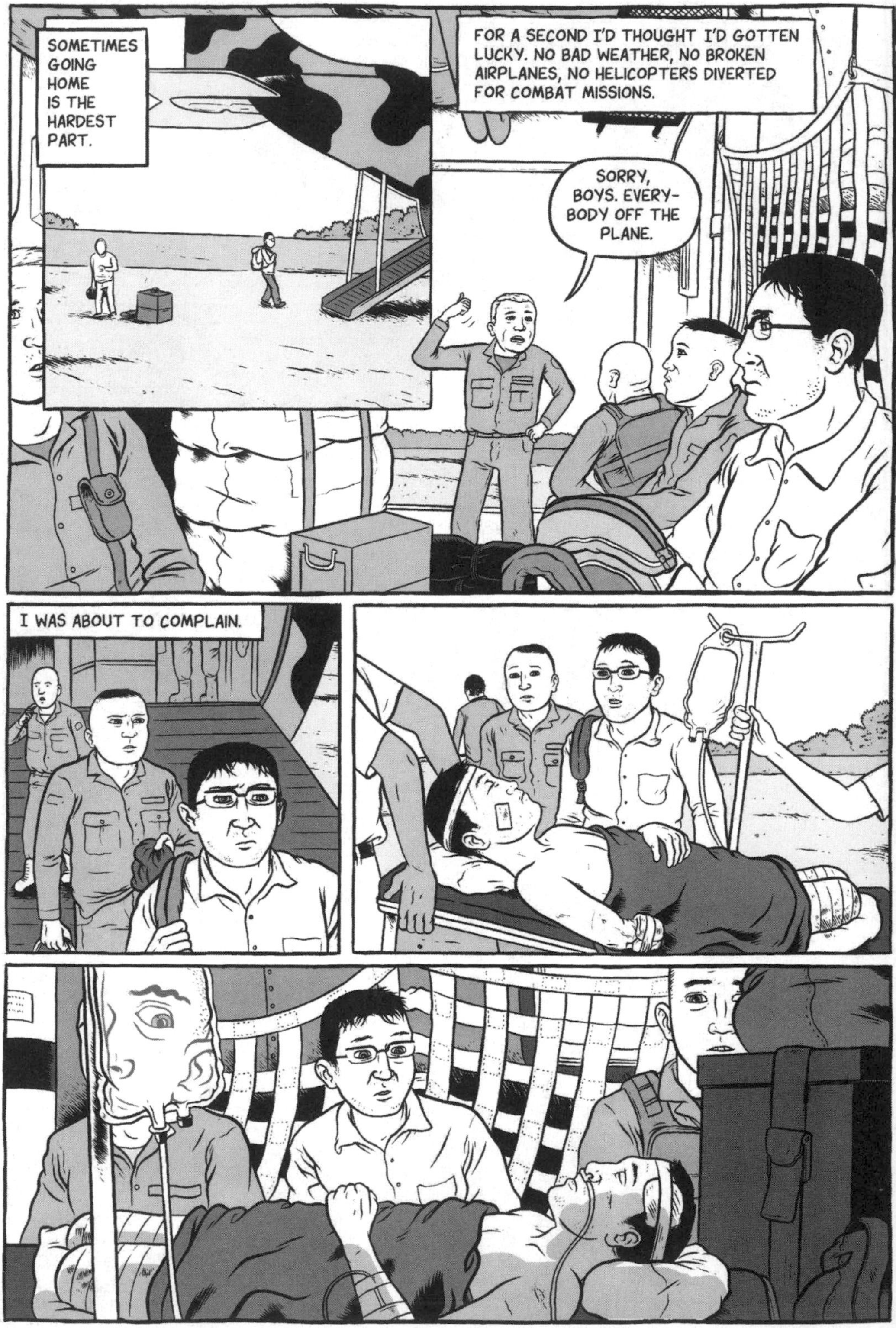
SOMETIMES GOING HOME IS THE HARDEST PART.
FOR A SECOND I'D THOUGHT I'D GOTTEN LUCKY. NO BAD WEATHER, NO BROKEN AIRPLANES, NO HELICOPTERS DIVERTED FOR COMBAT MISSIONS.
SORRY, BOYS. EVERY-BODY OFF THE PLANE.
I WAS ABOUT TO COMPLAIN.

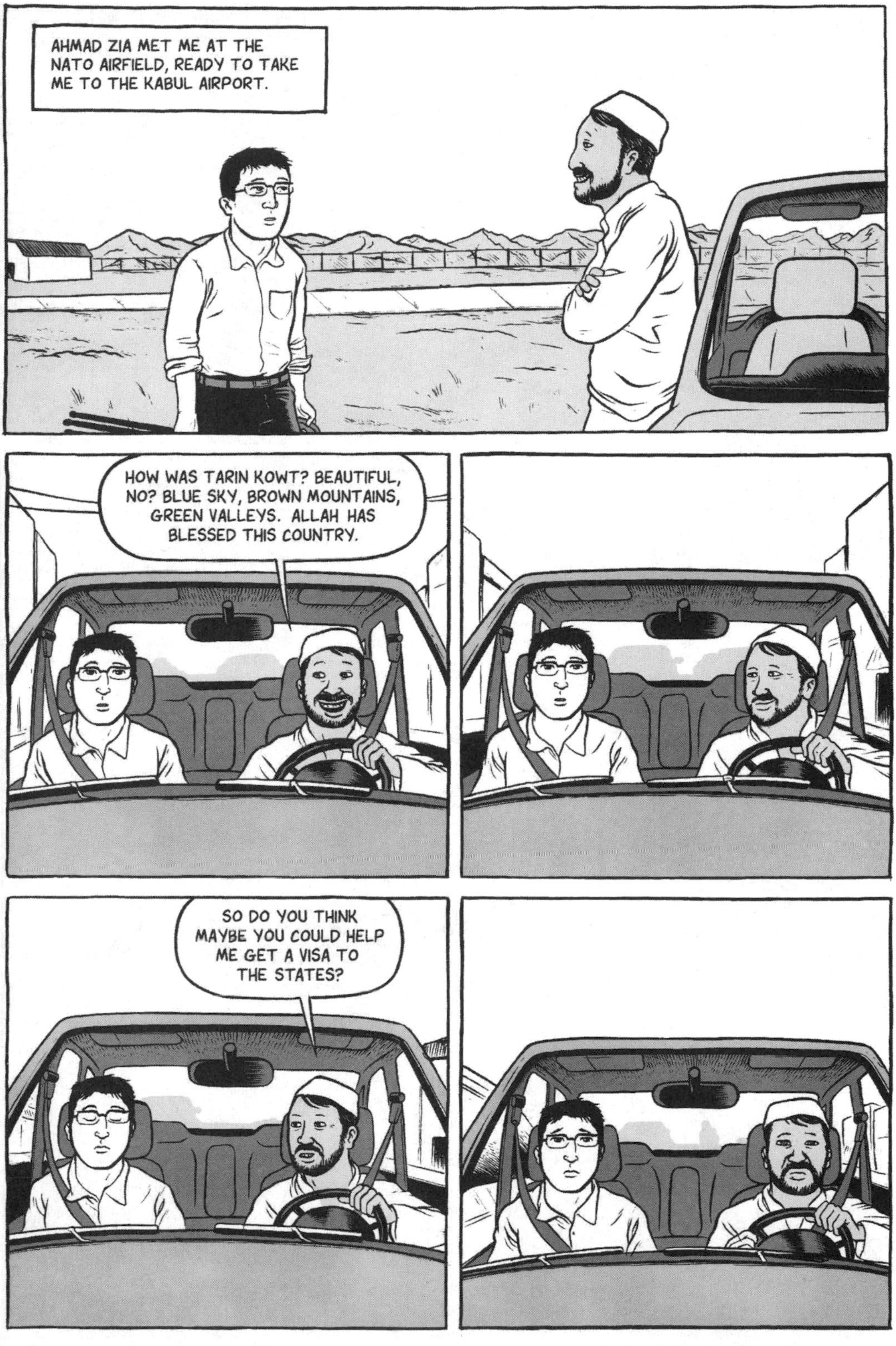
AHMAD ZIA MET ME AT THE NATO AIRFIELD, READY TO TAKE ME TO THE KABUL AIRPORT.
HOW WAS TARIN KOWT? BEAUTIFUL, NO? BLUE SKY, BROWN MOUNTAINS, GREEN VALLEYS. ALLAH HAS BLESSED THIS COUNTRY.
SO DO YOU THINK MAYBE YOU COULD HELP ME GET A VISA TO THE STATES?

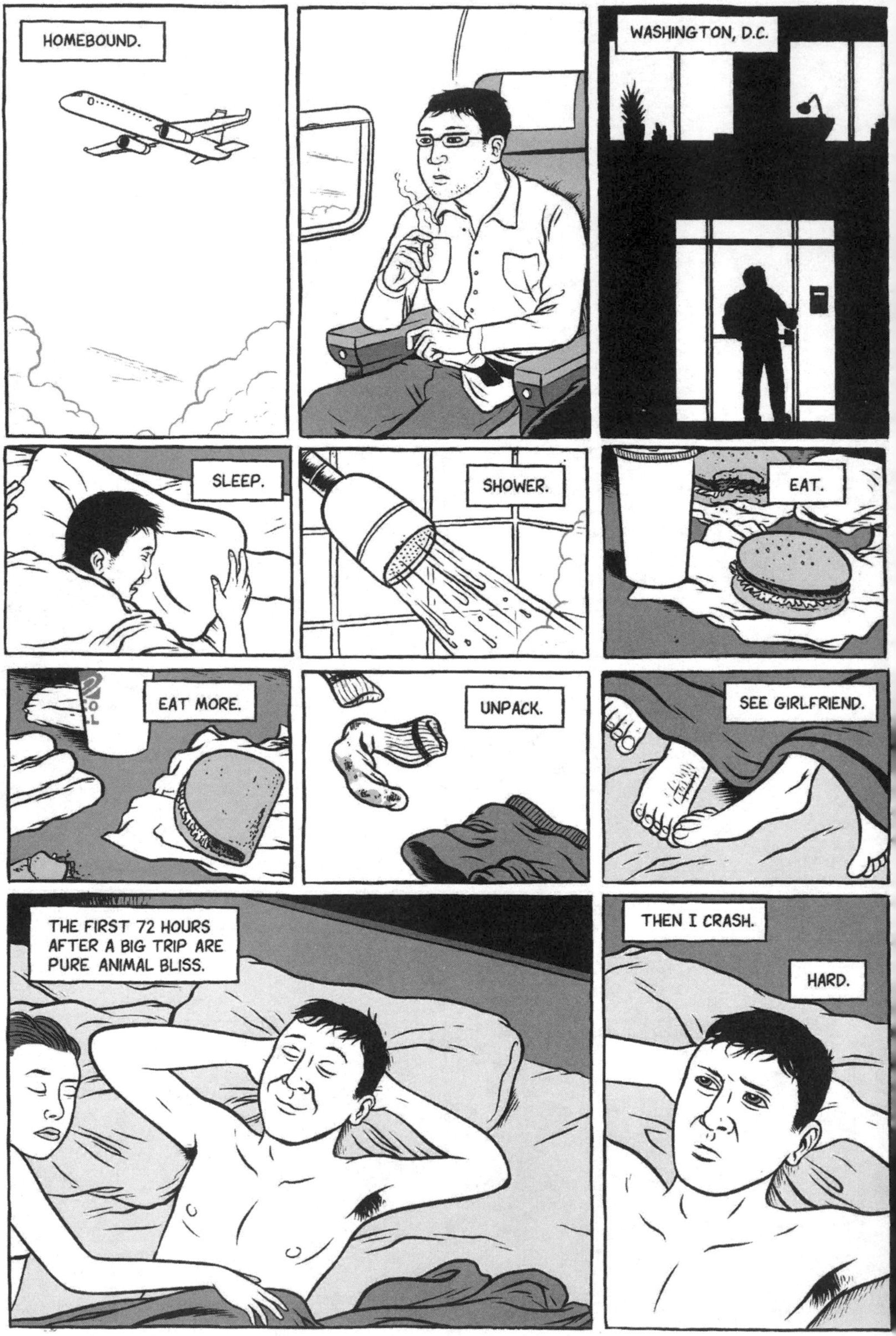
HOMEBOUND.
WASHINGTON, D.C.
SLEEP.
SHOWER.
EAT.
EAT MORE.
UNPACK.
SEE GIRLFRIEND.
THE FIRST 72 HOURS AFTER A BIG TRIP ARE PURE ANIMAL BLISS.
THEN I CRASH.
HARD.

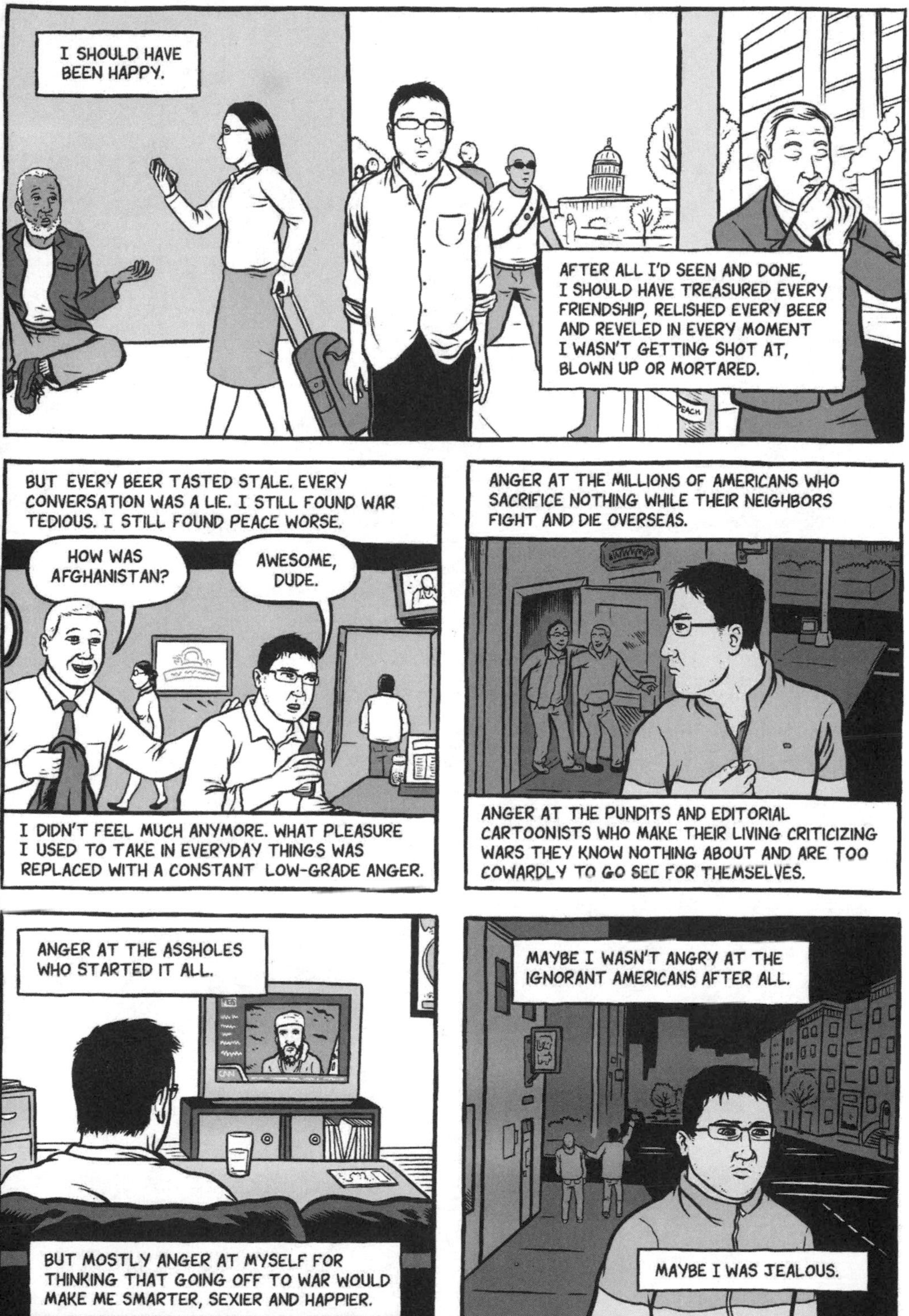
I SHOULD HAVE BEEN HAPPY.
AFTER ALL I'D SEEN AND DONE, I SHOULD HAVE TREASURED EVERY FRIENDSHIP, RELISHED EVERY BEER AND REVELED IN EVERY MOMENT I WASN'T GETTING SHOT AT, BLOWN UP OR MORTARED.
BUT EVERY BEER TASTED STALE. EVERY CONVERSATION WAS A LIE. I STILL FOUND WAR TEDIOUS. I STILL FOUND PEACE WORSE.
HOW WAS AFGHANISTAN?
AWESOME, DUDE.
I DIDN'T FEEL MUCH ANYMORE. WHAT PLEASURE I USED TO TAKE IN EVERYDAY THINGS WAS REPLACED WITH A CONSTANT LOW-GRADE ANGER.
ANGER AT THE MILLIONS OF AMERICANS WHO SACRIFICE NOTHING WHILE THEIR NEIGHBORS FIGHT AND DIE OVERSEAS.
ANGER AT THE PUNDITS AND EDITORIAL CARTOONISTS WHO MAKE THEIR LIVING CRITICIZING WARS THEY KNOW NOTHING ABOUT AND ARE TOO COWARDLY TO GO SEE FOR THEMSELVES.
ANGER AT THE ASSHOLES WHO STARTED IT ALL.
BUT MOSTLY ANGER AT MYSELF FOR THINKING THAT GOING OFF TO WAR WOULD MAKE ME SMARTER, SEXIER AND HAPPIER.
MAYBE I WASN'T ANGRY AT THE IGNORANT AMERICANS AFTER ALL.
MAYBE I WAS JEALOUS.

SOMALIA

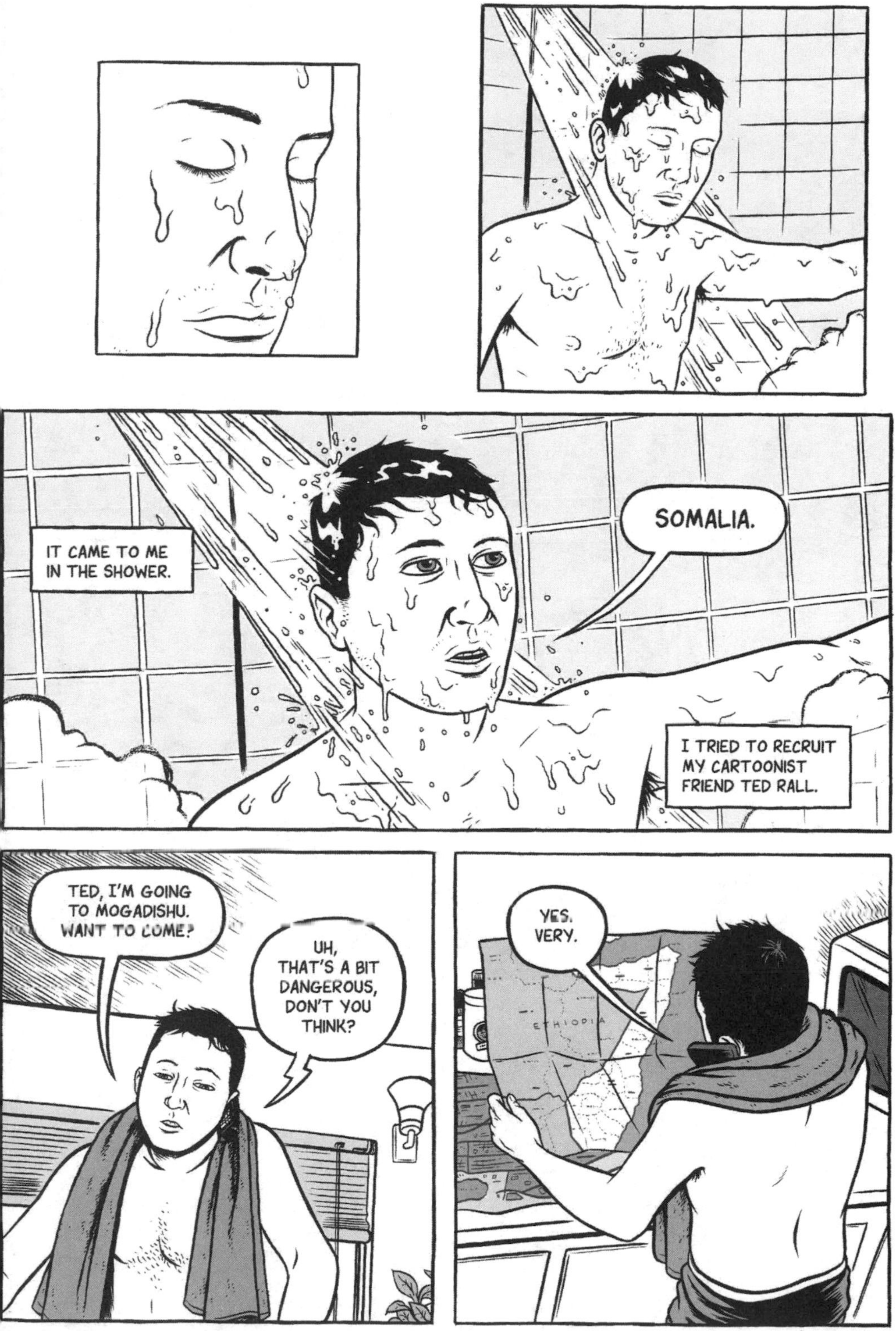
IT CAME TO ME IN THE SHOWER.
SOMALIA.
I TRIED TO RECRUIT MY CARTOONIST FRIEND TED RALL.
TED, I'M GOING TO MOGADISHU. WANT TO COME?
UH, THAT'S A BIT DANGEROUS, DON'T YOU THINK?
YES. VERY.
ETHIOPIA

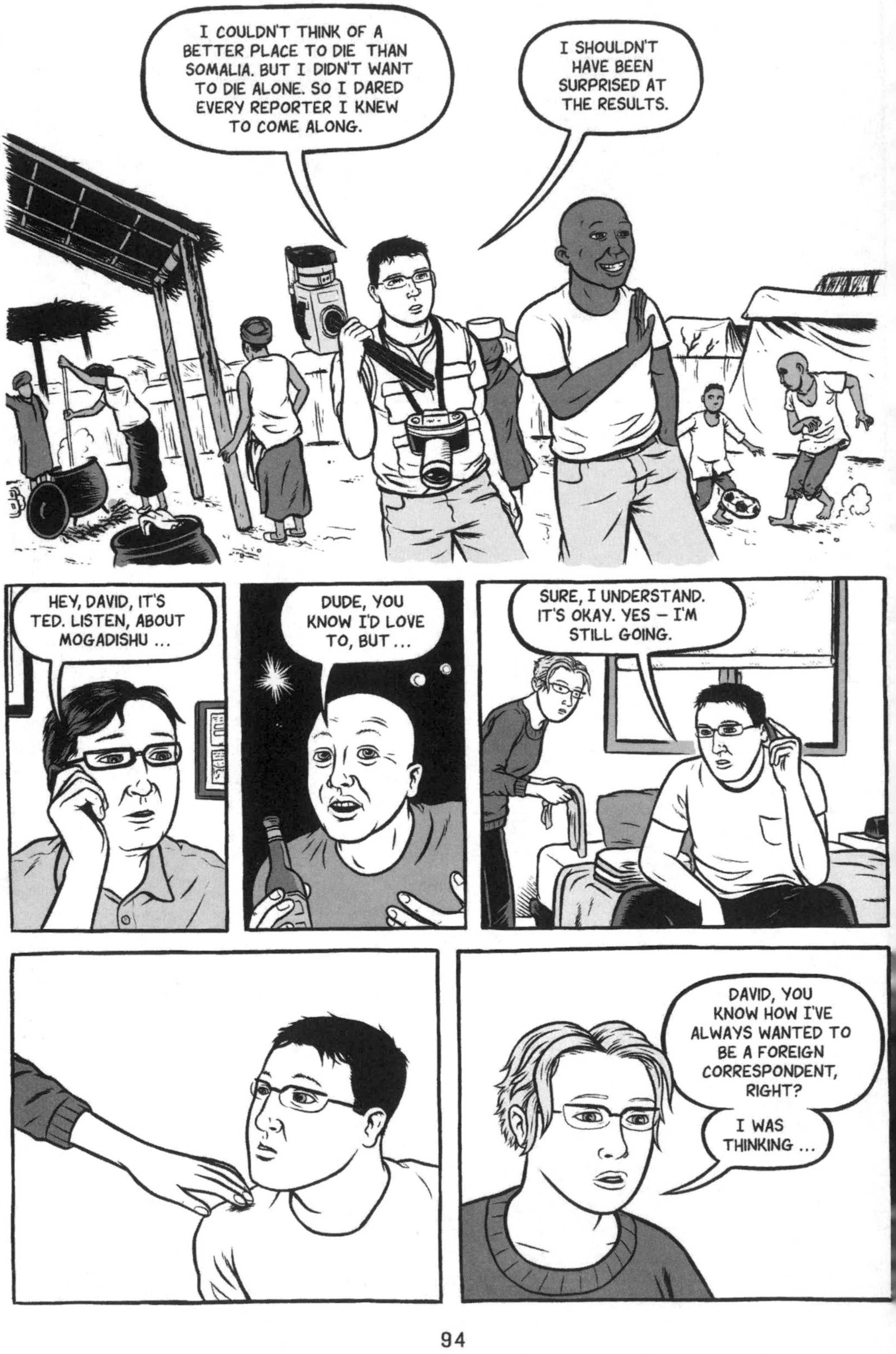
I COULDN'T THINK OF A BETTER PLACE TO DIE THAN SOMALIA. BUT I DIDN'T WANT TO DIE ALONE. SO I DARED EVERY REPORTER I KNEW TO COME ALONG.
I SHOULDN'T HAVE BEEN SURPRISED AT THE RESULTS.
HEY, DAVID, IT'S TED. LISTEN, ABOUT MOGADISHU ...
DUDE, YOU KNOW I'D LOVE TO, BUT ...
SURE, I UNDERSTAND. IT'S OKAY. YES – I'M STILL GOING.
DAVID, YOU KNOW HOW I'VE ALWAYS WANTED TO BE A FOREIGN CORRESPONDENT, RIGHT?
I WAS THINKING ...

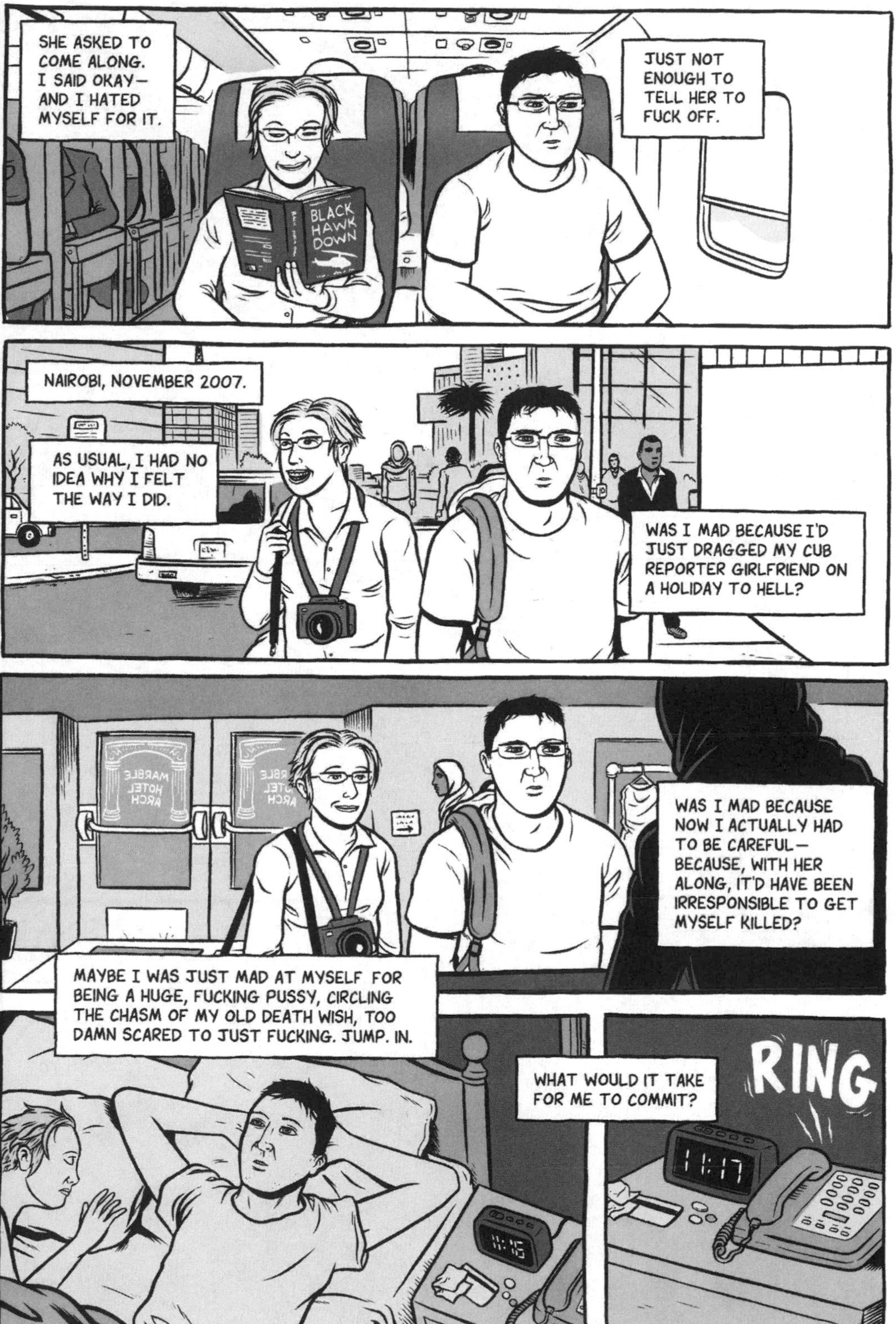
SHE ASKED TO COME ALONG. I SAID OKAY— AND I HATED MYSELF FOR IT.
JUST NOT ENOUGH TO TELL HER TO FUCK OFF.
BLACK HAWK DOWN
NAIROBI, NOVEMBER 2007.
AS USUAL, I HAD NO IDEA WHY I FELT THE WAY I DID.
WAS I MAD BECAUSE I'D JUST DRAGGED MY CUB REPORTER GIRLFRIEND ON A HOLIDAY TO HELL?
WAS I MAD BECAUSE NOW I ACTUALLY HAD TO BE CAREFUL— BECAUSE, WITH HER ALONG, IT'D HAVE BEEN IRRESPONSIBLE TO GET MYSELF KILLED?
MAYBE I WAS JUST MAD AT MYSELF FOR BEING A HUGE, FUCKING PUSSY, CIRCLING THE CHASM OF MY OLD DEATH WISH, TOO DAMN SCARED TO JUST FUCKING. JUMP. IN.
WHAT WOULD IT TAKE FOR ME TO COMMIT?
RING
11:17

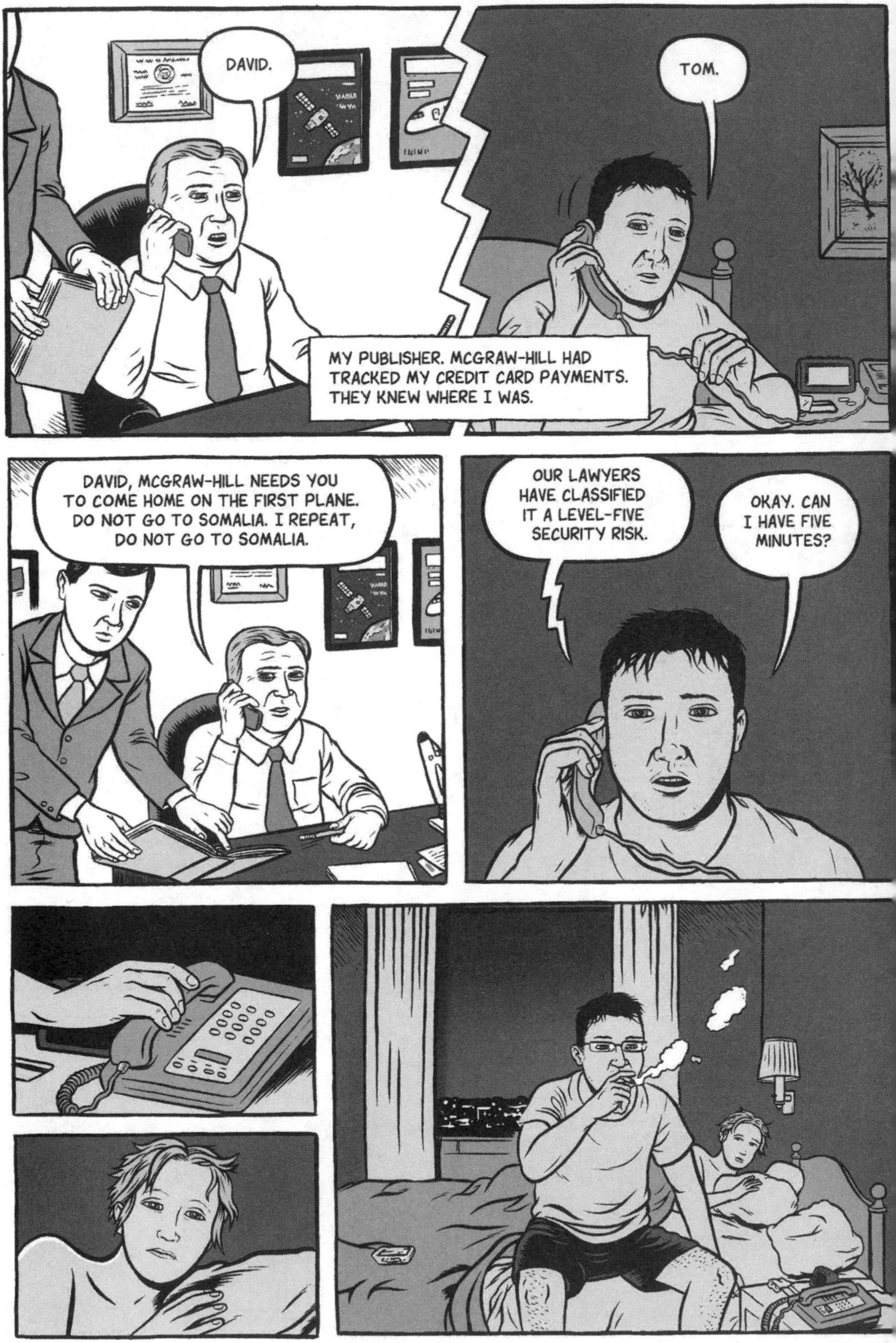
DAVID.
TOM.
MY PUBLISHER. MCGRAW-HILL HAD TRACKED MY CREDIT CARD PAYMENTS. THEY KNEW WHERE I WAS.
DAVID, MCGRAW-HILL NEEDS YOU TO COME HOME ON THE FIRST PLANE. DO NOT GO TO SOMALIA. I REPEAT, DO NOT GO TO SOMALIA.
OUR LAWYERS HAVE CLASSIFIED IT A LEVEL-FIVE SECURITY RISK.
OKAY. CAN I HAVE FIVE MINUTES?

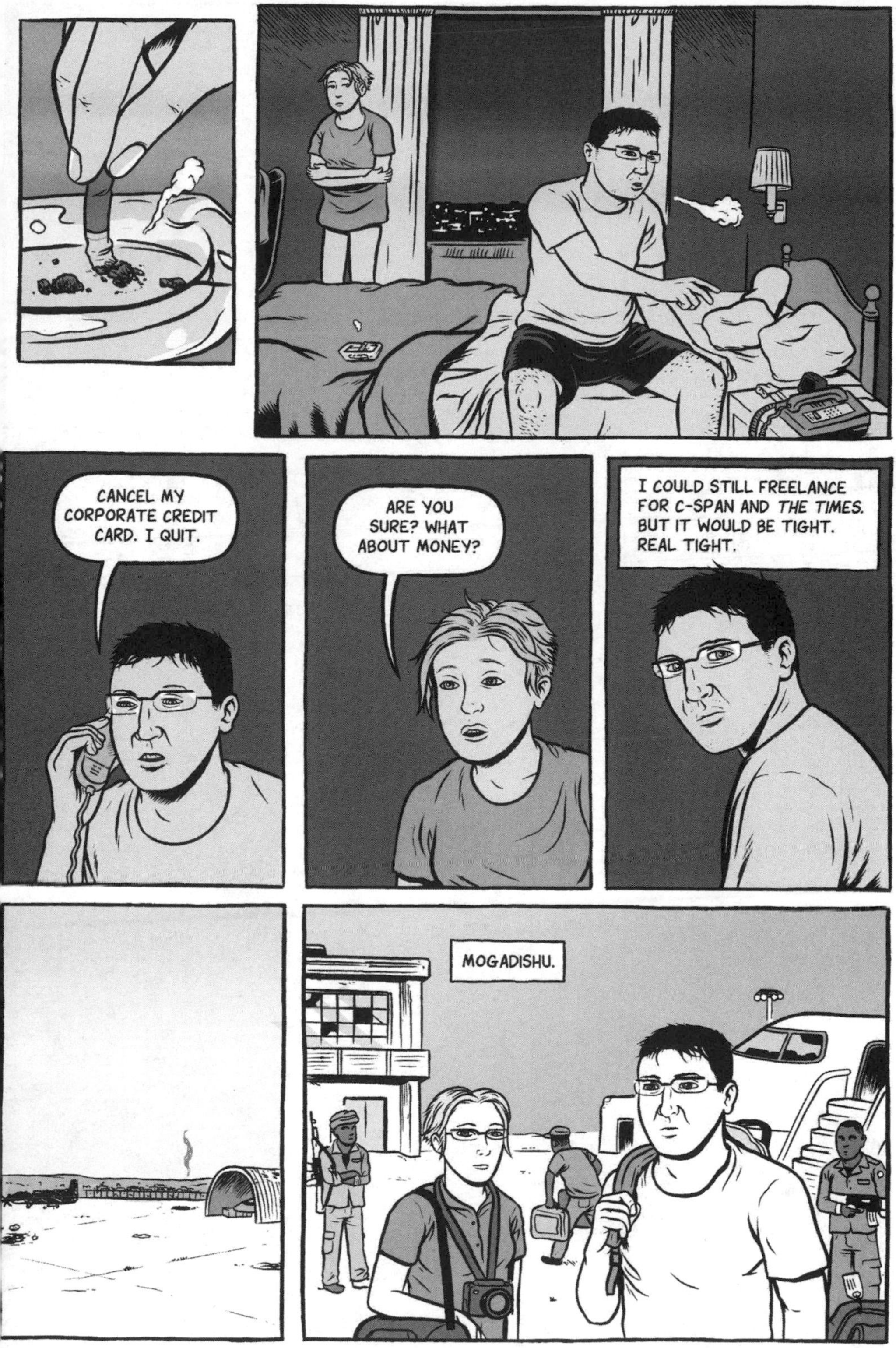
CANCEL MY CORPORATE CREDIT CARD. I QUIT.
ARE YOU SURE? WHAT ABOUT MONEY?
I COULD STILL FREELANCE FOR C-SPAN AND *THE TIMES.* BUT IT WOULD BE TIGHT. REAL TIGHT.
MOGADISHU.

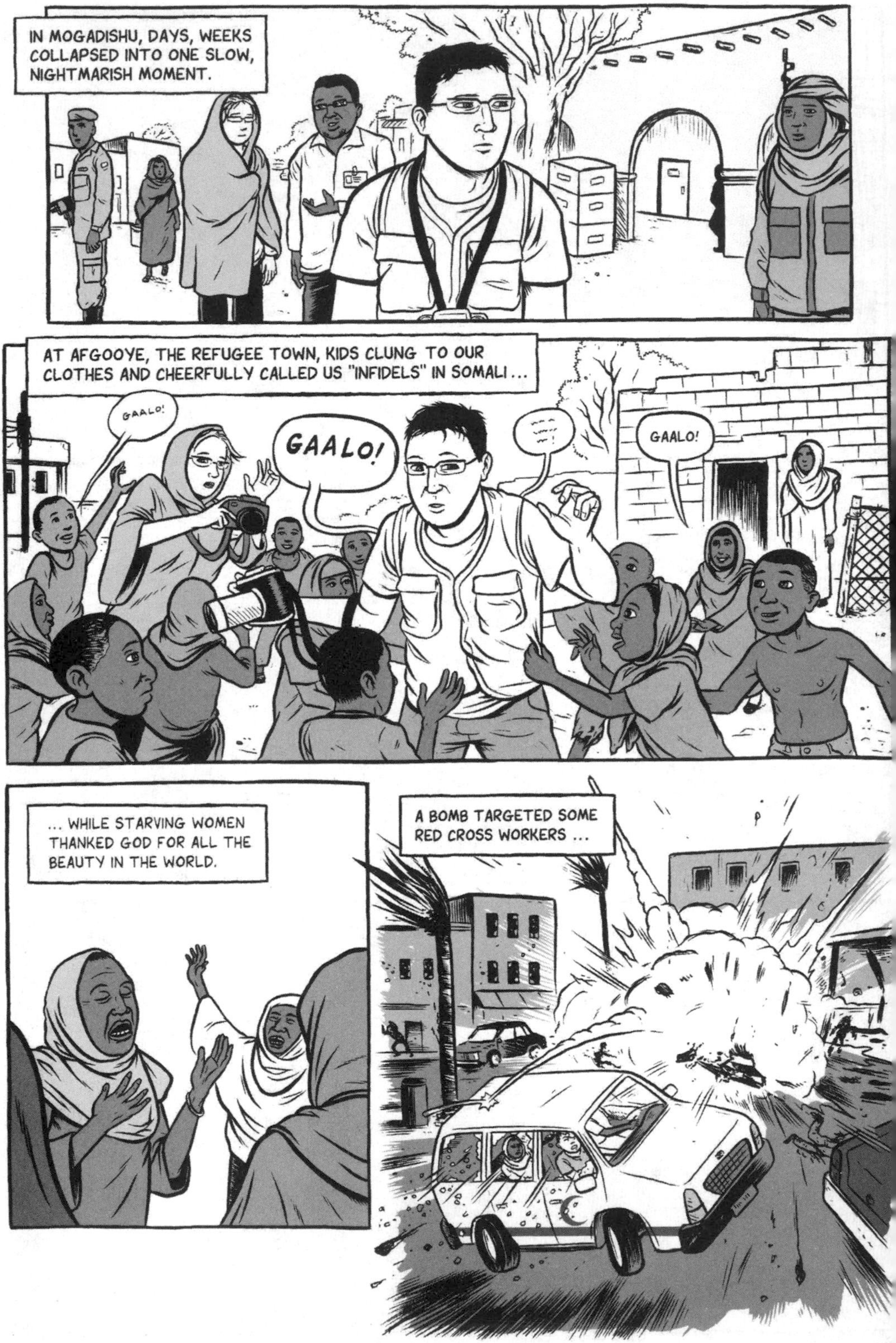
IN MOGADISHU, DAYS, WEEKS COLLAPSED INTO ONE SLOW, NIGHTMARISH MOMENT.
AT AFGOOYE, THE REFUGEE TOWN, KIDS CLUNG TO OUR CLOTHES AND CHEERFULLY CALLED US "INFIDELS" IN SOMALI ...
GAALO!
GAALO!
GAALO!
... WHILE STARVING WOMEN THANKED GOD FOR ALL THE BEAUTY IN THE WORLD.
A BOMB TARGETED SOME RED CROSS WORKERS ...

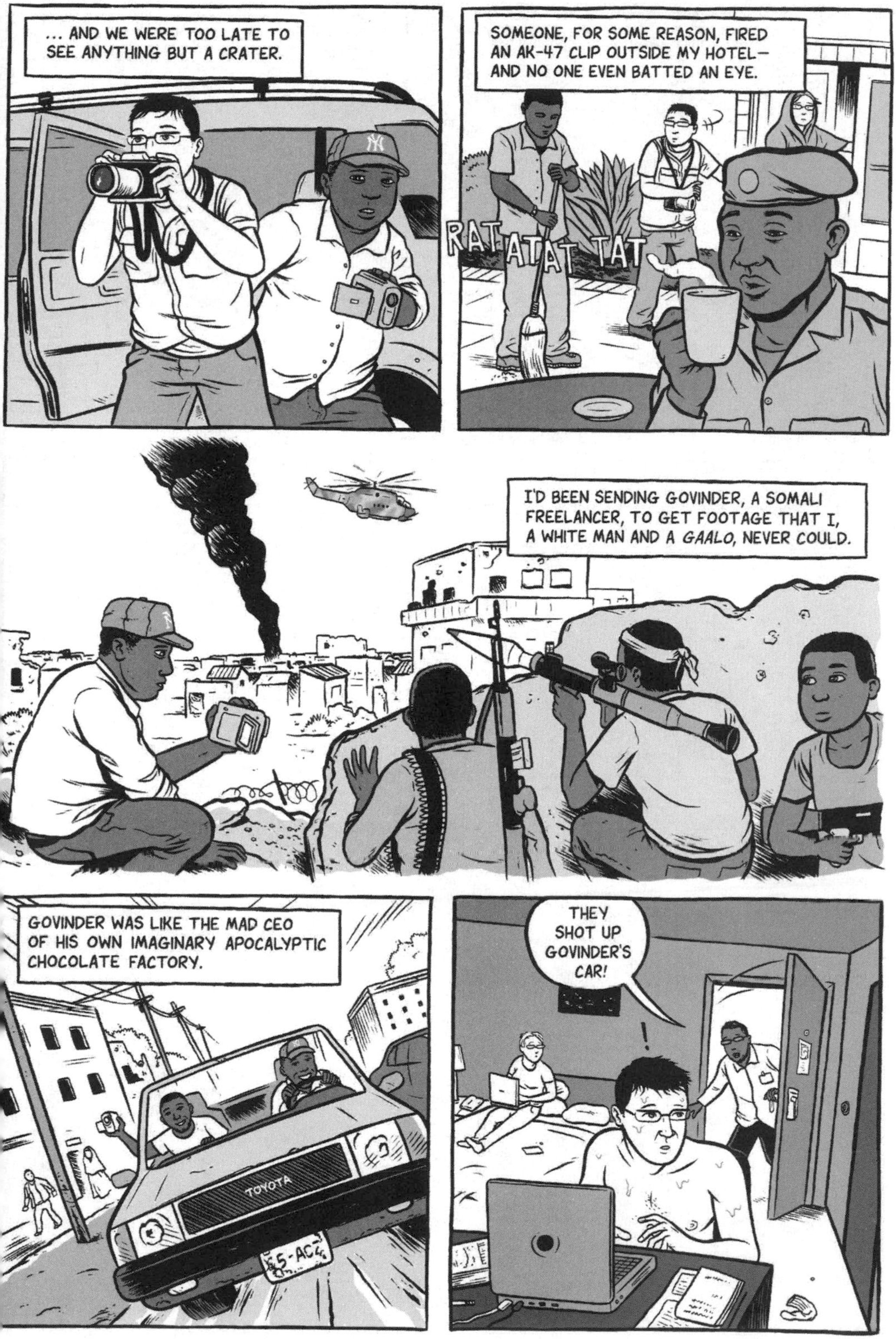
... AND WE WERE TOO LATE TO SEE ANYTHING BUT A CRATER.
SOMEONE, FOR SOME REASON, FIRED AN AK-47 CLIP OUTSIDE MY HOTEL— AND NO ONE EVEN BATTED AN EYE.
RAT ATAT TAT
I'D BEEN SENDING GOVINDER, A SOMALI FREELANCER, TO GET FOOTAGE THAT I, A WHITE MAN AND A *GAALO*, NEVER COULD.
GOVINDER WAS LIKE THE MAD CEO OF HIS OWN IMAGINARY APOCALYPTIC CHOCOLATE FACTORY.
TOYOTA
5-AC2
THEY SHOT UP GOVINDER'S CAR!
!

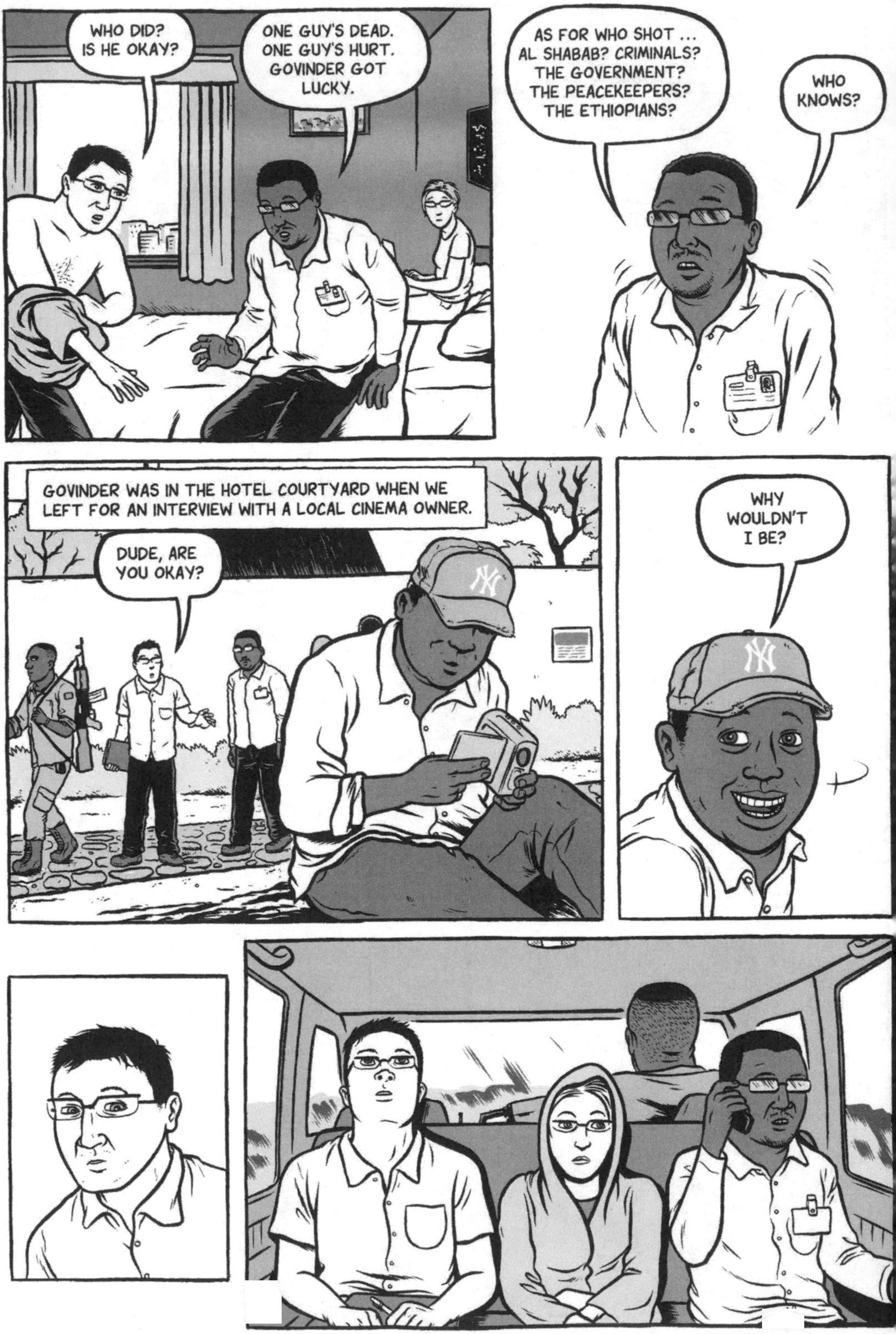
WHO DID? IS HE OKAY?
ONE GUY'S DEAD. ONE GUY'S HURT. GOVINDER GOT LUCKY.
AS FOR WHO SHOT ... AL SHABAB? CRIMINALS? THE GOVERNMENT? THE PEACEKEEPERS? THE ETHIOPIANS?
WHO KNOWS?
GOVINDER WAS IN THE HOTEL COURTYARD WHEN WE LEFT FOR AN INTERVIEW WITH A LOCAL CINEMA OWNER.
DUDE, ARE YOU OKAY?
WHY WOULDN'T I BE?

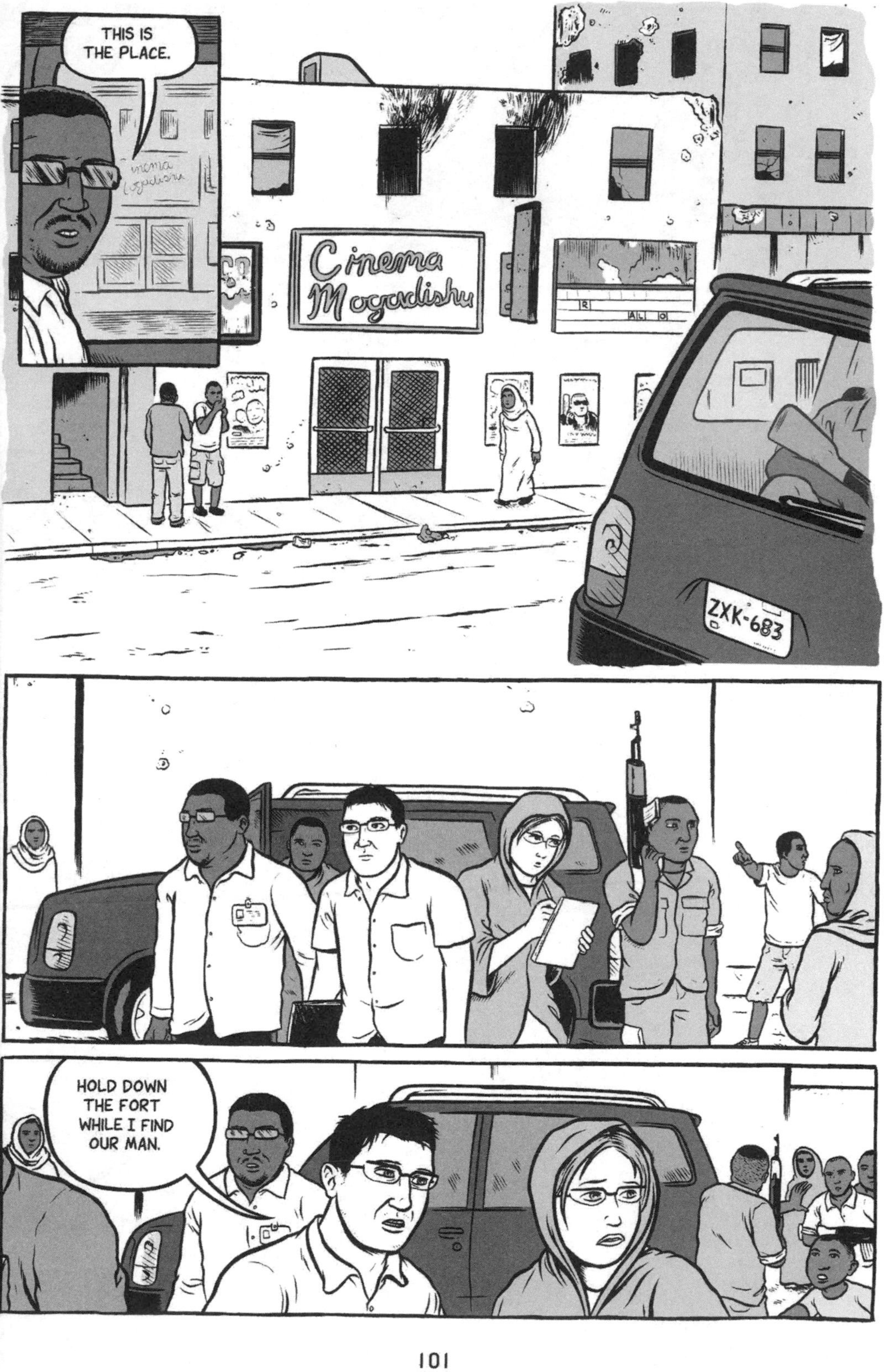
THIS IS THE PLACE.
Cinema Mogadishu
ZXK-683
HOLD DOWN THE FORT WHILE I FIND OUR MAN.

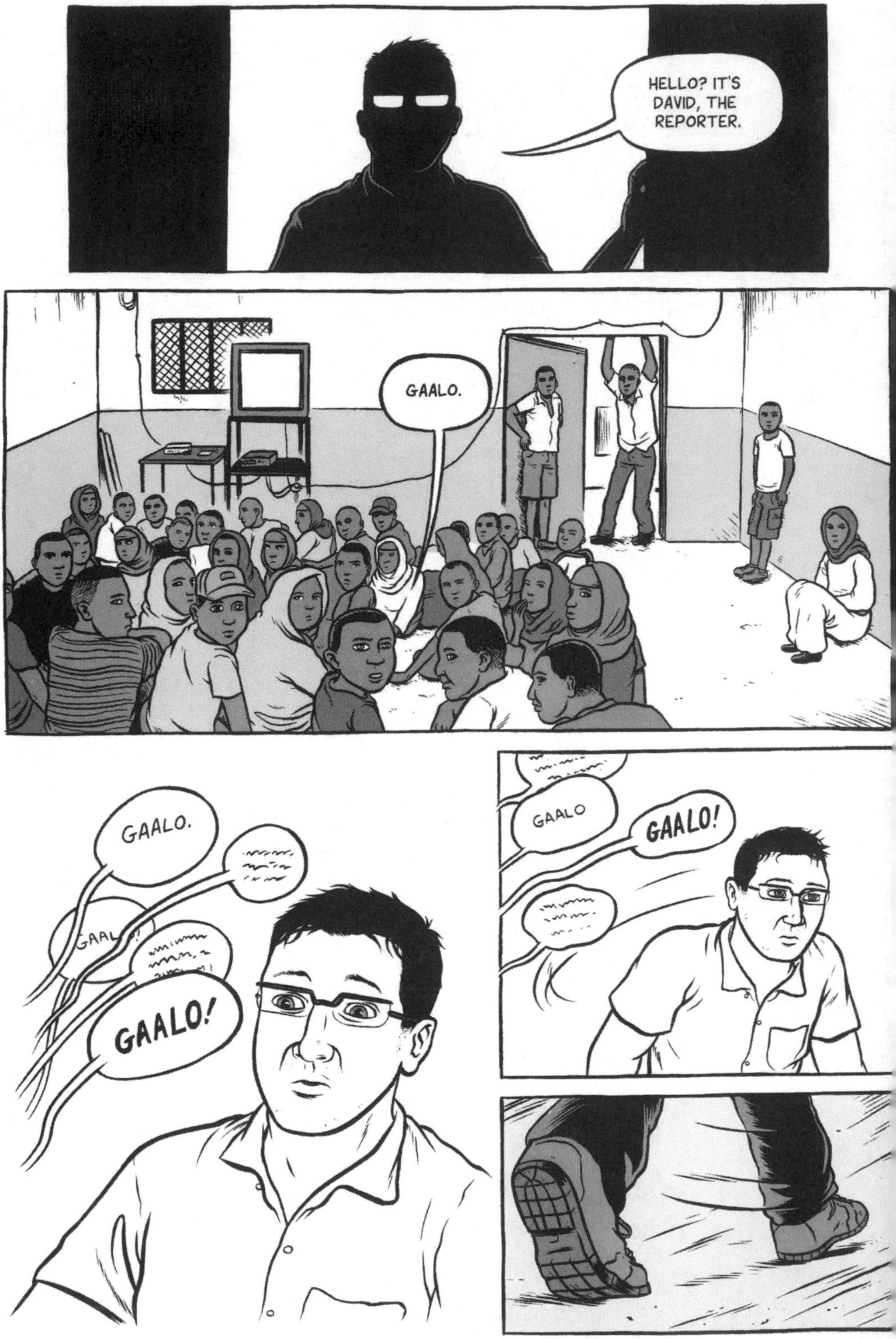
HELLO? IT'S DAVID, THE REPORTER.
GAALO.
GAALO.
GAALO!
GAALO
GAALO!

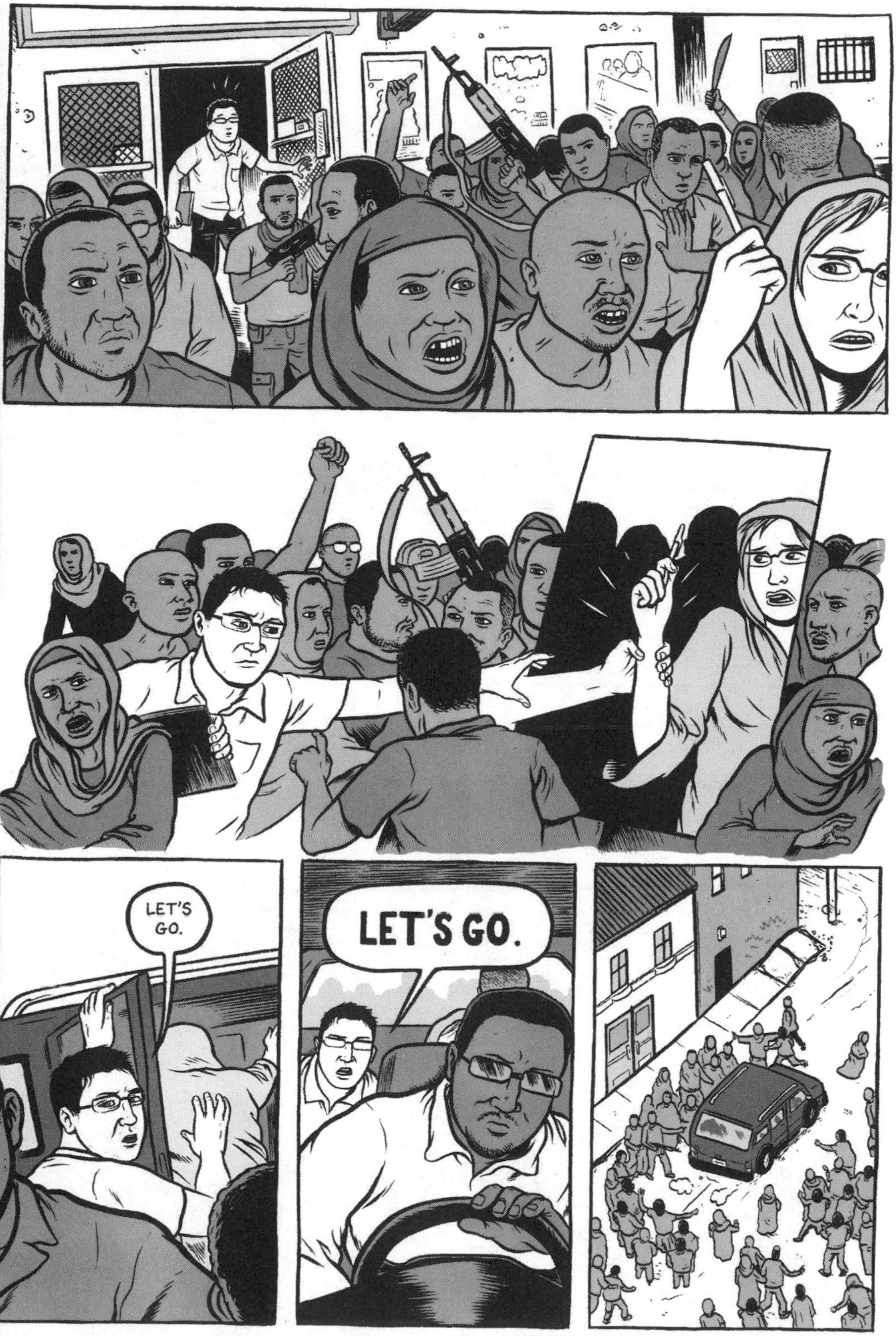
LET'S GO.
LET'S GO.

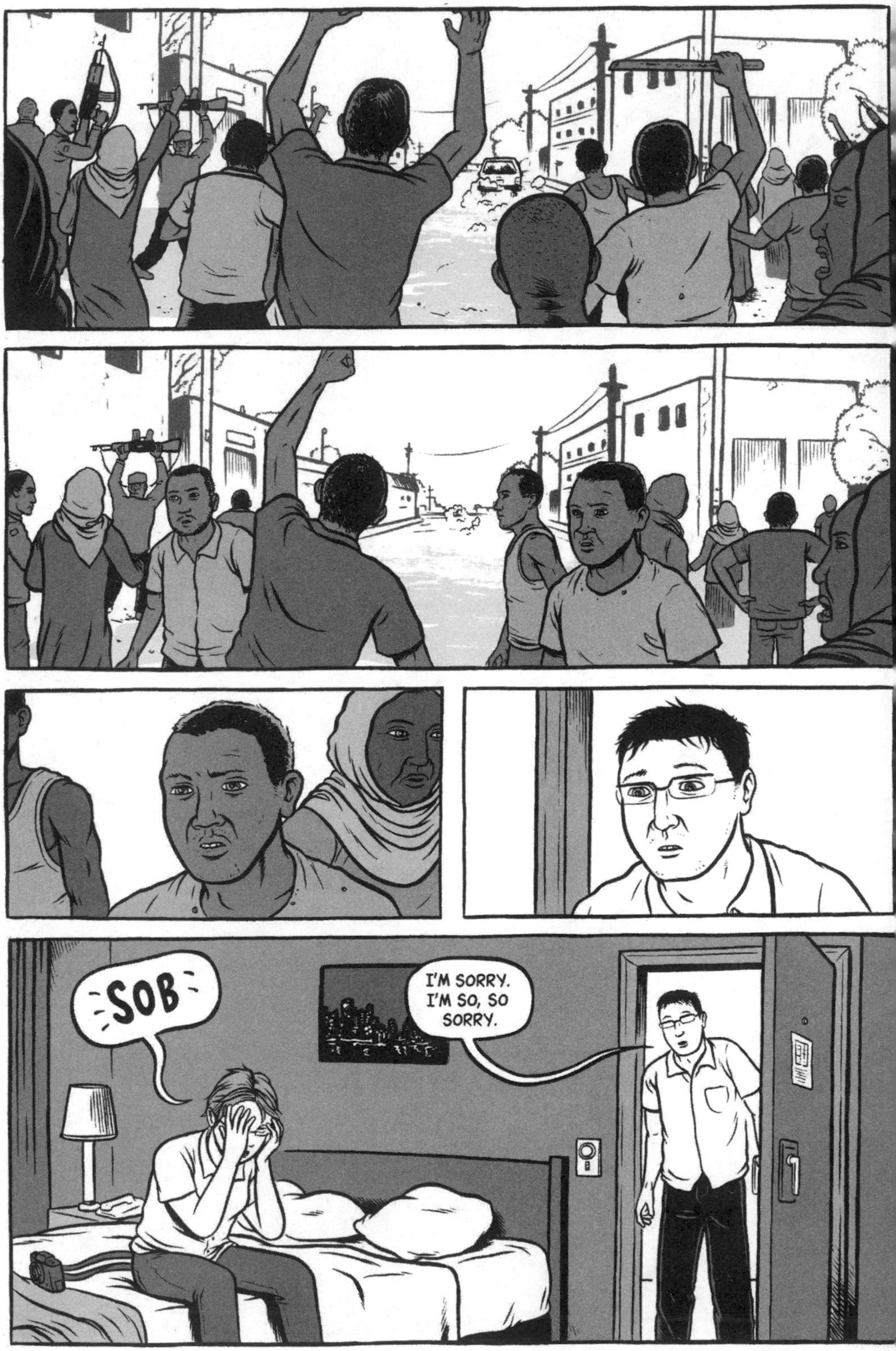
SOB
I'M SORRY. I'M SO, SO SORRY.

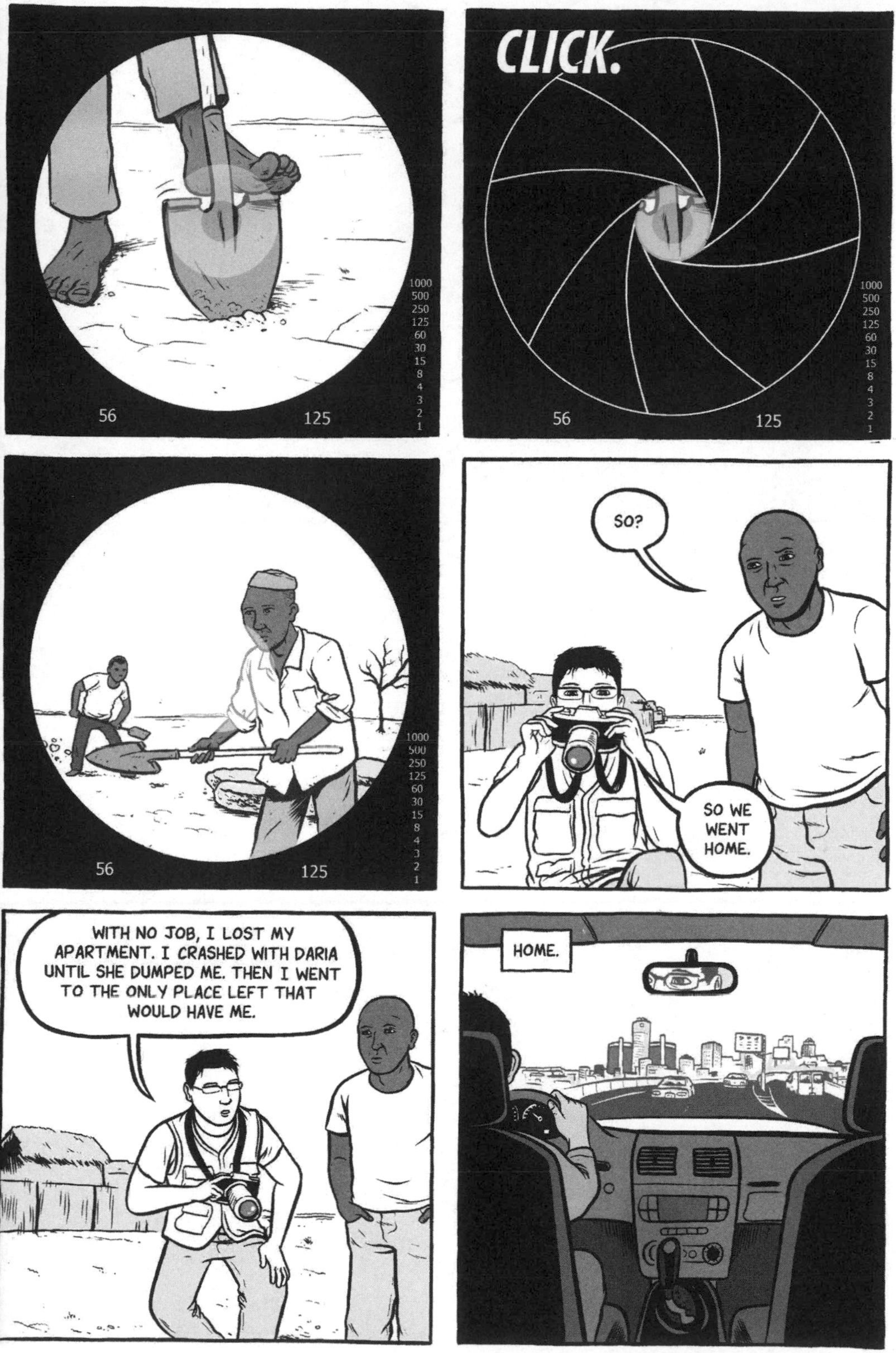
56
125
1000
500
250
125
60
30
15
8
4
3
2
1
CLICK.
56
125
1000
500
250
125
60
30
15
8
4
3
2
1
56
125
1000
500
250
125
60
30
15
8
4
3
2
1
SO?
SO WE WENT HOME.
WITH NO JOB, I LOST MY APARTMENT. I CRASHED WITH DARIA UNTIL SHE DUMPED ME. THEN I WENT TO THE ONLY PLACE LEFT THAT WOULD HAVE ME.
HOME.

DETROIT

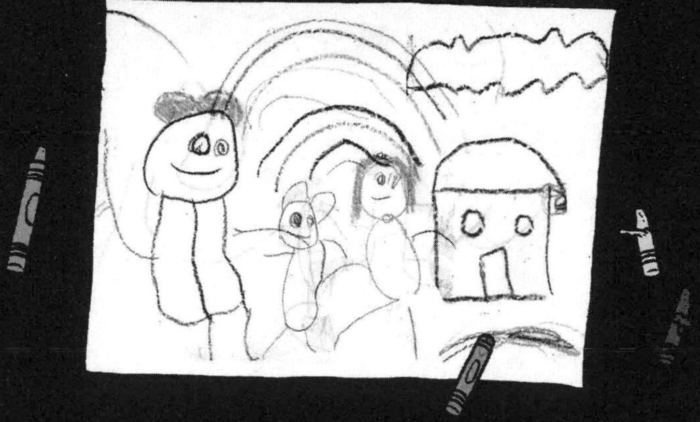

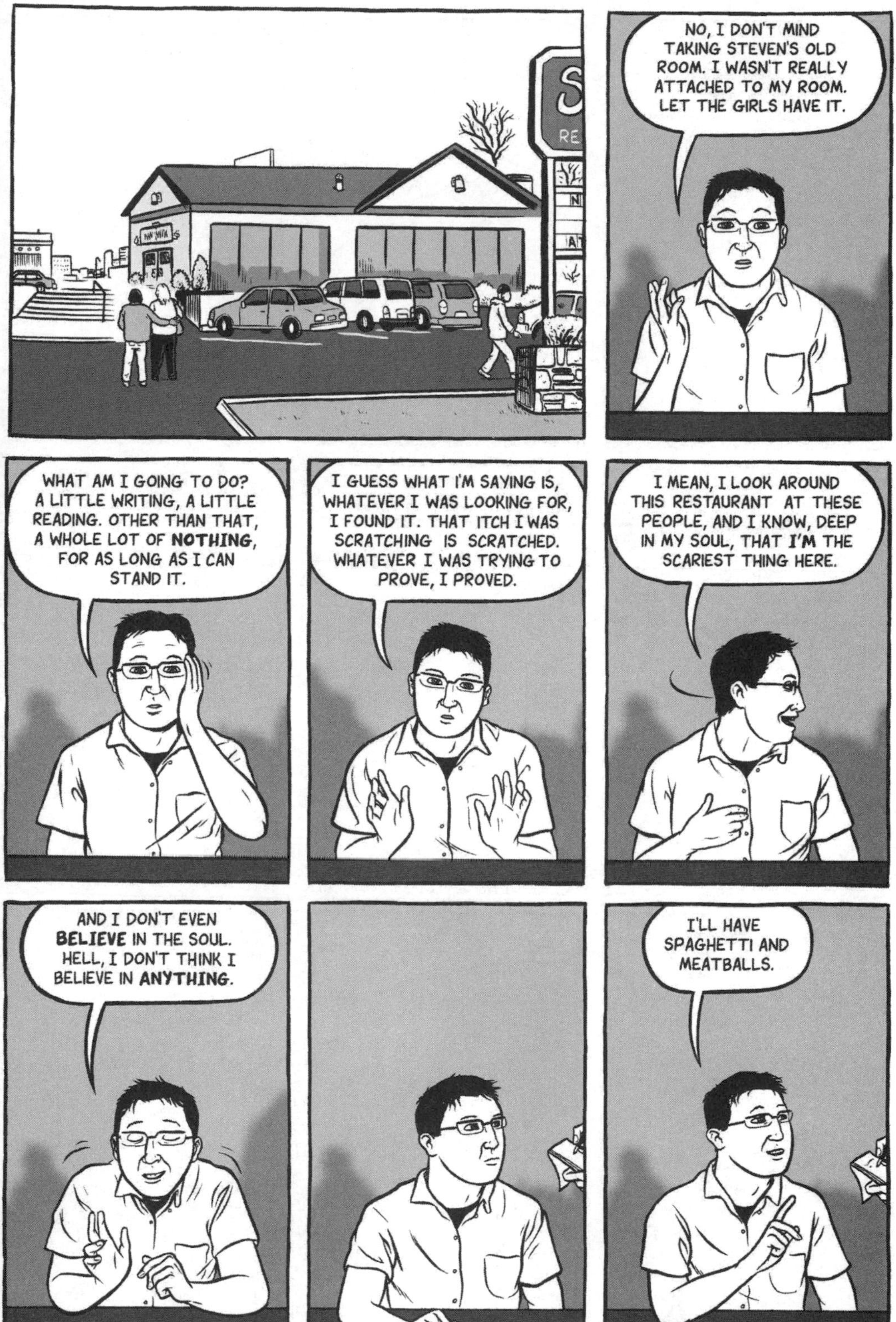
NO, I DON'T MIND TAKING STEVEN'S OLD ROOM. I WASN'T REALLY ATTACHED TO MY ROOM. LET THE GIRLS HAVE IT.
WHAT AM I GOING TO DO? A LITTLE WRITING, A LITTLE READING. OTHER THAN THAT, A WHOLE LOT OF **NOTHING**, FOR AS LONG AS I CAN STAND IT.
I GUESS WHAT I'M SAYING IS, WHATEVER I WAS LOOKING FOR, I FOUND IT. THAT ITCH I WAS SCRATCHING IS SCRATCHED. WHATEVER I WAS TRYING TO PROVE, I PROVED.
I MEAN, I LOOK AROUND THIS RESTAURANT AT THESE PEOPLE, AND I KNOW, DEEP IN MY SOUL, THAT **I'M** THE SCARIEST THING HERE.
AND I DON'T EVEN **BELIEVE** IN THE SOUL. HELL, I DON'T THINK I BELIEVE IN **ANYTHING**.
I'LL HAVE SPAGHETTI AND MEATBALLS.

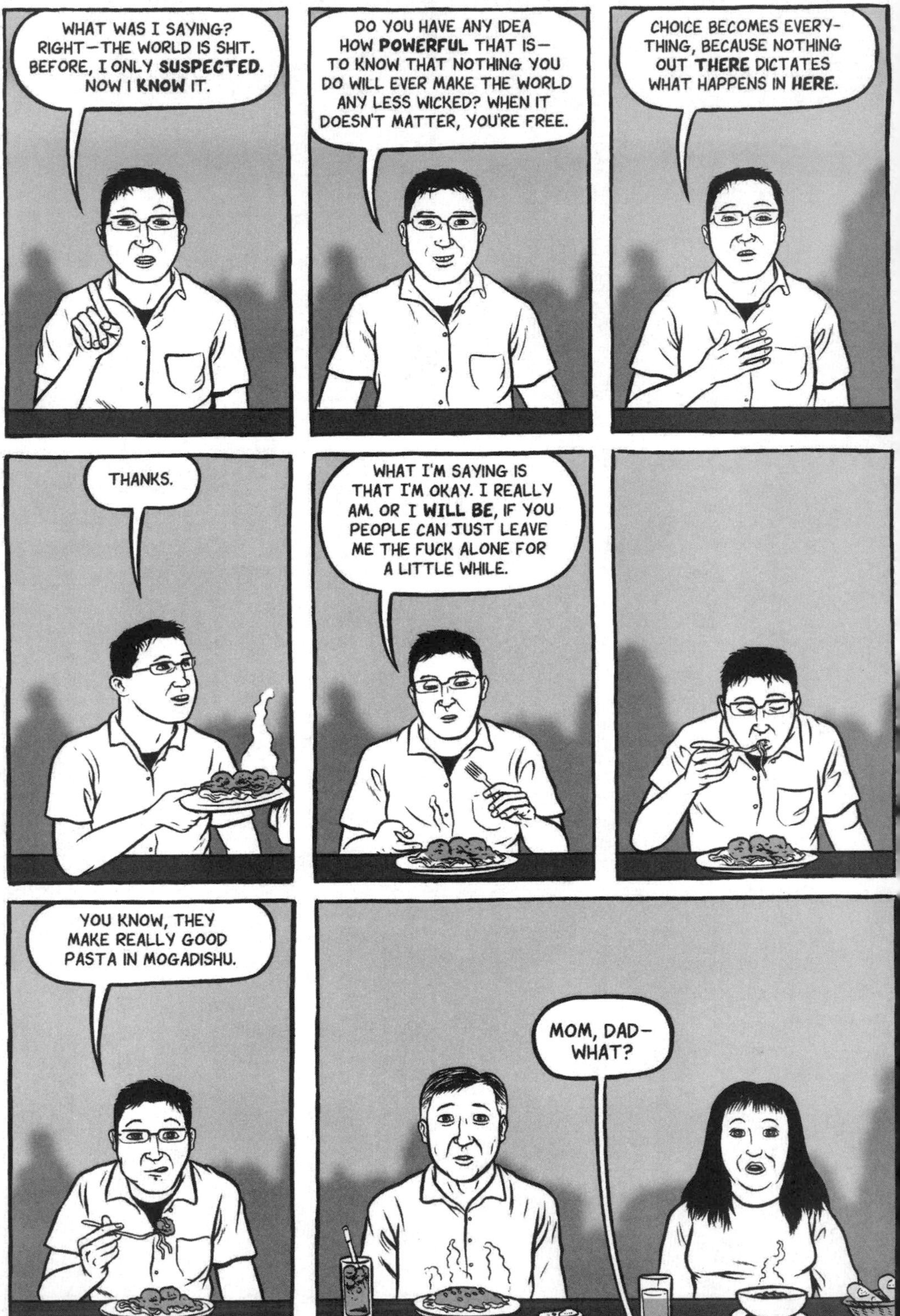
WHAT WAS I SAYING? RIGHT—THE WORLD IS SHIT. BEFORE, I ONLY **SUSPECTED**. NOW I **KNOW** IT.
DO YOU HAVE ANY IDEA HOW **POWERFUL** THAT IS—TO KNOW THAT NOTHING YOU DO WILL EVER MAKE THE WORLD ANY LESS WICKED? WHEN IT DOESN'T MATTER, YOU'RE FREE.
CHOICE BECOMES EVERYTHING, BECAUSE NOTHING OUT **THERE** DICTATES WHAT HAPPENS IN **HERE**.
THANKS.
WHAT I'M SAYING IS THAT I'M OKAY. I REALLY AM. OR I **WILL BE**, IF YOU PEOPLE CAN JUST LEAVE ME THE FUCK ALONE FOR A LITTLE WHILE.
YOU KNOW, THEY MAKE REALLY GOOD PASTA IN MOGADISHU.
MOM, DAD—WHAT?

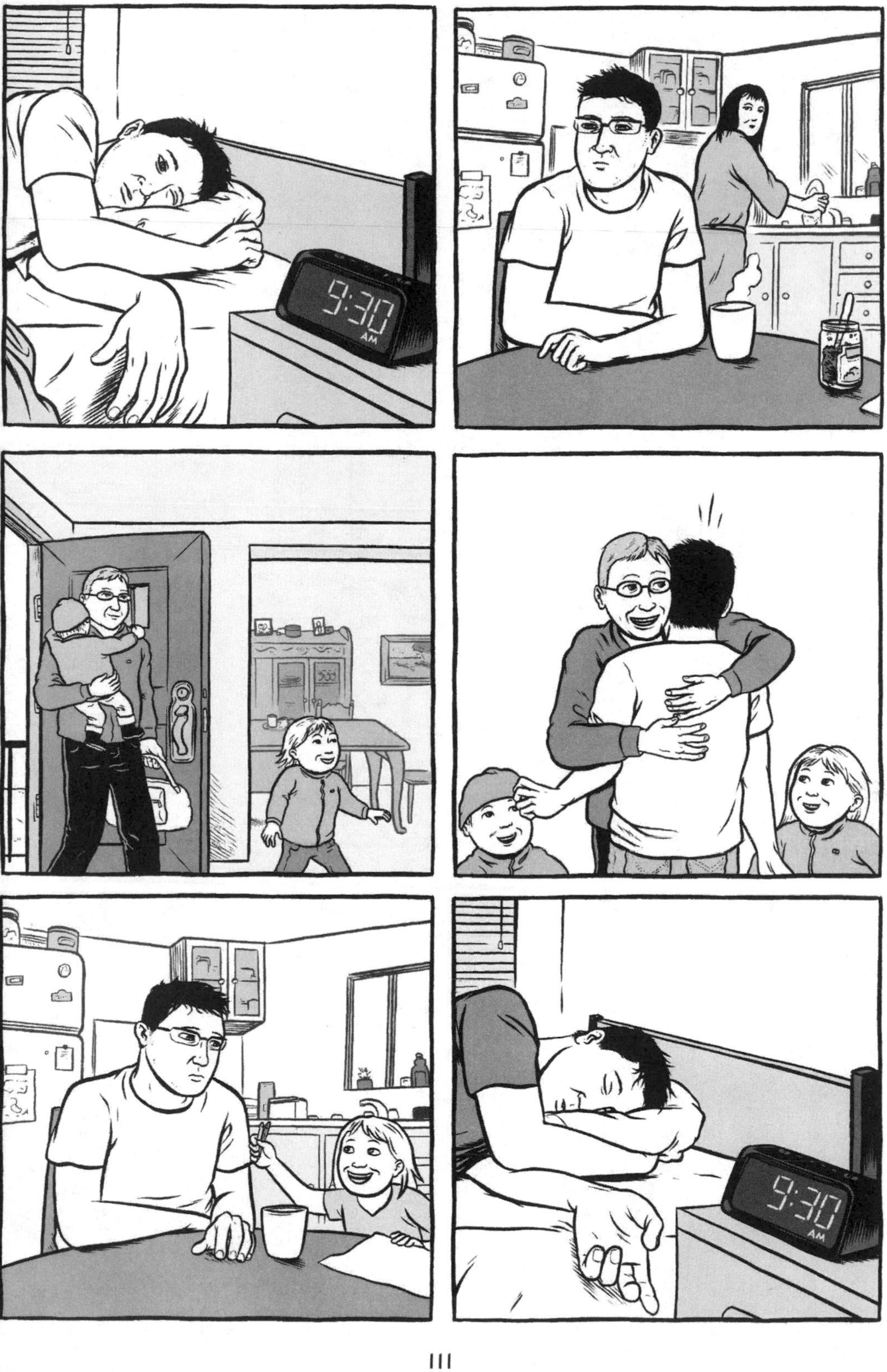
9:30
AM
9:30
AM

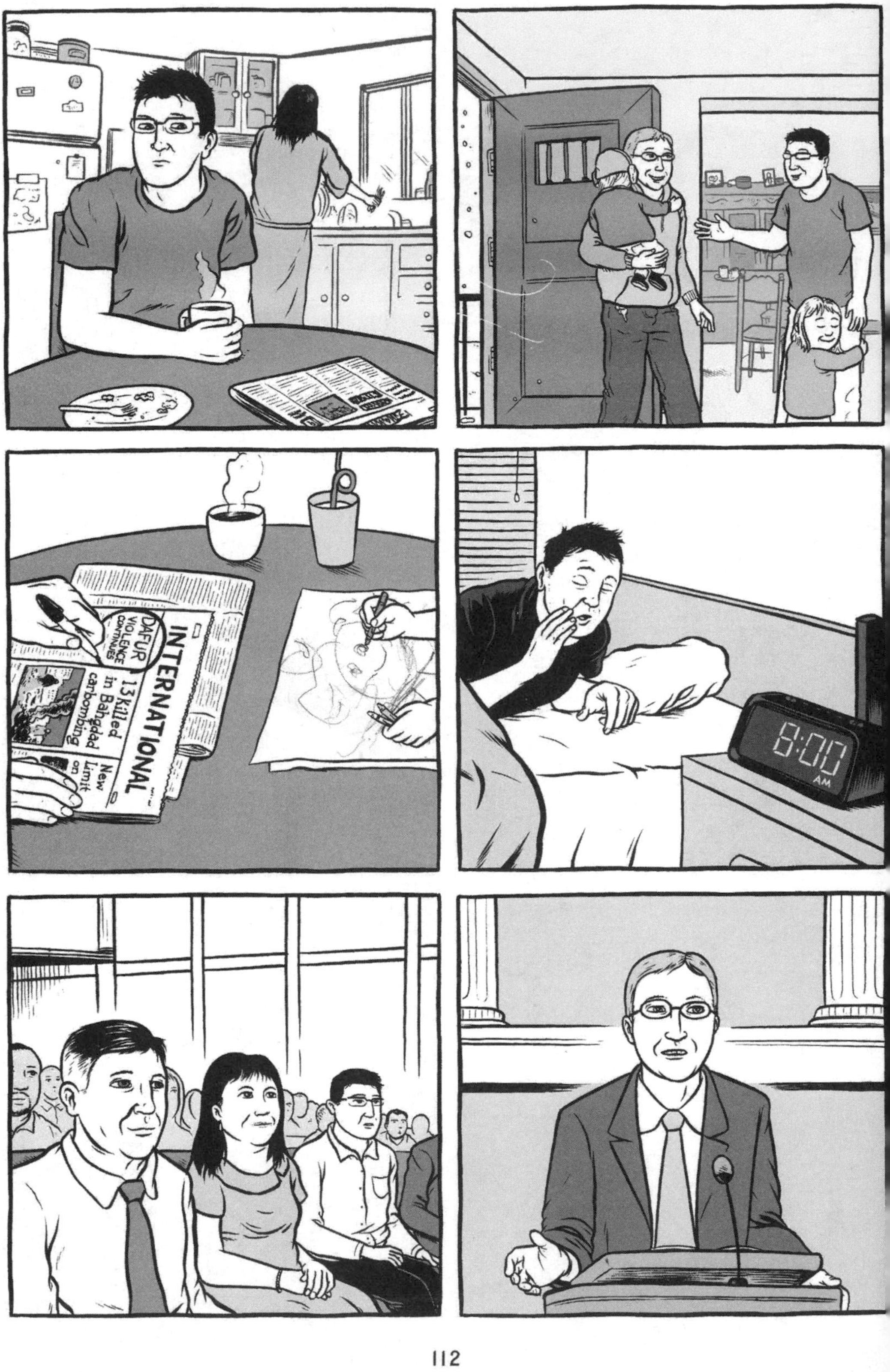
INTERNATIONAL
DAFUR VIOLENCE CONTINUES
13 Killed in Bahgdad carbombing
New Limit on
8:00 AM

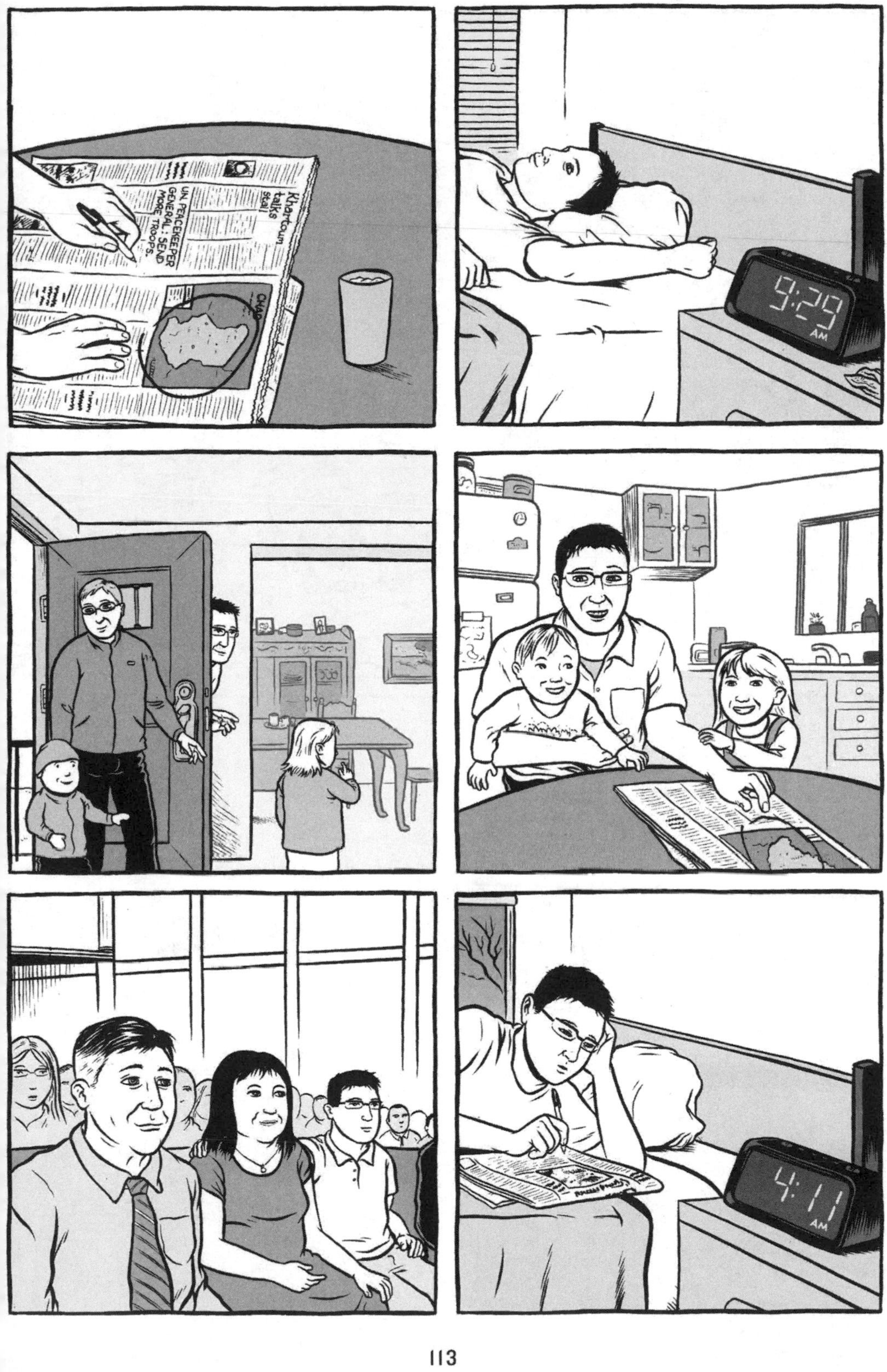
Khartoum talks stall
UN PEACEKEEPER GENERAL: SEND MORE TROOPS.
CHAD
9:29 AM
4:11 AM

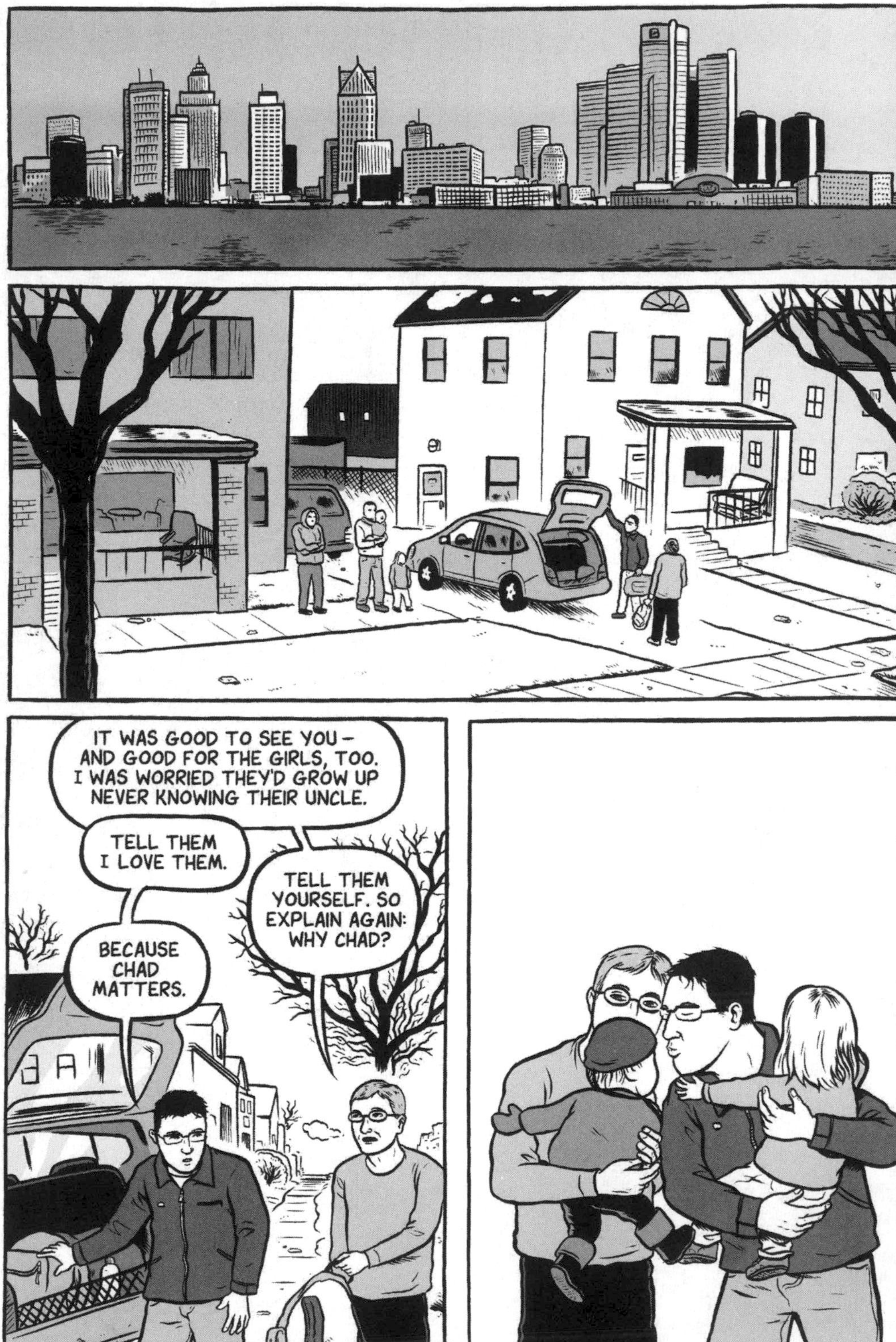
IT WAS GOOD TO SEE YOU – AND GOOD FOR THE GIRLS, TOO. I WAS WORRIED THEY'D GROW UP NEVER KNOWING THEIR UNCLE.
TELL THEM I LOVE THEM.
TELL THEM YOURSELF. SO EXPLAIN AGAIN: WHY CHAD?
BECAUSE CHAD MATTERS.

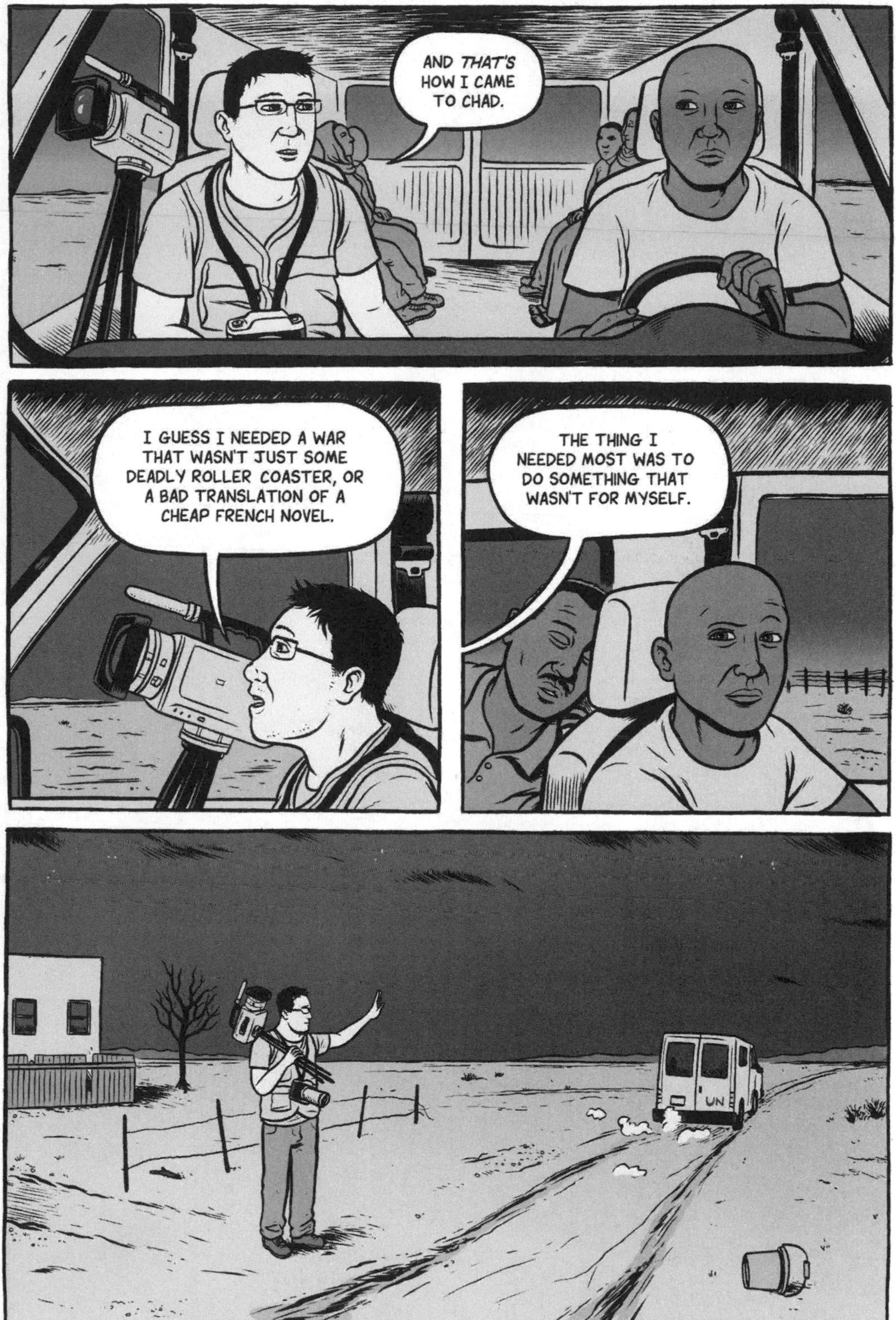
AND THAT'S HOW I CAME TO CHAD.
I GUESS I NEEDED A WAR THAT WASN'T JUST SOME DEADLY ROLLER COASTER, OR A BAD TRANSLATION OF A CHEAP FRENCH NOVEL.
THE THING I NEEDED MOST WAS TO DO SOMETHING THAT WASN'T FOR MYSELF.
UN

EPILOGUE

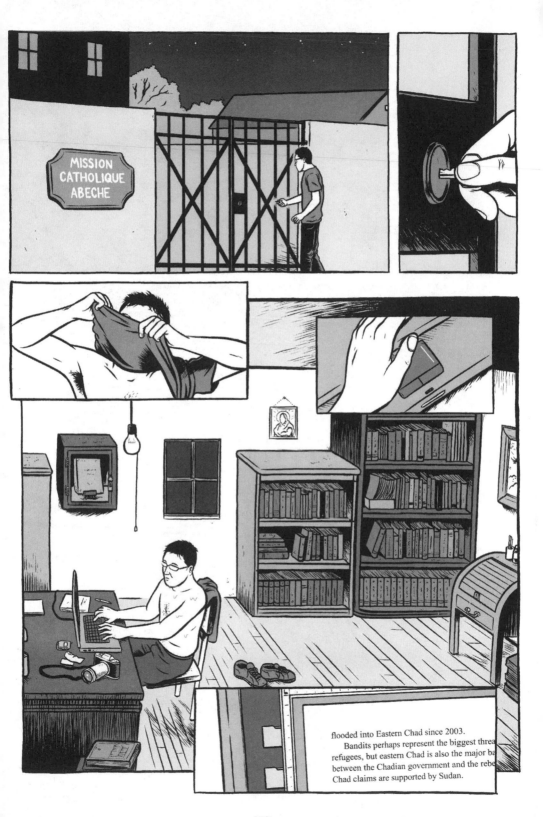

MISSION CATHOLIQUE ABECHE

flooded into Eastern Chad since 2003.

Bandits perhaps represent the biggest threat to refugees, but eastern Chad is also the major battle between the Chadian government and the rebels. Chad claims are supported by Sudan.

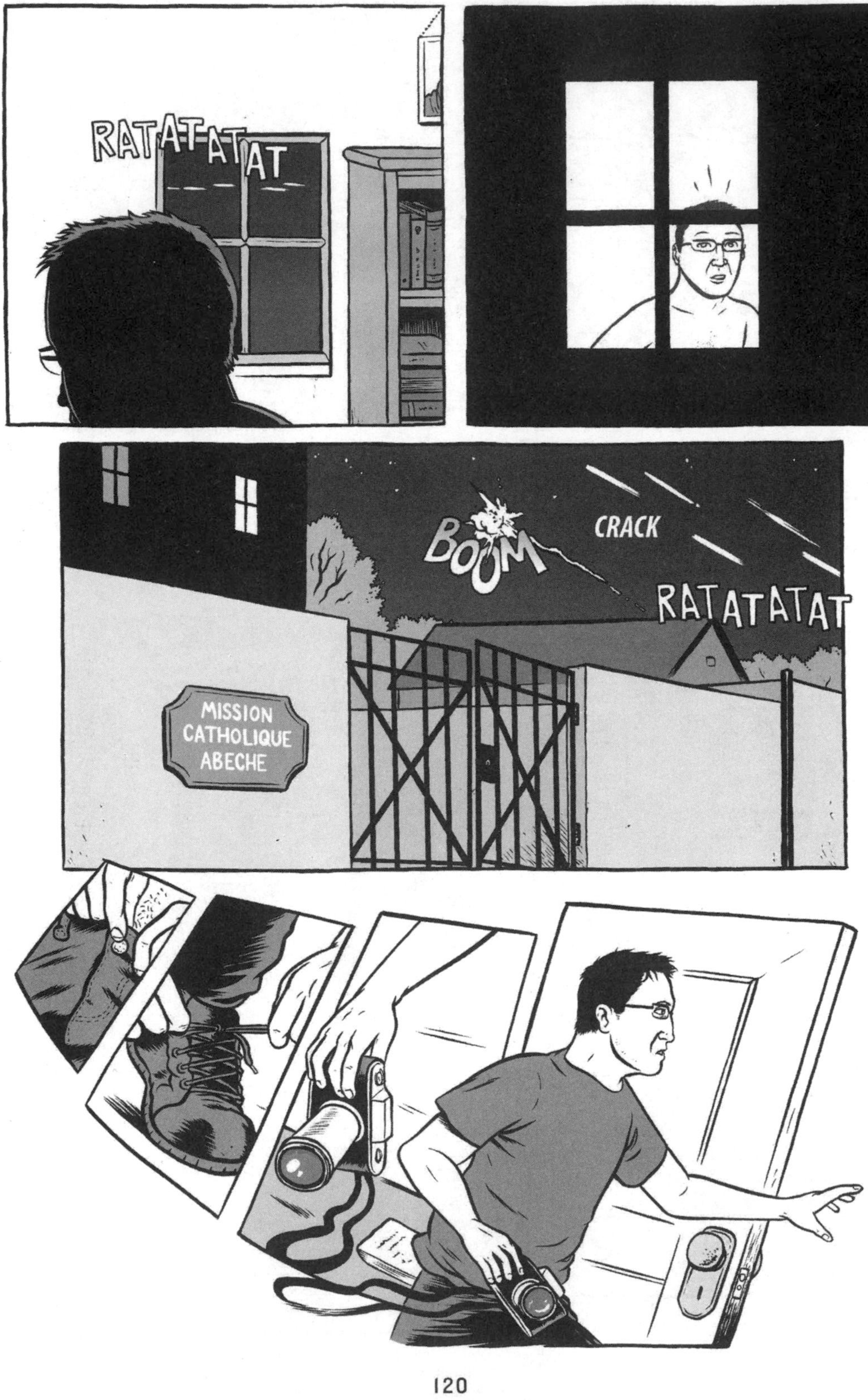
RATATATAT
BOOM
CRACK
RATATATAT
MISSION CATHOLIQUE ABECHE

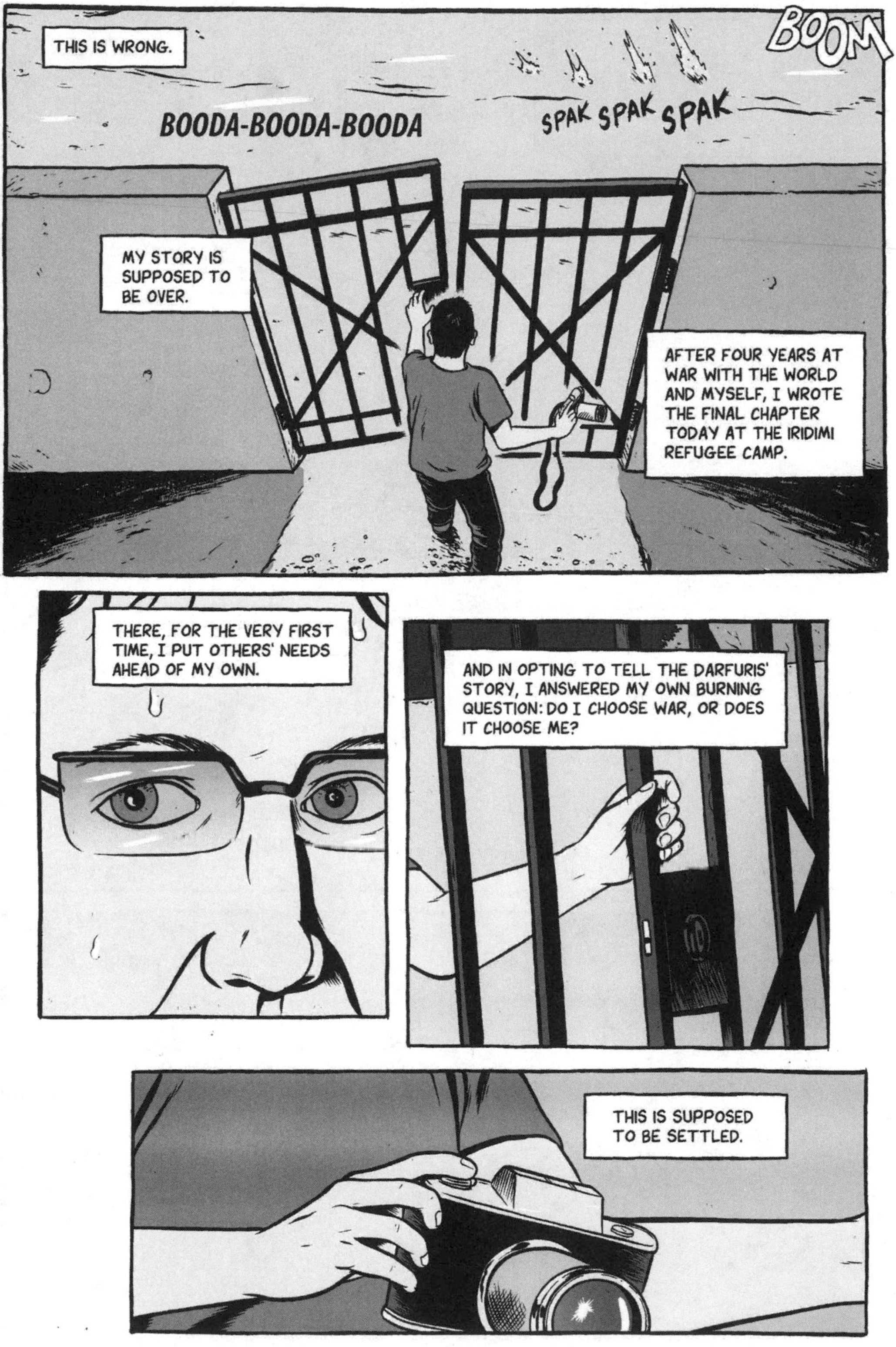
THIS IS WRONG.
BOOM
BOODA-BOODA-BOODA
SPAK SPAK SPAK
MY STORY IS SUPPOSED TO BE OVER.
AFTER FOUR YEARS AT WAR WITH THE WORLD AND MYSELF, I WROTE THE FINAL CHAPTER TODAY AT THE IRIDIMI REFUGEE CAMP.
THERE, FOR THE VERY FIRST TIME, I PUT OTHERS' NEEDS AHEAD OF MY OWN.
AND IN OPTING TO TELL THE DARFURIS' STORY, I ANSWERED MY OWN BURNING QUESTION: DO I CHOOSE WAR, OR DOES IT CHOOSE ME?
THIS IS SUPPOSED TO BE SETTLED.

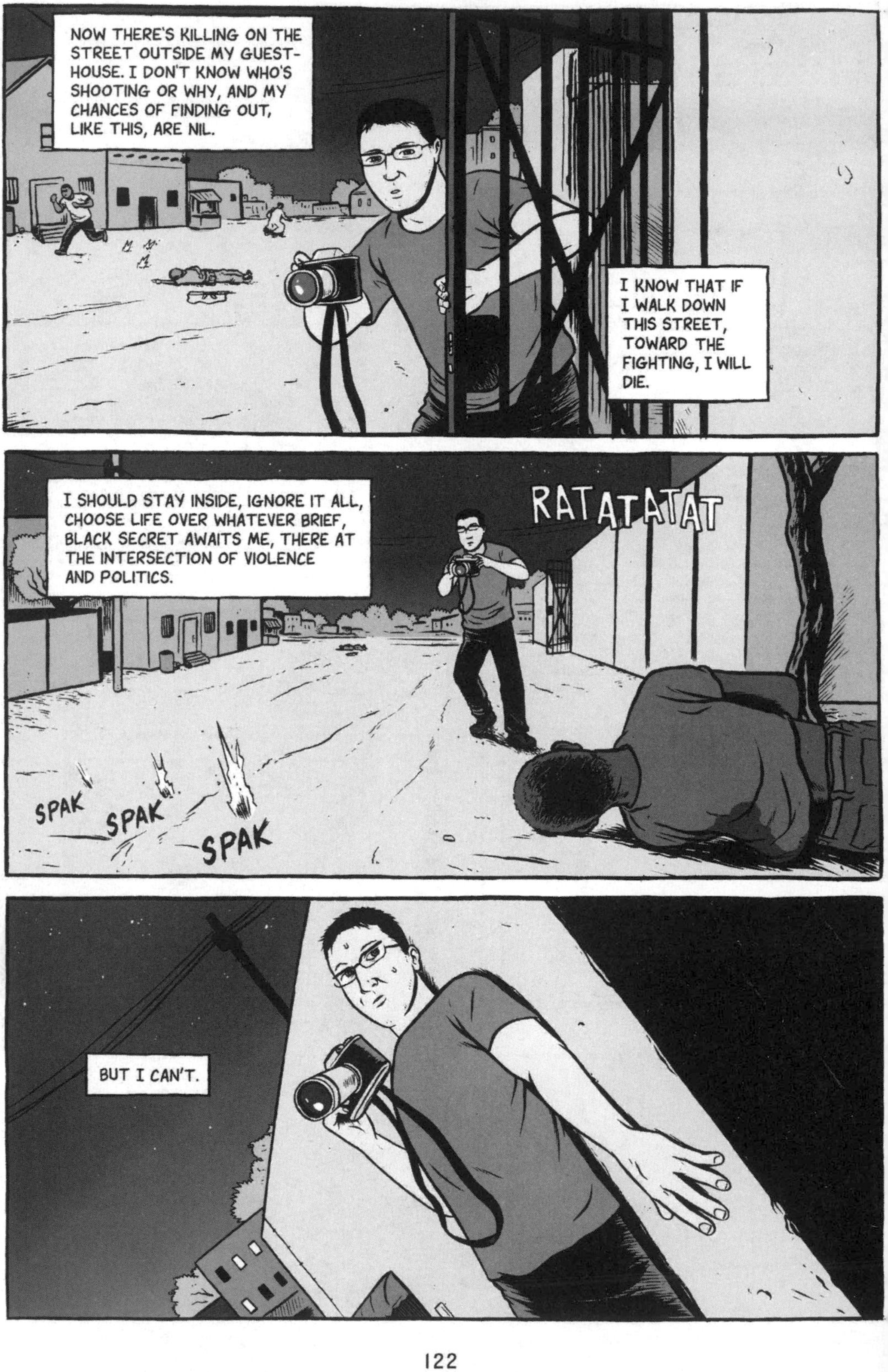
NOW THERE'S KILLING ON THE STREET OUTSIDE MY GUEST-HOUSE. I DON'T KNOW WHO'S SHOOTING OR WHY, AND MY CHANCES OF FINDING OUT, LIKE THIS, ARE NIL.
I KNOW THAT IF I WALK DOWN THIS STREET, TOWARD THE FIGHTING, I WILL DIE.
I SHOULD STAY INSIDE, IGNORE IT ALL, CHOOSE LIFE OVER WHATEVER BRIEF, BLACK SECRET AWAITS ME, THERE AT THE INTERSECTION OF VIOLENCE AND POLITICS.
RATATATAT
SPAK
SPAK
SPAK
BUT I CAN'T.

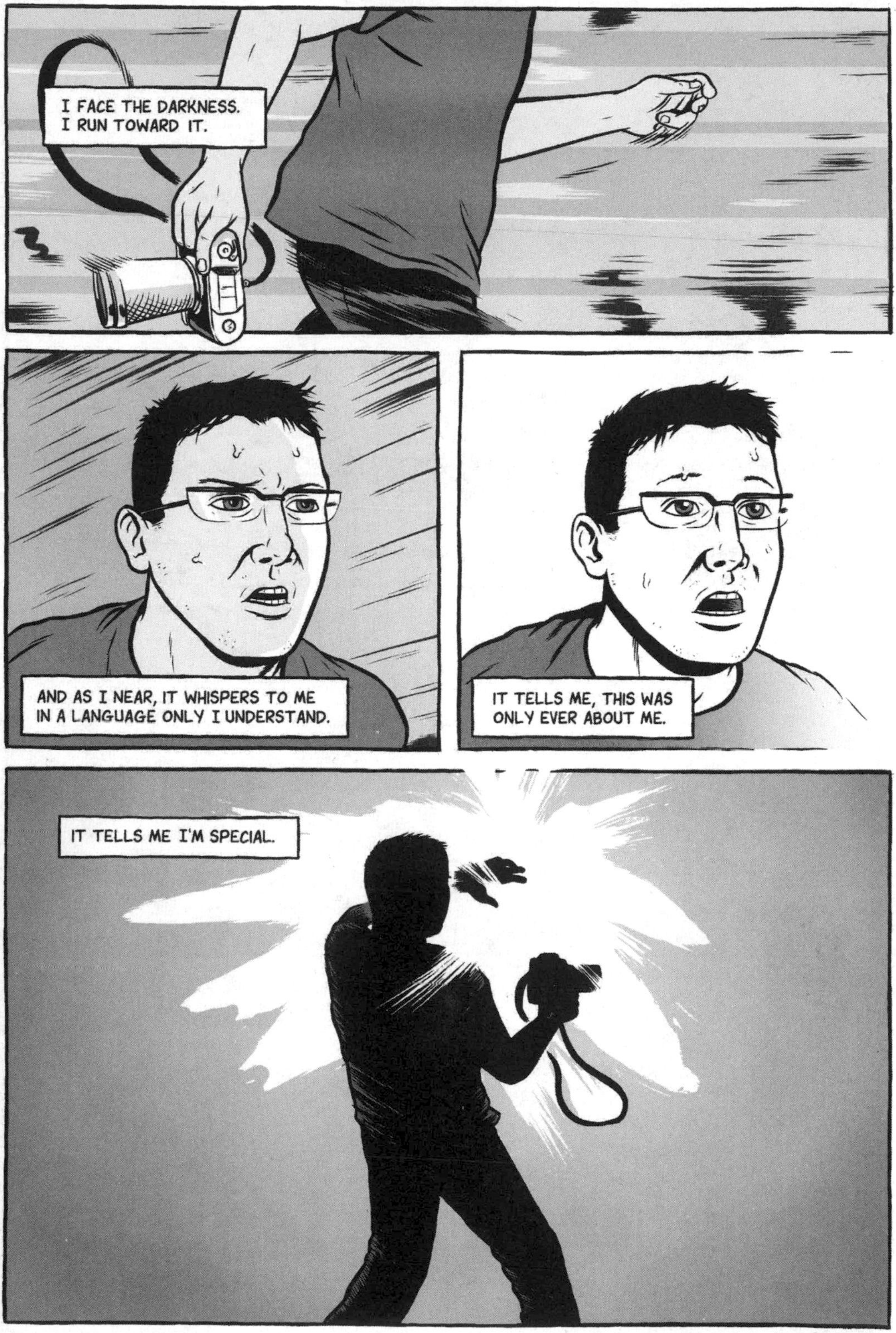
I FACE THE DARKNESS.
I RUN TOWARD IT.
AND AS I NEAR, IT WHISPERS TO ME
IN A LANGUAGE ONLY I UNDERSTAND.
IT TELLS ME, THIS WAS
ONLY EVER ABOUT ME.
IT TELLS ME I'M SPECIAL.

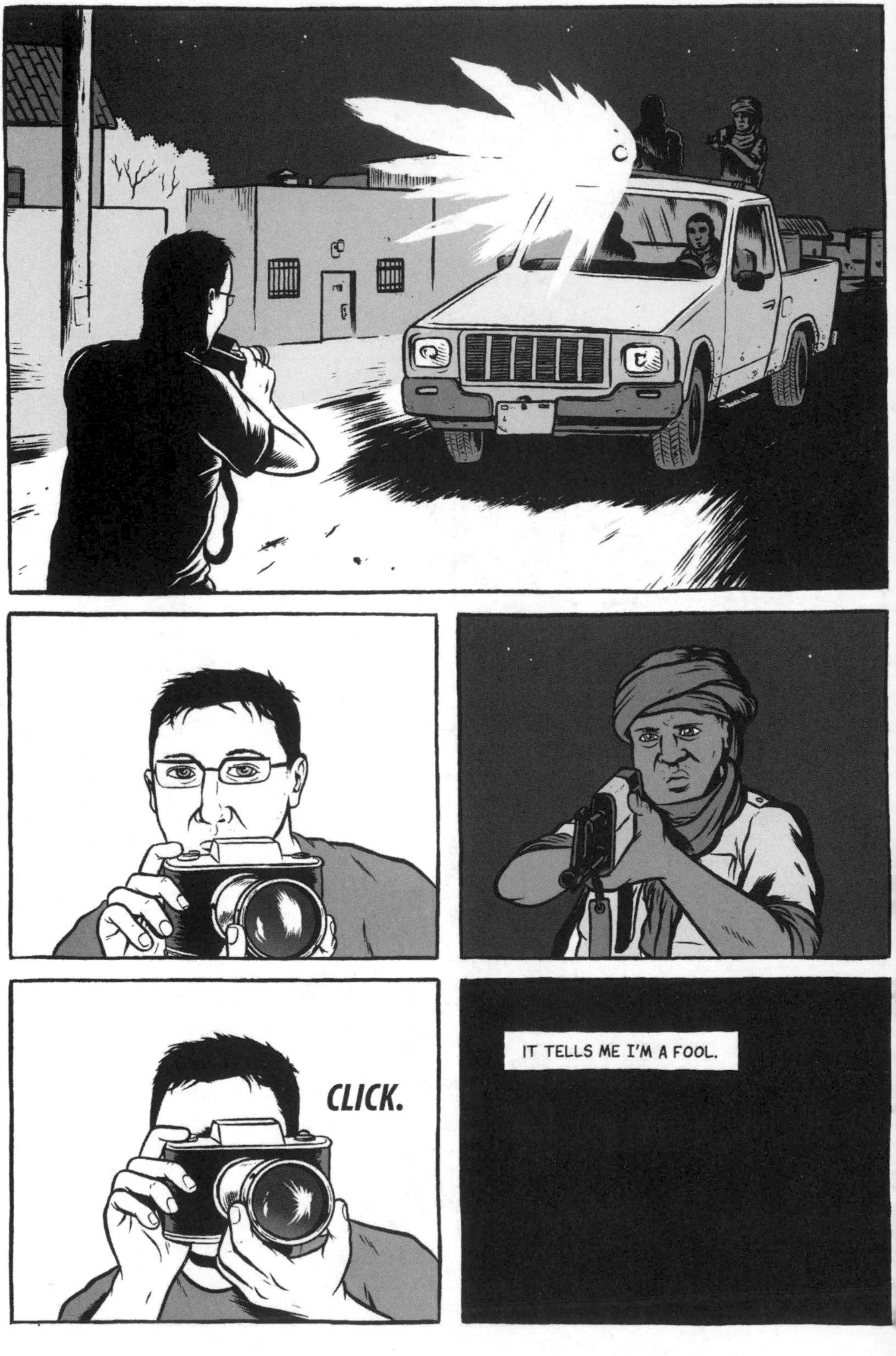
CLICK.
IT TELLS ME I'M A FOOL.

AFTERWORD

So I didn't die. Not really. The Chadian soldiers at the intersection in Abeche pointed their weapons at me, demanded to know who I was, seized my documents and threatened to kill me. But they didn't.

Neither did the mob of deserting child soldiers I fell in with after extricating myself from that intersection. The mob's ring leader—a hollow-faced sixteen-year-old boy—chased me through midnight Abeche with a knife, but I outran him, even with my cameras shoved in the crotch of my pants to protect them.

Nor did I die in Nicaragua, Kenya, Djibouti, off the Somali coast hunting for pirates or in Logar province, Afghanistan, where the Taliban blew up the truck behind mine in a U.S. Army convoy and pinned us down for twenty minutes with rockets and gunfire.

"I'm good luck," I now tell the soldiers I spend half my life with. They don't believe that. Neither do I. A lucky man wouldn't feel the way I do. A lucky man would be happy to be alive. Me? I feel like my body survived that night in Abeche, but something inside me succumbed to the violence it had always craved. Be careful what you wish for, I guess.

The more of the world I see, the less sense it makes. The more different people I meet, the less I believe in their humanity. The older I get, the less comfortable I am in my own skin. We are a world at war, sometimes quietly, often not. We are the cleverest monsters, and we deserve everything we've got coming.

Everything falls apart. Everyone dies in time. In the great, slow reduction of our lives and history, the things we can believe in shrink into a space smaller than our own bodies. To preserve them, for as long as you might, arm yourself, and be afraid.

David Axe
Columbia, South Carolina
November 2009

David Axe is a freelance war correspondent based in Columbia, South Carolina. Since 2005 he has reported from Iraq, Lebanon, East Timor, Afghanistan, Somalia, Chad and other conflict zones. A former staff writer for *Defense Technology International*, he has also contributed to *The Village Voice*, *The Washington Times*, C-SPAN, *Wired*, *Esquire*, *Popular Science*, *Popular Mechanics*, Voice of America and many others. He is the author of several books, including the graphic novel *War Fix* and the nonfiction books *Army 101* and *War Bots*.

Matt Bors is a nationally syndicated editorial cartoonist and illustrator based in Portland, Oregon. His work has appeared in newspapers and magazines across the country, including *The Nation*, *The Los Angeles Times*, *The Village Voice*, *The Stranger* and *The Boston Phoenix*. He also contributes local cartoons to *The Oregonian*. This is his first graphic novel.